MW01118109

Civic Service Worldwide

Civic
Service
Worldwide

Impacts and Inquiry

Foreword by Amitai Etzioni

Edited by
Amanda Moore McBride and Michael Sherraden

M.E.Sharpe
Armonk, New York
London, England

Library of Congress Cataloging-in-Publication Data

Civic service worldwide : impacts and inquiry / edited by Amanda Moore McBride and
Michael Sherraden.
    p. cm.
    Includes bibliographical references and index.
    ISBN-13: 978-0-7656-1640-1 (cloth : alk. paper)
    ISBN-10: 0-7656-1640-8 (cloth : alk. paper)
  1. Labor service. 2. National service. 3. Young volunteers in community development.
I. McBride, Amanda Moore, 1971– II. Sherraden, Michael W. (Michael Wayne), 1948–

HD4869.C58 2007
361.2′6—dc22

                                                                              2006012759

Printed in the United States of America

The paper used in this publication meets the minimum requirements of
American National Standard for Information Sciences
Permanence of Paper for Printed Library Materials,
ANSI Z 39.48-1984.

BM (c) 10   9   8   7   6   5   4   3   2   1

This book is dedicated to
Franklin Thomas and Susan Berresford,
visionary leaders of the Ford Foundation who have
promoted civic service around the world.

Contents

III. Civic Service Across the Life Course

IV. Civic Service Across Borders

V. Impacts and Inquiry

Foreword

Civic Service Analysis Has Come of Age

Amitai Etzioni

Local, national, and international civic service is again a hot topic in the wake of the 2003 U.S. invasion of Iraq (Dionne, Drogosz, and Litan 2003; Schulman 2002; Wilhelm and Williams 2002; Dionne and Drogosz 2003; Galston 2001). Questions are raised about the distribution of the burden of military service among various social groups, the need for a draft, and the need for alternative services (Lind 2002; Glastris 2002; Etzioni 2002; Confessore 2003). There is, however, a group of dedicated scholars who have studied the conditions under which civic service thrives, year in and year out, whether or not the subject is popular. The solid work of these scholars is well represented in this volume.

Most important, both for the world of action and that of study, the analysis of civic service has come of age. Civic service has long been rhapsodized. It has been credited with ennobling people and making society better for it; with serving the poor and the ill; with saving the environment, reducing public costs, and lifting the nation's spirit; and even with finding peaceful alternatives to war. Too often these blessings were poorly documented, giving the whole enterprise an aura of unreality. No more. The studies collected here fully qualify as social science research, and they deal candidly with challenges and not merely successes. They show that civic service studies have matured.

Before I discuss what I consider the main challenges to civic service, a few words on its unique profile. It constitutes a highly communitarian line of action by serving both the person and the community. Communitarians differ from each other as do other schools of thought. I refer here to those who see the essence of a good society as a carefully crafted balance between autonomy and social order, in which the social order is based as much as possible on moral suasion (Etzioni 1996; Communitarian Network). Many other activities enrich individuals or corporations at the expense of the community—for instance, environmental exploitation. Others require personal sacrifices or risks to serve the common good—liver donation by live donors, for example. Civic service makes people and communities better for it.

People who serve lead more meaningful lives and are more socially and politically aware than others. They are less isolated, better informed, and more connected than many others. Civic engagement promotes democratic values and political participation. Individuals who are aware of and involved in social issues have a greater sense of human sympathy and responsibility and are more minded toward diverse interests and collective action. Moreover, the societies they serve are the richer for it (Galston 2003; Bok 2001; Carnegie Foundation 2003; Ehrlich 2003). Civic service allows societies to pursue many goals that otherwise would be left unattended or poorly attended. Furthermore, it reduces divisiveness among people of divergent social backgrounds. Civic service enables people to find common ground that bridges cultural and political differences because it focuses on community strengthening (Joseph 2004; Diversity Within Unity). For all this and more, see the essays here collected.

Civic service, though, faces a whole raft of challenges that should not be taken lightly. I here briefly outline them as challenges for future research and service planning. Before I proceed, I should note that they all jointly point to one common conclusion: Civic service best starts on a small scale with a narrow agenda, and on a voluntary basis, before it expands, embraces more goals, and becomes—if at all—mandatory. I refer to these limited beginnings as thin starts.

Make Work

Those who have never participated in or studied civic service may be inclined to think that every hospital, school, and welfare service has volumes of work that needs doing but for which they have no hands, and hence, if offered rows of civic service participants, the organizations would be overjoyed. This is often not the case. Much of the work requires some skill and experience. Those who come to serve may not have these. Labor union (and many nonunionized) workers fear that free or low-cost labor will jeopardize their jobs, and thus they oppose or undermine civic service. All work must be organized; someone must lay out what needs to be done, supervise those who do it, and so on. Many an overworked organization does not have extra supervisory personnel. Management may be afraid to rely on civic service volunteers and thus assign them trivial work, which in turn alienates them and makes them work poorly, which further leads management not to entrust them with meaningful work.

All these matters can be handled by proper training of volunteers, by joint planning with the beneficiary organization, by providing a civic service infrastructure of supervision, and by other measures needed to ensure reliable, quality work. These in turn require effort, investment, and time. Hence the hypothesis that, when civic service is newly introduced to a community, it will develop more effectively if it starts modestly and grows rather than going to full scale from the start.

Face Costs

A wit once suggested that for economists everything has a price and for sociologists nothing has a price. One can read many a fine study of civic service without finding a mention of the costs involved. Indeed, in several treatments of the subject it is implied that civic service is all a gain: It provides a service such as helping take care of patients in a nursing home, without charge to the nursing home, a net gain. However, people who participate in civic service must be recruited, fed, housed, clothed, insured, covered medically, transported, and supervised—and in some cases rewarded for their service, say with college tuition.

The resulting costs vary a great deal, depending on how elaborate the living standard, infrastructure, and rewards are. They can be quite substantial. For instance, the costs of introducing universal national service to the United States have been estimated to run well over $50 billion (Bandow 1994). Aside from needing to provide some assessment of the costs of various programs, one must address the question of the source of these funds: are they going to be taken from some other program, to which they have been previously dedicated? Or will taxes be raised for this purpose? Or will the program rely on large-scale donations? And will these, if available, drain those available to other goals? And is national service more valuable than these other endeavors?

To keep the costs low and to minimize competition with other social goals that compete over scarce resources, it is best not to piggyback other missions on civic service. Take, for instance, income transfer (from those well endowed to those less privileged), arguably a noble goal but one that is not integral to civic service. Hence, if one sets up recruitment to civic service in such a way that it draws largely from those less well off, allowing people to do minimal service (say a few hours a week, from home) and then providing the graduates with several years of ample college tuition, one advances income transfer considerably, advances civic service not so well, and above all hugely drives up the costs of the whole enterprise. One can strongly favor income transfer (or other social goals), but its costs should not be charged to the civic service budget, or it will tend to become so high that it will undermine civic service.

The first goal of civic service should be civic service. Add-ons best stay limited, at least initially.

Social Mixer

Civic service promises to bring people of different social backgrounds together, under conditions that do not privilege those already privileged, and thus it contributes to community building. It can do so, but not just by throwing a bunch of inner-city youngsters and lower-class whites from Appalachia and Ivy League graduates together or by joining people of different nationalities on the other side of a mountain or ocean. Communicating across subcultures or cultures is for most a learned skill and not an inborn one—hence the need to teach it, and hence the need for coaches. New civic service units are thus best equipped with social organizers who are skilled in opening channels of communication and interaction among people who have different habits, tastes, viewpoints, and, above all, life experiences. When social organizers are well prepared and available, civic service still requires time and effort, well worth investing, to fulfill this community-building promise.

In Toto

The list of challenges with which civic service researchers and practitioners vie is not trivial. However, the challenges have to be first acknowledged before they can be analyzed and mastered. In the infancy of civic service, they were often glossed over. No longer. Hence we should expect a much more robust civic service, albeit at least initially more modest in scope of members and goals, than the one its early pioneers envisioned.

References

Bandow, D. 1994. *National Service: The Enduring Panacea* (Cato Policy Analysis 130). Washington, DC: Cato Institute. www.cato.org/pubs/pas/pa130.html.

Bok, D.C. 2001. Easing political cynicism with civic involvement. *Chronicle of Higher Education* 47 (27): B7–B11.

Carnegie Foundation. 2003. *Educating Citizens: Preparing America's Undergraduates for Lives of Moral and Civic Responsibility.* San Francisco: Jossey-Bass.

Communitarian Network. www.communitariannetwork.org.

Confessore, N. 2003. G.I. woe. *Washington Monthly,* March. www.washingtonmonthly. com/features/2003/0303.confessore.html.

Dionne, E.J., Jr., and K.M. Drogosz. 2003. The promise of national service. www. brookings.edu/comm/policybriefs/pb120.htm.

Dionne, E.T., Jr., K.M. Drogosz, and R.E. Litan, eds. 2003. *United We Serve: National Service and the Future of Citizenship.* Washington DC: Brookings Institution Press.

Diversity Within Unity. www.gwu.edu/~ccps/dwu_positionpaper.html.

Ehrlich, T. 2003. Civics and the spirit of liberty. *Christian Science Monitor,* May 13. www.csmonitor.com/2003/0513/p09s02-coop.html.

Etzioni, A. 1996. *The New Golden Rule: Community and Morality in Democratic Society.* New York: Basic Books.

———. 2002. For a homeland protection force. *Responsive Community* 12 (2): 50–52.

Galston, W. 2001. Can patriotism be turned into civic engagement? *Chronicle of Higher Education* 48 (12): B.16.

———. 2003. Civic education and political participation. *Phi Delta Kappa* 85 (1): 29–33.

Glastris, P. 2002. A new draft for a new time. *Responsive Community* 12 (2): 40–43.

Joseph, J.A. 2004. Soft power in a world of hard power: The globalization of community service. Comments presented at the CYZYGY Annual Conference, June 2, Boston, Massachusetts.

Lind, M. 2002. National service is essential to our security. *Chronicle of Philanthropy,* April 4.

Schulman, B. 2002. The new public spirit. *Responsive Community* 12 (2): 30–35.

Wilhelm, I., and G. Williams. 2002. An appeal for action. *Chronicle of Philanthropy,* February 7. www.leadershiponlinewkkf.org/emerging/news/actionappeal.asp.

Preface and Acknowledgements

In 2001, the Ford Foundation initiated a program of research, information, and policy and program development known as the Global Service Institute (GSI). GSI was conceived as an ever-growing set of interconnected individuals and organizations, a network of scholars, technical experts, policy makers, and practitioners around the world. The research and information agendas of GSI are facilitated by the Center for Social Development (CSD) at Washington University in St. Louis. Innovations in Civic Participation in Washington, DC, facilitate the policy and program agendas. The Ford Foundation has been a longtime supporter of civic service. This steady commitment is evident across the organization, from presidents Franklin Thomas and Susan Berresford to vice presidents and program officers in all three major divisions of the foundation. The impetus for creating GSI was a sense that service is developing globally, but that the knowledge base is very limited. The hope and intention is that increasing the quality and depth of knowledge, and sharing this information worldwide, will inform and undergird policy and program developments in civic service.

CSD has five primary objectives for GSI. These objectives structure our work in knowledge development. This book, *Civic Service Worldwide: Impacts and Inquiry,* illustrates all five objectives:

1. Build a foundation for civic service as a field of knowledge and inquiry
2. Plan, convene, and attend service-related conferences
3. Conduct innovative civic service research
4. Increase capacity for civic service scholarship and application
5. Expand and enhance the GSI information network

In this book, scholars demonstrate that civic service is an emerging global phenomenon, with a nascent knowledge base that will require the objective and critical tools of social science if it is to advance. Volunteerism overall has received scholarly attention only in the last three decades. Research on civic service, as a type of volunteerism, is even more recent and limited. A rough descriptive landscape has been defined, but more rigorous research is required to guide programs and policies. To move the field in this direction, this book attempts to better specify the meaning of civic service and its possible effects, along with providing theories that may help to explain those effects.

This volume is a continuation of a global debate and discussion on forms and effects of civic service, which began in earnest with CSD's 2002 international conference in Buenos Aires called "Toward a Global Research Agenda on Civic Service." The goals of the conference were to assess the history and status of civic service in eight regions of the world, review the civic service knowledge base in each, and identify questions for future research. These papers resulted in a special issue of *Nonprofit and Voluntary Sector Quarterly* that we edited in 2004. In 2003, CSD hosted a follow-up conference in St. Louis, titled "Civic Service Worldwide: Impacts and Inquiry." The goals of this conference were to specify forms of service and likely impacts, identify promising theoretical approaches, and facilitate interdisciplinary exchange. Over sixty scholars, practitioners, policy makers, and funders from twenty-eight countries attended. Following a process of review and revision, the chapters in this book have evolved from papers originally presented and discussed at this conference.

We gratefully acknowledge staff at CSD—Irina Novikova, Ella Boyd, Timothy Broesamle, Jenny Kraus Smith, and Lissa Johnson—who helped coordinate the conference in St. Louis, which provided the venue for lively discussion and debate, enriching the resulting book. Valuable assistance in the preparation of the book has been provided by Kathy McCabe at CSD and editorial staff at M.E. Sharpe, including Elizabeth Granda and Harry Briggs. We are grateful to M.E. Sharpe for moving civic service knowledge and discussion forward through this publication.

Civic Service Worldwide

I

CONTEXT

1

Building Knowledge on Civic Service Worldwide

Amanda Moore McBride and Michael Sherraden, with Margaret Lombe and Fengyan Tang

Amitai Etzioni, professor at George Washington University and founder of the communitarian movement, states in his foreword to this book that the analysis of "civic service has come of age." Civic service today is a prevalent social phenomenon that is touted as an expression of citizenship and used as a tool for addressing a diverse range of social issues—assisting in disasters, tutoring children, preserving ecosystems, and spurring economic development. But service is not a panacea nor is it an unqualified public good. In fact, we do not know very well what forms civic service takes and what effects civic service generates. The authors in this book provide examples across a range of service forms and social issues. As a context for this research, we present in this chapter a conceptualization of civic service and provide an overview of the book by discussing the forms and nature of civic service and the role of theory in guiding development of evidence.

Ongoing, occasional, and episodic volunteering tends to be the focus of scholarship on volunteerism (Carson 1999; Van Til 1988). These forms of volunteerism may result from individual initiative and may or may not require a program structure. There may be no defined endpoint: The individual may volunteer for the same organization for decades or only for a single day. Examples of these forms of volunteering include serving as a board member or committee chair for an organization or engaging in a community service day on behalf of your employer. But what about more formal, intensive volunteering, which occurs through structured programs? We refer to this volunteerism as *civic service.*

In a global assessment of the status and forms of civic service world-wide, 210 programs were found in 57 countries (McBride, Benítez, and Sherraden 2003). Across these programs, service tends to be full-time and averages about seven months in duration, though duration differs by form of service. These programs have been in existence an average of twenty-one years and a median of thirteen years, suggesting that civic service is a recent development in volunteerism. Diverse forms of service were also identified through this assessment, including community, national, and international service. Service-learning is a pedagogical approach used at primary, secondary, and university levels that focuses on community service, instruction, and reflection (Billig 2000). National service channels eligible citizens across a given country in service to the nation-state, but national service may or may not be sponsored by government. The National Youth Service Corps in Nigeria, AmeriCorps in the United States, and Katimavik in Canada are examples. International service refers to technical or nontechnical service performed outside of the server's home country. Examples include Voluntary Service Overseas in the United Kingdom, Japanese Overseas Cooperation Volunteers, the Peace Corps in the United States, and Canada World Youth.

Over the last decade, research and publication on civic service have increased, especially in Western Europe and the United States. Most research has focused on service-learning and national service (Grantmaker Forum on Community and National Service 2000; Perry and Imperial 2001; Perry and Thomson 2004). Service scholarship in other nations is just emerging (McBride and Sherraden 2004). As a global phenomenon, comparison of the forms and effects of civic service can inform program and policy development, hopefully increasing efficiency and effectiveness. But addressing these questions comparatively will require common conceptual categories and agreed upon definitions of operational features.

Civic Service as a Construct

Civic service is a complex phenomenon. It is comprised of multiple dimensions and, hence, many possible variables in research, which complicate inquiry. Key dimensions of volunteerism have been identified, and these can help establish boundaries and specify the nature of civic service. Differences in forms of volunteerism can be distinguished by structure; auspices and organizational host; intended beneficiaries and activities; compulsory or voluntary nature; time commitment; and remuneration or recognition (Cnaan and Amrofell 1994; Cnaan, Handy, and Wadsworth 1996). We apply these dimensions to civic service, illustrating our conceptualization of civic service and comparing it to traditional conceptions of volunteerism.

Structure

Civic service is implemented through programs operated by private, non-profit, or public organizations. Programs are marked by inputs, activities, and outputs, usually planned and implemented within a goal or objective framework. Programs are designed to seek designated ends through dedicated resources applied in a systematic way. In civic service programs, a service *role* is specified and then filled by an individual (Morrow-Howell et al. 2003). The *server* can be thought of as the primary input, the essential *vehicle* for delivery of the service. The role is defined with expectations about service performance and eligibility criteria for participation. Expectations and criteria may vary in scope and intensity in different service contexts. Programs may target servers of certain age groups, geographic areas, and skill levels. Structured orientation, training, supervision, and mentoring accompany most civic service programs.

Auspices and Organizational Host

Governments at local, provincial, national, or international levels may sponsor civic service. Governments may sanction and support the programs and may even implement them. However, in most national service, nonprofit or nongovernmental organizations implement and host the service program by recruiting, training, and managing the servers. In fact, nonprofit organizations are often both the creators and the hosts of service (McBride, Benítez, and Sherraden 2003). Schools and universities may also serve as the auspices for a service-learning program, working with a community-based host such as a nonprofit organization. There may be complex collaborative arrangements, especially among international service programs where there are *sending* and *hosting* organizations and where government provides endorsement or other support, for example, the European Voluntary Service (McBride, Benítez, and Danso 2003).

Intended Beneficiaries and Activities

Beneficiaries of volunteer programs may be strangers, neighbors, relatives, and/or the volunteers themselves (Cnaan and Amrofell 1994). Civic service programs are commonly characterized by a dual focus on the *servers* and the *served* (McBride, Benítez, and Sherraden 2003). Both are to benefit from the experience. Civic service programs are often distinguished by a public orientation, such that the *anonymous other* is a primary beneficiary; for example, those who might benefit from trees and trails. The targets of service may be individuals, families, organizations, communities, nations, or the world. Civic service programs are oriented toward a range of social and economic issues. Servers may tutor children, care for the aged, or re-locate families after a disaster. They may engage in program development or program evaluation (McBride et al. 2003). Servers may restore village common spaces or promote sustainable agriculture (Eberly and Sherraden 1990; McBride, Benítez, and Sherraden 2003; Sherraden 2001b). The range of service activities is highly diverse.

Compulsory or Voluntary Nature

Volunteering in its truest and narrowest sense is noncoerced action (Van Til 1988). However, participation may sometimes be compulsory in national service and service-learning programs. In the global assessment of civic service mentioned above, of the 210 programs identified, only 4 percent were compulsory (McBride, Benítez, and Sherraden 2003). While this assessment excluded service-learning programs, the results suggest that compulsion may be a less prevalent feature of service than is sometimes believed (Clotfelter 1999).

Time Commitment

Cnaan and Amrofell (1994) identify frequency and amount of time devoted to volunteer episodes as key attributes of the experience. Civic service is an intensive form of long-term volunteering. McBride, Benítez, and Sherraden (2003) find that 81 percent of civic service programs require a full-time com-mitment, equivalent to thirty-five hours or more per week. The remaining programs were flexible. Duration of the average service role is about seven months, and the median is five months. Workcamps may last for a month; service-learning programs may require 100 or 200 hours of community service during a semester; national and international service programs may require one or more years of service.

Remuneration or Recognition

Remuneration is a primary boundary for defining the contours of volunteerism (Carson 1999). Altruism is considered a prerequisite, so if benefits beyond a sense of well-being and societal belonging accrue to the individual, then the basis of volunteerism may be questioned. Nevertheless, many volunteer programs reimburse volunteers for task-related expenses. In civic service programs, levels of remuneration and recognition may be more extensive. There is an explicit intention to affect the server, so the programs may provide formal recognition or rewards that invest in the capacity of the server. Some programs reward service with educational credit and scholarships. National service programs typically offer awards or financial supports such as transfers that can be used for advanced education, homeownership, and small business capitalization. However, these stipends are not equivalent to market wages, thus distinguishing full-time, compensated service from employment (McBride, Benítez, and Sherraden 2003).

In sum, we suggest that civic service is distinct but related to traditional conceptions of volunteering. It is highly structured and formal. The time requirements are intense and long-term, and it is not always voluntary, which would place it on the fringe of voluntary action. We characterize this structured intervention as civic service. Based on this conceptualization, civic service can be generally defined as "an organized period of substantial engagement and contribution to the local, national, or world community, recognized and valued by society, with minimal monetary compensation to the participant" (Sherraden 2001c, 2).

We attach the descriptor *civic* to connote that the action performed is not what is traditionally considered military service or government civil service. Others may refer to it, using a related term, as *citizen* service (Clinton 2003). We also refer to the person performing this action as a *server* instead of a volunteer, though Eberly and Gal (Chapter 2), for example, refer to the person in the service role as a *cadet*. We readily acknowledge that translation of *civic service* into other languages sometimes does not result in the same idea (Pawlby 2003, 129–138; Tapia 2003, 139–148). In fact, the term *civic service* has yet to enter social scientific nomenclature, though the Israeli government has begun to use the term (Knafo 2005) as have various European countries (Association of Volunteer Service Organizations 2005).

This conceptualization and terminology have become starting points for global discussion about civic service (McBride and Sherraden 2004). But there is extensive debate about what volunteerism is and is not, with no clear consensus among scholars or citizens (Anheier and Salamon 1999; Carson 1999; Cnaan and Amrofell 1994; Cnaan, Handy, and Wadsworth 1996; Salamon and Sokolowski 2001). Moreover, historical, cultural, and legal determinants of volunteerism in any given nation or culture further compound the discussion (Carson 1999; Handy et al. 2000). We suggest, however, that the above conceptualization of civic service acknowledges and allows for variation and can promote measurement across cultural contexts, such that these dimensions and differences can be assessed empirically.

For example, in many developing countries, the line between volunteerism and civic service is blurred. What would constitute substantial engagement? Is it one week, full-time, or one day a week for several months? The issue of commitment is raised often in the Global South, where programmatic-based volunteerism is not well developed and there may be few constraints on the server role. Also, how does service-learning fit into the civic service construct? In some parts of the world, service-learning is the most prevalent from of organized service, but commitment and impacts may be limited. And what of *minimal* compensation? Some international service volunteers receive more in stipends than most people earn from labor in the countries where the volunteers serve. Can this be considered volunteerism? Moreover, volunteerism may not be the most appropriate operational reference in political contexts where *voluntary* work has in fact been obligatory, most often under communist or other authoritarian regimes (Kuti 2004). Some emerging scholarship argues for valuation of all work—whether voluntary or not, whether paid or not—so that it is monetized and acknowledged for its public and private benefits (Anheier et al. 2003).

These important questions and issues reflect the nascent state of knowledge in civic service as well as in volunteerism overall. By construing civic service as a form of volunteerism, the spirit of service is captured and a number of its dynamics are connected to a larger body of scholarship. As J. Davis Smith suggests, "we can perhaps best see civic service and volunteering as distinct concepts but with a strong element of overlap" (2004, 66S). In our view, civic service is part of volunteerism but distinctive. The goals at this juncture in civic service scholarship are to name and define the phenomenon being studied and to isolate its dimensions as variables that can be compared across service forms and contexts.

Civic Service Forms, Nature, and Impacts

Civic service programs and policies are designed with development goals in mind. In the language of the applied social sciences, civic service is a social intervention oriented toward the development of the servers and improvements in social and economic conditions, but the degree to which any particular service form focuses on these goals may differ. For example, national service programs tend to approach service developmentally. They may be less likely than international service programs to require servers to have specific characteristics, with a goal of increasing their skills and knowledge. This suggests that service forms differ functionally (Sherraden and Eberly 1982, 179–187). What outcomes do these service forms aim to promote? Service outcomes can be broadly classified as occurring at individual, organizational, and community levels (Davis Smith and Ellis Paine, Chapter 11). Service scholarship tends to focus on individual-level outcomes with scant attention paid to organizational and community-level outcomes (McBride et al. 2003; Perry and Thomson, Chapter 5). Below we define different service forms and possible impacts, foreshadowing the chapters that follow.

National Service: Evolution, Policy, and Potential

In essence, national service has existed since governments first organized the masses to construct public goods (Menon, McBride, and Sherraden 2003, 149–158). National service also has roots in military service, with the ultimate goal being preservation of the nation-state. Today national service in some parts of the world is morphing into international service as political boundaries become more complex, as in the European Union (AVSO 2005). In other countries, national service programs—especially those implemented under the auspices of governments—are wavering with political tides, with programs being scaled back or expanding. Connections among national service, citizenship, and military service have resurfaced in the United States. Reviews of research suggest that national service may have great potential to foster civic engagement and employability effects for young people (Abt Associates 2004; Perry and Thomson 2004). In some instances, national service may actually provide *employment* for underemployed youth (Tserendorjiin, Tumurbaatariin, and Gantumur 2005; Sherraden 1979). It may be used as a career path much like the university and the military, especially for disadvantaged youth (Stoneman 2002). In multiethnic states, it may be used to bring young people from different groups together to promote cultural integration and tolerance. Chapters in this volume trace the history and forms of national service, highlighting their weaknesses and potential.

Don Eberly of the International Association for National Youth Service and Reuven Gal of the Carmel Institute for Social Studies in Israel describe the roots and evolution of civic service from military service. The chapter focuses on national service in Germany, China, Israel, Nigeria, and the United States, identifying a modern trend and potential path for the evolution and expansion of voluntary national service.

Africa has long been a leader in national service, though some programs have faded in recent years. Ebenezer Obadare of the University of Kansas addresses national service theories and impacts throughout Africa, focusing on the Nigerian National Youth Service Corps. He describes how political regime and status of democracy may mediate development and effects of national service. Obadare encourages a critical stance toward the assessment of national service and its possible effects.

Based on recent research, Nicole Fleischer and Reuven Gal from the Carmel Institute for Social Studies in Israel advance an inclusive perspective of national service and its potential effects on conditions within a multiethnic state. They use examples from research conducted with national service participants in Israel, describing how service can be structured to effect bonding social capital but perhaps not bridging social capital. They discuss the challenges and potential for a universal national youth service scheme in Israel.

James Perry and Ann Marie Thomson (2004) of Indiana University present a summary of their metareview of over 100 research studies on national and community service in United States. They conclude that possible effects of service are wide-ranging, but methods in most studies do not allow definitive assessments of impacts. Perry and Thomson suggest that more rigorous research is needed, research that can address direct and unanticipated effects of service, as well as mediating factors related to the implementation context; for example, organizational effectiveness and cultural issues.

Civic Service Across the Life Course

At the Center for Social Development (CSD), our analytical perspective is service as a phenomenon that can be viewed across the life course. A young person today may be involved in a service-learning program during secondary school, an international service experience in college, and a stint of national service following college graduation (McBride et al. forthcoming). This person may then focus on career and family, returning to service in later adulthood and in retirement (Morrow-Howell et al. 2003). Applying a long-term perspective to global demographic changes, it is likely that older adults will be an important vehicle for social change through service programs (Hinterlong et al. 2005). These developments are already under way in many countries. In this view, a lifelong ethic and practice of service may become common.

Service-learning is emerging in many countries. International service-learning opportunities are also prevalent, sometimes used for citizenship and democratic training. Research on service-learning is relatively advanced, but is dominated by studies at the university level in the Global North. Comparative research would be informative, and even within the United States, little is known about service-learning across primary and secondary levels.

Judith Torney-Purta and her colleagues, Jo-Ann Amadeo and Wendy Klandl Richardson from the University of Maryland, present a comparative study of civic education conducted through the International Association for the Evaluation of Education Achievement. They discuss relationships between the co-occurrence of civic education and volunteering and a range of civic indicators. Across nations, the findings suggest that education and service may mutually reinforce civic engagement.

María Nieves Tapia, from the Latin American Center for Service-Learning (CLAYSS) in Argentina, grounds a conceptualization of service-learning in its diverse forms in Central and South America. She describes the prevalence and possible effects of service-learning in primary, secondary, and university environments. Tapia suggests that, in Central and South America, emphasis may be placed on the effects of the service-learning projects on the people and communities that are served, which may contrast with service-learning in North America, where emphasis is usually on the benefits to the servers.

Nancy Morrow-Howell of Washington University in St. Louis and Fengyan Tang of the University of Pittsburgh highlight the global potential for elder service from an institutional theoretical perspective and draw comparisons between forms and effects of youth service and elder service. They propose that elder service may be more flexible and that elders may be motivated less by what they gain from service and more by what they can contribute, based on their knowledge and skills.

Civic Service Across Borders

International service may be the most prevalent but least studied form of civic service worldwide (McBride, Benítez, and Danso 2003; McBride and Daftary 2005; Smith and Elkin 1981; Woods 1981). With complex roots in missionary service and international aid, international service has diverse goals and administrative structures. International service programs may be technical (servers must be experts), nontechnical (servers do good work), or learning-oriented (servers are connected to course work). In terms of structure, some programs are regionally based; for example, the Nigerian Technical Aid Corps is composed of African development experts serving Africans, and the European Voluntary Service Scheme is made up of youth from European nations serving other Europeans. Some programs, such as Experiment in International Living, are focused on development of global citizens, operating a large network of servers and hosts across multiple continents. Despite these rather ambitious arrangements and goals, international service has also been path-dependent and sometimes marked by elitism, state interests, and imperialism (McBride and Daftary 2005, Rockliffe 2005; Simpson 2004).

However, in a more globalized world, international service may acquire a new prominence, with potential to promote global citizenship, youth development, transnational social policy, and peace and tolerance (Grusky 2000; Heddy 2000; Sherraden 2001a; Sherraden and Benítez 2003).

Margaret Sherrard Sherraden of the University of Missouri-St. Louis and Washington University in St. Louis considers the potential of international service as social policy. She presents a conceptualization of international service as transnational service, and analyzes operational differences in program forms worldwide. In support of this framework, she describes research on the North American Community Service Project, which was an explicit attempt at co-ownership and co-management across Canadian, Mexican, and American borders.

Ronald Pitner of Washington University in St. Louis applies concepts and theories from social psychology to civic service programs designed to bring individuals from different groups together. His chapter addresses group differences, which may be greatest in international service programs that, by design, involve different cultural groups. His ideas, however, also apply to national service programs with goals of cultural integration among diverse groups. Pitner focuses on ethnonational differences, but suggests that any group difference may be applicable. He notes that, when individuals from different groups work on a project or task together, the project itself may represent a superordinate goal that enables participants to transcend differences and emphasize similarities. In this way, service may increase tolerance and cooperation.

Toward Theory and Comparative Evidence

As the chapters in this book demonstrate, civic service is a complex phenomenon that can take many different forms and has diverse goals and implementation arrangements—all of which are embedded within particular social, economic, political, and historical contexts. The evidence in these chapters helps to better specify the phenomenon, isolating variables of concern and suggesting the most likely areas of impact as well as potential unintended and sometimes negative outcomes. The chapters add a great deal to the emerging landscape of the possible forms and effects of civic service worldwide (McBride and Sherraden 2004). How can we capitalize on this existing knowledge? We suggest that the field can articulate and pursue common lines of inquiry, assessing what the most likely and productive effects of service are and what program and policy structures may be most effective and efficient within a given nation or culture.

Justin Davis Smith and Angela Ellis Paine of the Institute for Volunteering

Research in the United Kingdom discuss the conceptual and operational nuances of civic service and the importance of isolating its composite variables. They reinforce the multiple levels of impact and categorize and aggregate diverse impacts under the broad concept of capital. They define five types of capital: economic, physical, human, social, and cultural. Davis Smith and Ellis Paine also suggest common outcomes and highlight complexities in comparative research.

In our view, these complexities may be reduced through targeted inquiry guided by theory. Theory is the cornerstone. If there is an idea about relationships between phenomena—why and how they are related—then a theory is implied. In social scientific inquiry, theory informs the structure and application of research because it specifies context and interaction. When a theory is subject to empirical test, it can enhance understanding, explanation, and even prediction. Theory helps us to develop, implement, and study social interventions, and theoretically driven research makes efficient knowledge development possible. Theory allows social scientists to communicate more clearly their defined concepts, proposed relationships, and evidence regarding the nature of those relationships (Sherraden 1998).

In a review of forty-two civic service studies, McBride et al. (2003) report that only fifteen of the forty-two studies use a theoretical perspective. Of these, the majority offers a theoretical framework for conceptual and organizing purposes; very few use applied theory for explanation or prediction. As in other work (Sherraden et al. 2001, 260–284), our inclination is toward a traditional use of deductive reasoning, with an emphasis on application. Accordingly, we suggest that the service knowledge base is in need of testable hypotheses and systematic inquiry. Theories tested against empirical reality can move the knowledge base beyond anecdotes, exploration, and description to comparable evidence and verification. Because of the diverse suggested effects of civic service, the study of service is inherently interdisciplinary (McBride et al. 2003). As demonstrated in this book, theories from social psychology, education, and political science can all be fruitfully applied.

As we have stressed elsewhere (McBride and Sherraden 2004), civic service may be a promising social intervention, but the knowledge base is in its early childhood. Applied social science requires clear conceptualization, definitions, proposed relationships, and explanations for why those relationships exist. Theoretical specification requires identification of distinct independent variables (for civic service) and dependent variables (for the impacts of service) (Sherraden 1998). We offer the following questions as guideposts for considering the scientific implications of this book:

- If civic service is a construct, then what variables measure its occurrence, and which variables influence the intended outcomes?

- How does the service program reflect and interact with cultural, social, economic, and political contexts in which it is developed and implemented? What contextual features mediate the intended outcomes?
- How does the program interact with characteristics of the individual servers to motivate and sustain service performance and maximize effects?
- What are the likely long-term impacts of service on the servers and on the service targets and host communities?

In order to answer these questions, it will be necessary to apply and develop useful theories. Hypotheses regarding specific influences and effects of service must be clearly specified. Looking ahead, we summarize and conclude this book by advancing an institutional perspective on civic service that may offer tentative answers to these questions in the form of clear propositions and testable hypotheses. The reader can decide whether these might be useful or what alternative conceptualizations might be productive in building the knowledge base on civic service.

References

Abt Associates. 2004. Serving country and community: A longitudinal study of service in AmeriCorps. www.nationalservice.org.

Anheier, H.K., E. Hollerweger, C. Badelt, and J. Kendall. 2003. *Work in the Non-Profit Sector: Forms, Patterns, and Methodologies.* Geneva: International Labour Office.

Anheier, H.K., and L.M. Salamon. 1999. Volunteering in cross-national perspective: initial comparisons. *Law and Contemporary Problems* 62 (4): 43–66.

Association of Voluntary Service Organizations (AVSO). 2005. *Youth Civic Service in Europe.* Pisa: University of Pisa Press.

Billig, S.H. 2000. Research on K–12 school-based service-learning: The evidence builds. *Phi Delta Kappan* 81: 658–664.

Carson, E.D. 1999. On defining and measuring volunteering in the Untied States and abroad. *Law and Contemporary Problems* 62 (4): 67–71.

Clinton, E.J. 2003. The duties of democracy. In *United We Serve: National Service and the Future of Citizenship,* ed. E.J. Dionne, K.M. Drogosz, and R.E. Titan. Washington, DC: Brookings Institution Press.

Clotfelter, C.T. 1999. Amateurs in public service: Volunteering, service-learning, and community service. *Law and Contemporary Problems* 62 (4): 1–16.

Cnaan, R.A., and L. Amrofell. 1994. Mapping volunteer activity. *Nonprofit and Voluntary Sector Quarterly* 23 (4) Supplement: 335–351.

Cnaan, R.A., F. Handy, and M. Wadsworth. 1996. Defining who is a volunteer: Conceptual and empirical considerations. *Nonprofit and Voluntary Sector Quarterly* 25 (3): 364–383.

Davis Smith, J. 2004. Civic service in Western Europe. *Nonprofit and Voluntary Sector Quarterly* 33 (4) Supplement: 64S–97S.

Eberly, D., and M. Sherraden, eds. 1990. *The Moral Equivalent of War?: A Study of Non-Military Service in Nine Nations.* New York: Greenwood Press.

Grantmaker Forum on Community and National Service. 2000. *The State of Service-Related Research: Opportunities to Build a Field.* Berkeley, CA: Grantmaker Forum on Community and National Service.

Grusky, S. 2000. International service-learning: A critical guide from an impassionate advocate. *American Behavioral Scientist* 43: 858–867.

Handy, F., R.A. Cnann, J.L. Brudney, U. Ascoli, L.C.M.P. Meijs, and S. Ranade. 2000. Public perception of "who is a volunteer": An examination of the net-cost approach from a cross-cultural perspective. *Voluntas: International Journal of Voluntary and Nonprofit Organizations* 11 (1): 45–65.

Heddy J. 2000. *ENVOL 2000: Final Evaluation Report.* Brussels: European Voluntary Service for Young People.

Hinterlong, J., A.M. McBride, F. Tang, and K. Danso. 2005. Elder volunteering and service: Global issues and outcomes. In *Civic Engagement and People Age 50 and Beyond,* ed. L. Wilson. New York: Haworth Press.

Knafo, D. 2005. National youth service in Israel. Keynote speech at the International Roundtable on Volunteerism and Service, Washington, DC, August 3.

Kuti, E. 2004. Civic service in Eastern Europe and Central Asia: From mandatory public work toward civic service? *Nonprofit and Voluntary Sector Quarterly* 33 (4) Supplement: 79S–97S.

McBride, A.M., C. Benítez, and K. Danso. 2003. Civic service worldwide: Social development goals and partnerships. *Social Development Issues* 25 (1/2): 175–188.

McBride, A.M., C. Benítez, and M. Sherraden. 2003. *The Forms and Nature of Civic Service: A Global Assessment* (CSD Report). St. Louis: Washington University, Center for Social Development.

McBride, A.M., J. Brav, N. Menon, and M. Sherraden. In review. Limitations of civic service: Critical perspectives.

McBride, A.M., and D. Daftary. 2005. *International Service: History and Forms, Pitfalls and Potential* (CSD Working Paper 05–10). St. Louis: Washington University, Center for Social Development.

McBride, A.M., M. Lombe, F. Tang, M. Sherraden, and C. Benítez. 2003. *The Knowledge Base on Civic Service: Status and Directions* (CSD Working Paper 03–20). St. Louis: Washington University, Center for Social Development.

McBride, A.M., S. Pritzker, D. Daftary, and F. Tang. In press. Youth civic service: A comprehensive perspective. *Journal of Community Practice.*

McBride, A.M., and M. Sherraden, eds. 2004. Toward an international research agenda on civic service. *Nonprofit and Voluntary Sector Quarterly* 33 (4) Supplement.

Menon, N., A.M. McBride, and M. Sherraden. 2003. Understanding service in the context of history and culture. In *Service Enquiry: Service in the 21st Century,* ed. H. Perold, S. Stroud, and M. Sherraden. Johannesburg: comPress.

Morrow-Howell, N., J. Hinterlong, M. Sherraden, F. Tang, P. Thirupathy, and M. Nagchoudhuri. 2003. Institutional capacity for elder service. *Social Development Issues* 25 (1/2): 189–204.

Pawlby, I. 2003. What should we call "civic service"? In *Service Enquiry: Service in the 21st Century,* ed. H. Perold, S. Stroud, and M. Sherraden. Johannesburg: comPress.

Perry, J., and M.T. Imperial. 2001. A decade of service-related research: A map of the field. *Nonprofit and Voluntary Sector Quarterly* 30 (3): 462–479.

Perry, J., and A.M. Thomson. 2004. *Civic Service: What Difference Does It Make?* Armonk, NY: M.E. Sharpe.

Rockliffe, B. 2005. International volunteering: An evolving paradigm. *Voluntary Action* 7 (2): 35–56.

Salamon, L.M., and W. Sokolowski. 2001. *Volunteering in Cross-National Perspective: Evidence from 24 Countries.* Working paper of the Johns Hopkins Comparative Nonprofit Sector Project, no. 40. Baltimore: Johns Hopkins Center for Civil Society Studies.

Sherraden, M. 1979. The Civilian Conservation Corps: The effectiveness of the camps. PhD diss., University of Michigan.

———. 1998. *Forming a Theoretical Statement: Doctoral Seminar on Social Work Theory and Knowledge.* Paper presented. St. Louis: Washington University, George Warren Brown School of Social Work.

———. 2001a. *Civic Service: Issues, Outlook, Institution Building* (CSD Perspective). St. Louis: Washington University, Center for Social Development.

———. 2001b. *Service and the Human Enterprise* (CSD Perspective). St. Louis: Washington University, Center for Social Development.

———. 2001c. *Youth Service as Strong Policy* (Working Paper 01–12). St. Louis: Washington University, Center for Social Development.

Sherraden, M., and D. Eberly. 1982. The impact of national service on participants. In *National Service: Social, Economic, and Military Impacts,* ed. M. Sherraden, and D. Eberly. New York: Pergamon Press.

Sherraden, M., N. Morrow-Howell, J. Hinterlong, and P. Rozario. 2001. Productive aging: Theoretical choices and directions. In *Productive Aging: Concepts and Challenges,* ed. N. Morrow-Howell, J. Hinterlong, and M. Sherraden. Baltimore: Johns Hopkins University Press.

Sherraden, M.S. 2001. *Developing Transnational Social Policy: A North American Community Service Program* (CSD Working Paper 01–10). St. Louis: Washington University, Center for Social Development.

Sherraden, M.S., and C. Benítez. 2003. *North American Service Pilot Project: Pilot Project Research Report* (CSD Report). St. Louis: Washington University, Center for Social Development.

Simpson K. 2004. "Doing development": The gap year, volunteer tourists, and a popular practice of development. *Journal of International Development* 16 (5): 681–692.

Smith, D.H., and F. Elkin. 1981. Volunteers, voluntary associations and development: An introduction. *International Journal of Comparative Sociology* 21(3/4): 1–12.

Stoneman, D. 2002. The role of youth programming in the development of civic engagement. *Applied Developmental Science* 6 (4): 221–226.

Tapia, M.N. 2003. Servicio and Solidaridad in South American Spanish. In *Service Enquiry: Service in the 21st Century,* ed. H. Perold, S. Stroud, and M. Sherraden. Johannesburg: Global Service Institute, USA and Volunteer and Service Enquiry Southern Africa comPress.

Tserendorjiin, E., B. Tumurbaatariin, and R. Gantumur. 2005. *Study of the Effects of the National United Nations Volunteers Program in Mongolia* (CSD Research Report 05–06). St. Louis: Washington University, Center for Social Development.

Van Til, J. 1988. *Mapping the Third Sector.* Washington, DC: Foundation Center.

Woods, D.E. 1981. International research on volunteers abroad. *International Journal of Comparative Sociology* 21 (3/4): 196–206.

2

From Military Service to Civic Service

The Evolution of National Youth Service

Donald J. Eberly and Reuven Gal

Throughout the twentieth century, there were parallels between developments in military service and national youth service. Early on, while armies mobilized large numbers of young people to fight wars, several people proposed the mobilization of young people for limited periods of civilian service. During the century, as advances in weaponry and technology led to the reduction in the size of armed forces, a number of countries mobilized young people for civilian service in various ways related to war and the military, and valuable lessons were learned from these programs. By the end of the twentieth century, new national youth service programs that drew on those lessons were founded to take advantage of the perceived benefits of national youth service rather than to provide a connection with military service. Given the frequent references to national youth service in this chapter, we refer to it with the acronym NYS; and given the variety of names applied to NYS participants, from corpers to zivies to volunteers, we refer to them generically as cadets.

Although this chapter is concerned only with the past and present century, it is worth noting that links between military and civilian service go back thousands of years. Nubian soldiers in the army of Old Egypt built monuments that still stand. The Incan army in South America built roads and irrigation systems. The soldiers of Etruria built aqueducts around Rome to supply water to the city, and later the Roman army built Hadrian's Wall and highways, some of which form the motorways of today's England (Glick 1967, 33–34). In the United States 200 years ago, President Thomas Jefferson assigned military officers Meriwether Lewis and William Clark to explore the Northwest Passage.

Transitions and Transformations in Military Organizations

In a historical perspective, the military model is ever-changing and transforming as a function of the changing environment, technology, and political situations, as Table 2.1 demonstrates. Charles Moskos, among other scholars in military sociology, claims that even within the last century the military organizations in almost all states and countries have undergone a major common transition. This transition can be captured in various characteristics, or armed-forces variables, ranging from the structure of the force to its approach toward homosexuals or conscientious objectors (COs). Arguably, the postmodern military could be characterized by diminishing support from the public. Also its orientation and ethos are more tolerant and flexible, thus making it not as distinct as it was in the past, and, finally, the motivation of the servicemen and -women is not necessarily patriotic, but rather stems from the desire for self-actualization and exposure to occupational opportunities (Moskos 2000).

The merging of the postmodern army stems, obviously, from the end of the Cold War and the collapse of the Soviet bloc and the Warsaw Pact, but it is also the result of vast economical, cultural, and societal changes occurring in the West, including globalization, weakening of the nation-state, increased standards of living, changes in the workplace, and erosion of traditional values (Haltiner 1998; Von Bredow 1999; Moskos, Segal, and Williams 2000). But perhaps the most striking transformation—and the most relevant to the present discussion—is the decline, almost disappearance, of the universal (mandatory or compulsory) conscription-based army. As of mid-2001, the only four countries left in Europe that still maintained hard-core conscript forces were Greece, Turkey, Finland, and Switzerland. It should be noted that Israel, too, still maintains a full mandatory service. Starting in the early 1960s and up to the recent time, all other North American and European countries have transformed their militaries into all-volunteer forces (AVFs) or are in the process of doing so (Haltiner 2003).

Furthermore, as can be seen in Figure 2.1, the overall participation ratio of servicemen and -women out of the entire population in fifteen Western European countries has diminished from around 5 percent in the 1970s and late 1980s to less than 3 percent in 2000 (Haltiner 2003). In several countries, such as Germany, France, Great Britain, and Holland, this percentage is below 0.5 percent (International Institute for Strategic Studies 2000).

Though less profound, this dual process of downsizing the armed forces and transforming from conscription to AVFs is also occurring in countries in Asia and Africa. For example, Thailand's armed forces had in 2001 reached 70 percent of their recruitment target from volunteers (*Bangkok Post* 2001), thus putting this country in the Type 1 (conscription ratio below 50 percent) category of Karl Haltiner's typology. A similar trend is taking place elsewhere in Asia.

Recent transformations of military organizations, however, apply not only to their size and structure, but also to their mission and orientation. Along with an increasing tendency to engage in peacekeeping and constabulary missions

Table 2.1

Armed Forces and Postmodern Society

Armed forces variable	Modern (pre–Cold War) 1900–1945	Late modern (Cold War) 1945–1990	Postmodern (post–Cold War) since 1990
Perceived threat	Enemy invasion	Nuclear war	Subnational (e.g., ethnic violence, terrorism)
Force structure	Mass army, conscription	Large professional army	Small professional (voluntary) army
Major mission definition	Defense of homeland	Support of alliance	New missions (e.g., peacekeeping, humanitarian)
Dominant military professional	Combat leader	Manager or technician	Soldier-statesman; soldier-scholar
Public attitude toward military	Supportive	Ambivalent	Skeptical or apathetic
Media relations	Incorporated	Manipulated	Courted
Civilian employees	Minor component	Medium component	Major component
Women's role	Separate corps or excluded	Partial integration	Full integration
Spouse and military	Integral part	Partial involvement	Removed
Homosexuals in military	Punished	Discharged	Accepted
Conscientious objection	Limited or prohibited	Routinely permitted	Subsumed under civilian service

Source: Moskos et al. (2000).

Figure 2.1   **Population Military Participation Ratio 1970–2000: Total Average of Fifteen Western European Conscript Armed Forces**

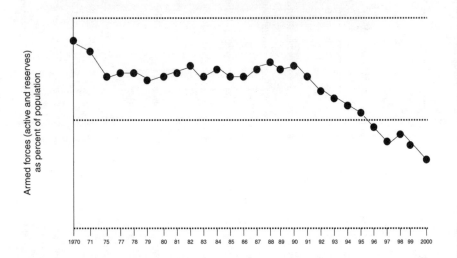

(rather than in all-out war), many military organizations today are involved in domestic and humanitarian missions, or, as the military jargon refers to them, military operations other than war (MOOTW). They include missions such as rescue operations, firefighting, refugee camps operations, and food supply. This trend of "military humanitarianism" (Weiss and Campbell 1991, 451–465) brings military service close to the civic service model, which includes all kinds of operations *but* war and, to use William James's term, constitutes the "moral equivalent of war" (James 1968). The evolution of military organizations, which has occurred throughout the last few decades, is directly related to the growth of NYS during these same decades. As armies shrink in size and move toward nonmilitary missions, more young people are available for organizations which are more civilian in the first place. However, this evolution of the military is not the only factor. Three men who advocated forms of NYS near the beginning of the twentieth century did not do so because they foresaw smaller armies or transformed military organizations; rather, William James, Eugen Rosenstock-Huessy, and Pierre Ceresole did so for psychological, moral, and religious reasons.

Development of the NYS Concept

Development of the NYS concept began with William James's essay "The Moral Equivalent of War," first given as a lecture at Stanford University in 1906. He called for a conscription of the whole youthful population to work on many of the toughest jobs. [They would go] to coal and iron mines, to freight trains, to fishing fleets in December, to dish-washing, clothes-washing, and window-washing, to road-building and tunnel-making, to foundries and stokeholes.... [Those who served] would have paid their blood-tax, done their own part in the immemorial human warfare against nature; they would tread the earth more proudly, the women would value them more highly, they would be better fathers and teachers of the following generation. (James 1968, 669)

Although James placed himself "squarely in the anti-militarist camp," he said that martial values such as "intrepidity, contempt of softness, and surrender of private interest" must be the enduring cement of society; and he noted that painful work would be "done cheerily because the duty is temporary and threatens not, as now, to degrade the whole remainder of one's life" (668–669).

A few years later Eugen Rosenstock-Huessy of Germany called for a work service corps. Writing to the Prussian Ministry of War, he argued "there were so many one [sic] and two-year recruits freed from military service for ridiculous reasons of health. They should all be collected together in a social service corps where they could practice living and learning how to live" (1978, 40). His proposal went nowhere immediately, but later he did organize a variety of short-term service corps efforts. Rosenstock-Huessy said he learned two major lessons from these experiments. First, they were much more successful when they involved young people from different strata of society rather than those from a homogeneous group. Second, he found that short-term workcamps had little impact. He wrote, "As war must be replaced by something as earnest or nearly as earnest, I must insist that it is necessary to sacrifice some period of time, a considerable period, a chapter of your life" (42).

The development of civic service continued in 1920 with the launching of Civil Service International and the voluntary workcamp movement. As the international secretary of the Fellowship of Reconciliation, Pierre Ceresole of Switzerland was the prime mover in the establishment of what is generally recognized as the first international voluntary workcamp. It was situated near Verdun, site of 1 million deaths in a yearlong battle in 1916. Ceresole, the son of a Swiss president, had strong Christian beliefs that led him to prison in both world wars for refusal to pay war taxes (Gillette 1968). Since 1920, numerous workcamps have brought together young people from many countries to assist in reconstruction and rehabilitation after wars and natural disasters.

Major NYS Initiatives

During the twentieth century, the countries with the largest NYS programs in proportion to population were related in various ways to the military and were found in different parts of the world, including the United States, Germany, China, Israel, and Nigeria. They were created and supported by governments. Each of them addressed one or more significant national problems and each yielded valuable lessons in the evolution of NYS.

The United States

President Franklin D. Roosevelt of the United States launched the Civilian Conservation Corps (CCC) in 1933. The CCC, America's largest and probably most successful NYS program, was dependent on the U.S. army for its basic administration. Military officers ran the CCC camps. Corps members got up to morning reveille, were assigned to mess duty, and performed daily drill without guns. Only civilian officials supervised their work projects. The CCC had an unexpected military linkage: Many of its former members entered military service early in World War II and easily adapted to the military lifestyle because of their experience in the CCC.

The purposes of the CCC were to perform important conservation work, alleviate a very high level of youth unemployment, and transfer money to very poor families. The CCC met its goals. From 1933 until its wartime demise in 1942, an average of 300,000 young men were at work in the CCC at any one time—a figure that represents about 30 percent of the male age cohort. The value of the work they did in projects such as planting billions of trees, building thousands of bridges, and laying more than 100,000 miles of minor roads, has been estimated at many times total program costs (Sherraden and Eberly 1982, 164–169); and the transfer of money to poor families was vital to basic sustenance as there was not the safety net of social security and welfare that came later.

It was not until 1960 that NYS received major endorsement again in America, this time in the form of a campaign speech in which John F. Kennedy proposed a Peace Corps. Kennedy received enthusiastic support from university campuses because he said he would consider making Peace Corps service an alternative to what was then a required military service (Eberly 1966, 51; 1961). As president, however, he backed away from that idea because he felt the draft was too hot an issue. One consequence was that some local draft boards—which exercised wide discretion in the treatment of persons called for the draft—exempted Peace Corps cadets from military service, others deferred them until they returned home, and still others drafted them while still in the Peace Corps.

Germany

Germany came by way of NYS accidentally. The post–World War II constitution stated, "No one shall be forced to do war service with arms against his conscience" (Kuhlmann and Likkert 1993, 98). So when military conscription returned in 1958, provision had to be made for COs. This provision led to a program of alternative service for COs, termed Zivildienst; German CO applicants had to convince a review panel that they were genuine COs. Only a handful of young men became COs.

However, the number gradually rose during the 1960s and the necessity of convincing a panel of one's genuineness in expressing a conscientious objection to war service led to complaints that the system discriminated in favor of well-educated people who could better present their convictions. In the 1970s West Germany took a number of measures to correct the situation. By the early 1980s, a young man had only to sign a paper saying he was a CO; he was then assigned to alternative civilian service instead of military service. When that practice was later found to be unconstitutional, it was replaced by the young man writing a letter giving his reasons for his request for CO status. About 85 percent of such requests were approved, and by 2000 there were some 180,000 young men classified as COs who were either serving in Zivildienst or awaiting assignment to it. The length of civilian service is one-third longer than military service.

According to the Federal Ministry of Defense, the proportion of young men available for conscription who enter Zivildienst is 38 percent, somewhat higher than the 30 percent going into military service. For comparison, two full-time volunteer service programs unrelated to military service—the Voluntary Social Year and the Voluntary Ecology Year—enroll about 1 percent of a single-year cohort of young people. Since 90 percent are young women, this means that nearly 2 percent of young women enroll in one of the programs.

There was also a dramatic shift in the public's view of NYS. As the number of young men performing civilian NYS at any one time rose from a few thousand in the 1960s to a plateau of about 130,000 by the mid-1980s, and as a larger percentage of the German public has become familiar with the work of the COs, the public attitude shifted from negative—viewing COs as deviants and draft-dodgers—to positive (Kuhlmann 1982, 146).

China

As with the Etruscans and Romans of old, China's largest NYS has been done by men in military service. Mao Zedong intended that virtually everyone in China be occupied in a way that served the greater good of the Chinese people. Thus, his statement that "there is no profound difference between the farmer and the soldier" might as easily be applied to the teacher or the fisherman or the factory worker (Glick 1967, 41). Such a broad definition of service complicates the task of identifying NYS activities as distinct from salaried employment.

Still, there can be little doubt that the young men of the People's Liberation Army (PLA) have provided an enormous amount of civilian service. From 1950 to 1984, the Chinese army constructed 8,000 miles of railway, planted hundreds of millions of trees, brought a million acres of land under irrigation, constructed forty iron and steel factories and twenty coal mines, provided medical assistance and public health education to much of the population, and responded to thousands of natural disasters (Sherraden and Eberly 1990, 36).

China also provides incentives for young people outside the military to do NYS kinds of activities. In its Poverty Alleviation Relay Project (PARP), university graduates are asked to go to the countryside to teach school for one or two years. They know that doing so greatly increases their chances of obtaining a desired job and decent housing on their return to the city. PARP costs the central government about US$900 per cadet-year, a sum that includes health care, some travel, and a stipend for things such as food and clothing. The locality where cadets serve normally provides housing and a bicycle (Hou 2002). The PARP is administered by the Chinese Young Volunteers Association (CYVA), established in 1994 to promote volunteer service activities. One of its programs is called One-on-One, in which young volunteers are individually linked with retired persons.

With 5 million college young people going to rural areas for short terms in 2001 to serve as team members providing health and education services, and many of the 68 million members of the Communist Youth League serving part-time locally in schools, neighborhoods, and factories, the youth service activities in China are very substantial (Wang 2004).

Israel

The evolution of NYS in Israel resembles that in China in some ways. Chairman Mao's dictum that there is no difference between a farmer and a soldier also applies to Israel. Soon after independence, the Knesset (Israeli parliament) passed a military service law declaring, "agricultural training will be an integral part of military service" (Glick 1967, 135). Even before the Jewish state was created in 1947, Jewish residents established various youth organizations and pioneer youth movements that they described to the British overlords as nothing more than Boy Scout troops. But much of the underlying rationale for these youth groups was to develop a cadre of young people who would be trained in military discipline, able to endure long route marches through the desert, and ready to defend the nation-state when the time came. With the birth of Israel and its frequent wars with its neighbors, Israel maintained a high state of military readiness combined with development of the land and other nation-building missions.

Both young men and young women serve in the Israeli Defense Forces on a compulsory basis. As recently as the 1980s conscription was almost universal and included most Jewish youth, both men and women (Arab youth are exempted). But by 2000, the number had edged toward 50 percent as the army became increasingly professionalized. The low participation rate concerns many Israelis who believe that service by young people is both vital to national development and a rite of passage to adulthood.

A number of NYS programs have developed over the years to meet this demand. Some 5,000 religious young women give a year or two of social service in Sherut Leumi (national service organizations). Another 1,000 young women of varied beliefs serve in Shlomit (a specific national service organization), which at the turn of the century included also a few Arabs and young men in their service projects. About the same number of women in the army are assigned to civilian service activities, sometimes alongside those in Sherut Leumi and Shlomit. In 2003, NYS included altogether some 7,000 young people in full-time, year-round service. Since all but a few of them are women, that equaled about 12 percent of the single-year cohort of young women.

Nigeria

Nigeria's NYS was the direct result of the civil war in the late 1960s, when one part of Nigeria—called Biafra—tried to break away from the rest of the country. Although Biafra failed in its effort to secede, Nigeria decided it must make efforts to foster national unity. University students and other youth groups called for a national youth scheme whose first projects would be the provision of relief in war-torn areas. After much debate, the head of state, General Yakubu Gowon, issued a decree in 1973 creating the National Youth Service Corps (NYSC) to develop common ties among the youth of Nigeria and to promote national unity. For its first quarter century, the NYSC was administered by the army, and then transferred to a succession of civilian ministries.

The NYSC requires all university graduates to serve for one year in a different part of the country from where they grew up. After an orientation period, NYSC cadets are posted to the place of assignment where they are expected not only to work for eleven months in a regular job, but also to initiate community development projects in the areas where they serve.

NYSC cadets serve in their professional areas. Agricultural graduates advise farmers on crops and pesticides while English majors teach high school English. The government provides stipends for them. After service, cadets are brought together again to discuss their experiences, to participate in a passing out parade, and to receive a Certificate of National Service that entitles them to be employed in Nigeria.

There seems to be a general acceptance among cadets of the value of NYSC as a means of nation-building. While many an entering cadet is not happy about being posted to a distant part of the country, a study of former corps members' attitudes to being posted away from their home areas showed that in retrospect only one in ten were negative (Akpan 1993, 295). The director-general of the NYSC reported in 2000 that "inter-tribal marriage, which would have once seemed strange, is increasingly common, and about a quarter of Corps members remain in the area of their Primary Assignment after it is finished" (Ogunkoya 2000, 31).

The NYSC operated effectively into the 1980s, when problems arose because of its increasing size and funding limitations. In 2002 the government instituted a major review of the NYSC that reaffirmed the philosophy and ideals of the Corps and prompted a number of changes in funding and logistics.

NYS Trends

In the last third of the twentieth century, three trends are discernible that have led to an increase in the number of NYS programs. These trends are the establishment of NYS programs based on the merits of NYS rather than some military reason, a gradual change in the nature of volunteer service, and an increasing recognition of the learning value of service experiences.

The Military Connection

A trend away from militarily linked NYS programs is apparent in each of the five countries reviewed above. While the initial NYS programs in each country had military linkages, the later ones do not. The United States' AmeriCorps (established in 1993), Germany's Voluntary Social Year (established in 1964), and China's Poverty Alleviation Relay Project (established in 1995) are unrelated to military service. Israel's Shlomit has a more tenuous linkage to the military than earlier NYS programs. Nigeria's National Youth Service Corps was shifted away from military control in the late 1990s and now comes under the Federal Ministry of Women's Affairs and Youth Development.

Another such example—though on a smaller scale than those described in the previous section—is to be seen in Indonesia. During its war of independence from 1945 to 1950, members of the Student Army served as schoolteachers when they were not engaged in battle. With independence in 1950, a number of those students proposed to the minister of education that all university students serve for a time as teachers. Although somewhat watered down in practice, their proposal led to the opening of dozens of secondary schools from 1950 to 1963, by which time sufficient numbers of teachers were being produced by teacher-training colleges. Later in the decade, a combined push by university students and government officials led to the creation of Kuliah Kerja Nyata (learning through real work), in which teams of about a dozen students and one or two professors worked for periods of up to six months on village development projects.

Among the programs founded primarily on the merits of NYS are the UK's Community Service Volunteers (established in 1961), India's National Service Scheme (established in 1969), Ghana's National Service Scheme (established in 1973), Costa Rica's Trabajo Comunal Universitario (established in 1975), Canada's Katimavik (established in 1977), Chile's Servicio Pais (established in 1995), and Vietnam's Organization of Young Intellectual Volunteers Participating in Rural and Mountainous Area Development (established in 1995). While cadets gain work experience and career exploration opportunities in all NYS programs, some programs are more specifically employment-oriented and include periods of skill training and classroom education as well as service. These include the Gambia's National Youth Service Scheme (1996) and Brazil's Servicio Civil Voluntario (2000).

Still, the military linkage has not disappeared. It may be seen in Europe, where Italy has recently formed an NYS as a response to the end of conscription and where Russia, Finland, Denmark, Spain, France, and Portugal have been considering NYS and in some cases testing it as well. Of course, there is another side to the coin: What happens if the draft returns? By the 1990s it was pretty well established in the United States that if there were a return to the military draft, it would be accompanied by an NYS option. The same is probably true for most European countries and a number of others as well.

The Nature of Volunteer Service

Second, just as military service has been transformed in the past hundred years, so has the perception and nature of volunteer service. In many non-Western countries it was seen as an obligation of members of an extended family or of a community. In Western countries, volunteer service was seen as a kind of noblesse oblige, in which rich people had an obligation to be generous to poor people.

The expanding role of volunteer service was given official recognition in the guidelines for International Year of Volunteers 2001: "IYV 2001 is for and about all kinds of volunteers everywhere; it is not limited to any one category of volunteer, whether formal or informal . . . domestic or international, unremunerated or modestly remunerated." The guidelines also pointed to "volunteer service schemes as accepted alternatives . . . to military conscription" (World Volunteer Web 2001).

In both Western and non-Western countries, the sense of obligation has expanded beyond family members and rich people. The governments of Nigeria and Ghana decided in 1973 that university graduates had an obligation to give a year of service, usually in their fields of study. In the United States, the sense of obligation has extended to secondary schools. For about the last fifteen years, a number of cities and states in America have made a period of community service a graduation requirement. As expected, civil libertarians challenged these actions on the grounds that they violated the constitutional restrictions on compulsory service. On appeal, the Supreme Court rejected that argument, essentially agreeing with the lower court decision that community service is as much a part of the educational process as the study of history or mathematics, which is also required for graduation.

Volunteer service is widening its scope. It has extended to those in the Peace Corps and the United Nations Volunteers who receive stipends, to those in educational institutions where service is seen as a vital part of the educational process, and to those in countries where service is seen as a responsibility of citizenship.

The Educational Linkage

Third, the strongest and probably most irreversible trend in recent decades has been the linkage between NYS and education. One of the earliest examples of this linkage is in Mexico, where in 1936 the government directed that all senior medical students serve for six months in the poorest communities. Servicio Social, as it was and is called, was so successful that it led to a doubling of the public health budget and ten years later to extension to students in other disciplines. Programs of full-time service linked with education have already been noted in the United States, Germany, China, Nigeria, Indonesia, and Vietnam.

Even larger numbers of young people are found in programs of part-time service linked with education. Service-learning, where students do part-time or short-term service in a way that is closely integrated with their studies, is offered in secondary schools in almost every country in South and North America; in many school systems it is a requirement. At the university level, Costa Rica's Trabajo Comunal Universitario is perhaps the strongest example of service-learning. Students typically work in villages in teams of ten to fifteen, accompanied by one or two professors. The professors help with the service project and conduct seminars one or more times per week in which the learning dimensions of the service experience are discussed.

Given the good sense, the momentum, and the low cost of service-learning, we think it likely that it will be widespread around the world in another twenty years or so. The major issue will be maintaining the quality of service-learning.

Lessons

Compared to many fields of human endeavor, rigorous research on NYS has been fairly limited. Still, it may be useful to put forward a number of observations based on what the two of us have studied and experienced over nearly a hundred years of combined interest in NYS. Each of the observations refers to NYS programs that are well designed and well administered.

NYS is good value for the money. Simply in terms of services rendered by cadets to persons in need and to the environment, we can expect the value of those services to exceed the cost of the program. The service impact of America's CCC has already been noted. Studies of more recent NYS programs generally show the value of services given by cadets to be of equal or greater value than program costs.

NYS also provides substantial benefits to the cadets who serve. The benefits include "work experience, career exploration, skills acquired, increased social maturity and self-esteem, increased awareness of the needs of others, and new understanding between ages, races, ethnic, and linguistic groups" (Eberly 1992, 38). For many cadets, the service experience is a rite of passage from adolescence to adulthood (Christopher 1996). The profile of benefits is different for each cadet, but if they could be quantified in monetary terms, we are fairly confident that the total value would be greater than program costs and, in some cases, greater than the value of services rendered.

Incidentally, it is the accumulation of benefits to the cadets that prevents NYS from becoming an exploitative program. Although their dollar incomes are below market wages, the sum of their psychic incomes and the value of their long-term benefits more than makes up the difference.

A corollary to the value of benefits received is found in the special case of service-learning. Although the service impact is below that of full-time NYS, service-learning students acquire some of the same values as those in NYS and their academic learning is strengthened by what they learn from their service experiences (Billig 2004, 12–17). The author of a large study of high school service-learning reported in 1987 that the study found

> participation in community service, internships, and other experiential learning programs in schools did increase the level of personal and social responsibility of participants, did result in more positive attitudes toward adults and others with whom they worked, and did increase their willingness to be active in the community. Nearly all students gained in terms of career information and exploration. They also showed modest increases in self-esteem. (Hedin 1987)

NYS can operate successfully on a large scale. There is any number of small youth service programs that have been successful, perhaps because of a particularly talented leader or a unique local situation, but that is not sufficient proof that they can function well on a large scale. NYS has operated successfully on a large scale with the CCC in the United States, Zivildienst in Germany, Sherut Leumi in Israel, and the National Youth Service Corps in Nigeria.

In order for NYS to achieve its potential, a period between nine months and two years of full-time service appears to be the optimal time span. Shorter periods fail to yield such benefits and longer periods may exploit the cadets, who risk burnout.

Nation-building is a primary reason for several NYS programs—especially those in China, Nigeria, Canada, and Vietnam—and appears to be an outcome of these NYS programs and of others designed for other purposes. Cadets become familiar with a part of their country they had not known before, and after giving a year or two of service cadets feel they have made an investment in their country. That encourages them to develop strong national loyalties, as has been true with veterans' organizations over the years.

In spite of the widely held belief that persons in compulsory NYS programs give inferior performances to those in volunteer programs, anecdotally, it is believed that this is not the case when cadets understand and accept the rationale for the compulsion. Thus, Nigerian cadets who are teaching school perform at the same level as the salaried employees teaching in the same school. The German members of Zivildienst doing the same jobs as members of the Voluntary Social Year perform them just as well.

It is likely that both communities and nations benefit from an increase in social capital and a reduction in crime, savings on welfare, unemployment payouts, and training courses. As yet, we do not have adequate research on these factors.

Directions for Research

In our view, the areas most in need of study involve longitudinal and comparative research. In the United States, stories abound of the number of former CCC cadets who have shown their grandchildren the national forest or other area where the cadet served with the boast, "That was the best year of my life." What is needed is to study NYS cadets together with control groups over an extended period to determine the extent to which the NYS experience influenced their career choices, employability, civic involvement, and other measures. Parallel studies should be made of the persons, communities, and nations served.

In doing these studies, it is important to assess not only the intended purposes of NYS, but also the unintended purposes that may derive from NYS. Such assessments would be a great boon to comparative studies because of the variety of purposes for which NYS has been designed. For example, it would appear to be difficult to compare the Vietnamese program, which is intended to influence cadets to take up jobs in rural and mountainous regions, with the German Zivildienst program, which is intended to make equitable a system of military conscription. However, an overall evaluation, which assesses the points raised in the previous section, would very likely show the extent to which the program outcomes correspond with each another.

Conclusion

If NYS is to attract a substantial proportion of young people, it must offer a strong incentive for service. Thus, large numbers of Americans joined the CCC because doing so provided some relief for the extreme poverty faced by their families. The Nigerian Youth Service Corps has a very high participation rate because refusal means that young people are not eligible for employment in Nigeria. In Germany, some young men are genuine conscientious objectors while others in Zivildienst find a period of civilian service a more agreeable option than a somewhat shorter period of military service. By contrast, NYS programs like Voluntary Social Year in Germany and Servicio Pais in Chile, which offer little external incentive but rely on the young person's inherent incentive to serve, have much smaller enrollments.

On the basis of what we have seen to date, it is safe to say that if NYS is to operate on a large scale throughout the world, there will have to be forms of the social contract that build NYS into the life of a country and of young people as integrally as the study of anatomy is woven into medical education. That social contract will vary among countries, which have different norms on matters such as individual choice, collective responsibility, remuneration, and acceptable kinds of service. Experiences with NYS in the twentieth century suggest that, in terms of the needs of individual countries, of society at large, and of young people the world over, NYS can successfully replace military service to a substantial extent. It could become in the twenty-first century as much an institution of society as military service was in the twentieth century.

References

Akpan, Edet A. 1993. Valedictory address of December 19, 1987. In *NYSC: Twenty Years of National Service,* ed. G. Enegwea, and G. Umoden. Lagos, Nigeria: Gabumo Publishing Company.

Bangkok Post. 2001. Military draft: Volunteers filling the ranks. April 13. www. bankokpost.com.

Billig, S.H. 2004. *The Research on K–12 Service-Learning: Growing to Greatness.* St. Paul, MN: National Youth Leadership Council.

Christopher, N.G. 1996. *Right of Passage: The Heroic Journey to Adulthood.* Washington, DC: Cornell Press.

Eberly, D.J. 1961. Peace Corps: Wishful thinking. *Michigan State News,* January 25, editorial.

———, ed. 1966. *A Profile of National Service.* New York: Overseas Educational Service.

———, ed. 1992. *National Youth Service: A Global Perspective.* Washington, DC: National Service Secretariat.

Gillette, A. 1968. *One Million Volunteers: The Story of Volunteer Youth Service.* Harmondsworth, UK: Penguin Books.

Glick, E.B. 1967. *Peaceful Conflict: The Non-military Use of the Military.* Harrisburg, PA: Stackpole Books.

Haltiner, K.W. 1998. The definite end of the mass army in Western Europe. *Armed Forces and Society* 25 (1): 7–36.

———. 2003. The decline of the European mass armies. In *Handbook of the Sociology of the Military,* ed. G. Caforio. New York: Kluwer Academic Press.

Hedin, D. 1987. Testimony before the House Committee on Employment Opportunities as it considers National Youth Service legislation, June 30, Washington, DC.

Hou, B.J. 2002. Interview by D.J. Eberly. Beijing, May 28.

International Institute for Strategic Studies. 2000. *The Military Balance, 2000–2001.* London: Oxford University Press.

James, W. 1968. The moral equivalent of war. In *The Writing of William James,* ed. J.J. McDermott. New York: Random House.

Kuhlmann, J. 1982. West Germany: The right not to bear arms. In *National Service: Social, Economic and Military Impacts,* ed. M.W. Sherraden, and D.J. Eberly. New York: Pergamon Press.

Kuhlmann, J., and E. Likkert. 1993. Federal Republic of Germany: Conscientious objection as social welfare. In *The New Conscientious Objection,* ed. C.C. Moskos, and J.W. Chambers II. New York: Oxford University Press.

Moskos, C.C. 2000. Toward a postmodern military: The United States as a paradigm. In *The Postmodern Military: Armed Forces After the Cold War,* ed. C.C. Moskos, D.R. Segal, and J.A. Williams. New York: Oxford University Press.

Moskos, C.C., D.R. Segal, and J.A. Williams, eds. 2000. *The Postmodern Military: Armed Forces After the Cold War.* New York: Oxford University Press.

Ogunkoya, K. 2000. The Nigerian experience in the role of National Youth Service. In *Building Citizenship and Society,* ed. R. Gal. Jerusalem: Carmel Institute for Social Studies.

Rosenstock-Huessy, E. 1978. *Planetary Service.* Essex, VT: Argo Books.

Sherraden, M., and D.J. Eberly. 1982. The economic value of service projects. In *National Service: Social, Economic and Military Impacts,* ed. M. Sherraden, and D.J. Eberly. New York: Pergamon Press.

Sherraden, M., and D.J. Eberly. 1990. China: Youth service during economic reform and the opening to the West. In *The Moral Equivalent of War: A Study of Non-*

military Service in Nine Nations, ed. D. Eberly, and M. Sherraden. Westport, CT: Greenwood Press.

Von-Bredow, W. 1999. New roles for armed forces and the concept of democratic control. Paper presented at the biennial conference of the Inter-university Seminar on Armed Forces and Society (IUS), October 22–24, Baltimore, Maryland.

Wang, M. 2004. E-mail message from the Chinese Young Volunteers Association to D.J. Eberly, November 19.

Weiss, T.G., and K.M. Campbell. 1991. Military humanitarianism. *Survival* 33 (5): 451–465.

World Volunteer Web. 2001. International Year of Volunteers 2001: Guidance notes. www.worldvolunteerweb.org/events/iyv/networking/guidance.htm.

II

NATIONAL SERVICE
POLICY, POTENTIAL, AND EFFECTS

_____ 3

The Effects of National Service in Africa, With a Focus on Nigeria

Ebenezer Obadare

The Civic Service Landscape in Africa

A reasonable appreciation of the state of national youth service on the African continent may be gleaned from sharply contrasting developments in three southern African countries: Botswana, South Africa, and Namibia. In April 2000, the government of Botswana decided to wind up the Tirelo Setshaba, the national service program that had been inaugurated in 1980 to "promote self-development, cross cultural exposure, and to build work experience for its participants" (Molefe and Weeks 2001).

The decision to terminate the program was actually made in 1998, the same year that the _Green Paper on National Youth Service_ was released in South Africa. The Green Paper's euphoria about the value of national service was clearly evident in its confident affirmation that "service occurs where development, structured learning and service to communities interact" (Mulaudzi 2000, 132).

The picture that comes to the observer from these developments is complicated: How can the disillusionment with national service in one country —Botswana—be reconciled with optimism in two others—South Africa and

Namibia? One way is to examine why the three countries have embarked on radically opposed trajectories at virtually the same time. A plausible explanation might be that Botswana, having implemented a program of national service for the better part of two decades, has exhausted the gamut of social advantages that national service has to offer, while South Africa for example, recently free following decades of apartheid minority rule, is yet to experience the same. Thus, while Botswana appears to have seen the limitations of national service as a mechanism for social engineering, South Africa and Namibia, it would appear, are merely waiting to discover the same. The logical deduction may be that national service, while laudable, almost always falls short of its founding goals.

However, this may be the wrong conclusion to draw, for evidence from the rest of the continent seems to indicate that the idea of national service is increasing in popularity. A review of the phenomenon in Africa reveals that in the past decade, in addition to South Africa, where plans for a national service program are already in an advanced stage, two other countries have floated and begun implementing the idea (Perold 2000)—Eritrea in 1994 and The Gambia, which actually received technical assistance from Nigeria in 1996. Given these developments, the development in Botswana would seem atypical indeed.

Of course this is not to suggest that all is well. National service has encountered serious problems at inception as well as during implementation and its presumed effects have come under scrutiny. On its own, this is not necessarily a bad development. In a majority of cases, criticism of national service on the continent has included brilliant ideas for its reinvention (as is currently the case in Nigeria, for instance), and proponents of national service have not been shy to incorporate some of these proposals in their bid to shore up existing programs. African states seem to have been cured of the rash optimism of the early postindependence era, when national youth service was seen as an automatic route to social development and national integration (Iyizoba 1982).[1]

Yet there is little doubt that the moral (and financial) investment in the phenomenon of national service remains high indeed, a situation that has been further encouraged by the global resurgence of both policy and scholarly interest in the institution over the past decade or so. This, in fact, is the overall context for the reflections in this chapter, the central aim of which is to examine the effects of national service in Africa (McBride, Benítez, Sherraden, and Johnson 2003).[2] While events in Botswana and South Africa and Namibia respectively seem to provide a timely continental impetus, the international environment appears to make the project doubly imperative.

National Service: Global Perspectives

> The global proliferation of service programs indicates a tacit
> presumption of their positive nature.
> —Brav, Moore, and Sherraden, *Limitations of Civil Service*

In David Selbourne's quasi-conservative volume *The Principle of Duty: An Essay on the Foundations of the Civic Order* (1994), we are offered an incisive critique of the contemporary liberal order, culminating in why, in the author's critical view, its moral foundations are in urgent need of reconstruction. Selbourne's disgust with the contemporary moral order is clearly evident in the surfeit of epithets with which he describes it. Thus, he variously laments the contemporary "civic breakdown, extensive dissolution of citizen feeling, ethical myopia, and social and civic disorder." He also regrets the current "civic turmoil and disaggregation" and "accelerated civic disaggregation." Stressing the imperative to "recompose the civic order," Selbourne argues that the "development of the modern politics of claims-to-dutiless-rights, in the form of claims to public provision and welfare," which "is not really a politics of rights at all but an economics of benefits," has led to the corruption of the contemporary liberal order (3–98).

The remedy for this untoward situation, he suggests, is a reinstatement of the ethos of duty. Selbourne argues "the performance of duty (to self, fellows, and the civic order) is the morally superior, as well as the historically prior constituent of human association, particularly when it is set against the claims of right" (3). Furthermore, he insists, "that which citizens owe by way of duty both to one another and to the civic order which they together compose is ethically and logically prior to the relation between themselves and *the state*" (5).

While classical philosophy has always struggled with the dilemma of finding the correct moral balance between practical, necessary obligation to one's political community and blind subordination to the same community, Selbourne unabashedly affirms the priority of duties over rights, and while he does not mention the word *service* directly, his is easily one of the most powerful statements of the contemporary case for a return to the idea. For him, the challenge for our times is not whether the principle of duty can withstand the ascendance of the neoliberal politics of rights, but "how individual self-realisation may be made compatible with civic order" (8).

Selbourne has written at a critical crossroads in global evolution, one in which globalizing markets and antigovernmental paranoia have obscured our civic vision (Barber 1998, 37–38). Whatever the character of the contemporary order, there seems to be a fair consensus that the collapse of both the

Soviet empire and its ideology in the late 1980s represents a critical moment in the remaking of world order (Chandhoke 1995; Huntington 1997). The official collapse of the socialist project in the former Soviet Union and its Eastern European satellites ushered in a market economy triumphalism, of which Fukuyama's "end of history" thesis remains arguably the most forceful articulation (Fukuyama 1992).

Scholarship continues to be divided between those who privilege external factors for the collapse of the Soviet experiment and those who accent factors that are endogenous to the former socialist societies. One factor, however, on which there seems to be some agreement is what Nairn calls the "re-animation of civil society," indicating the groundswell of critical public energy whose pressure on the Soviet regime partly occasioned its sensational collapse (1997, 75). As an idea, civil society has ever since enjoyed a fascinating, if intriguing, conceptual career, but one thing appears to be constant: its imagination as a possible answer to the failings of the state, be it the Stalinist states in Eastern Europe and the former Soviet Union, the one-party state in Africa, or what Reitzes refers to as the "overburdened welfare states of Western Europe" (1994, 102).

The contemporary revival of the idea of civil society is therefore partly grounded in a certain expectation: it will deliver on those fronts where the state has tried and failed. While this is largely correct, what drives civil society from region to region also, quite expectedly, varies. According to Marschall,

> in the developing world, after decades of failed, state-centered development strategies, the lesson was driven home that without the *participation of indigenous communities,* these strategies will not succeed . . . in post-communist countries, it has become clear that civil society is what makes democracy work . . . [while] . . . in Western consumer societies, there is a growing recognition of the need for a *renewal of civic value.* (1998, 31; emphasis added)[3]

Overall, the world seems to have entered a period of change with evolving perceptions of federal roles and citizen responsibilities. Indeed, the institution of civic service has even been touted as capable of offering a headway as humanity at large continues to search for enduring solutions to transnational problems, including those (like the threat of ecocide) that on the surface appear not to lend themselves to civic examination—thus, Sherraden's belief that "service offers considerable promise as an institution that can respond to the major challenges facing our species and planet" (2001, 10).

This is not to suggest that the phenomenon of service is new. Indeed, the notion of service in whatever form has been an integral part of the history of human communities from the earliest times (Moskos 1988; McBride, Benítez,

Sherraden, and Johnson 2003). What seems to be relatively new, however, is the increased "presumption of [its] positive nature" (Brav, Moore and Sherraden 2002, 1), and the growing realization of the possibility of service as a veritable means of enhancing citizenship (Rossant 1988).

This is the overall context for examining the effects of national service in Africa, especially as an increasing number of African countries are seriously considering developing their own national service programs. This examination should help identify both some of the problems encountered in the implementation of existing programs and practical solutions to them. In particular, it would seem that the rest of the continent has a lot to learn from the case of Nigeria (its own definite challenges notwithstanding), where, after thirty-odd years, the National Youth Service Corps (NYSC) has entered a crucial new phase. Before going ahead, a description of the sociopolitical context of national service in Africa is necessary.

National Service in Africa: Context and Issues

This section is prefaced with an admission and a caveat. The social and geographic canvas that this analysis covers is very broad indeed. Africa is a massive continent, and one may not be able to go beyond merely general insights even when it is obvious that exact knowledge of a particular situation is required. The researcher's situation is worsened by the relative dearth of comparative literature on national service on the continent. This poverty of comparative studies becomes all the more intriguing when it is realized that national service programs in many African countries have taken their inspiration and drawn useful lessons from sister countries' experiences. Two examples illustrate this point. The first is the case of the government of The Gambia, which sought technical assistance from the directorate of the Federal Ministry of Women's Affairs and Youth Development in Nigeria to set up its own program in 1996. Second, the report of the technical committee on the re-organization of the NYSC in Nigeria actually contains several direct references to the service experience of other African countries (Federal Ministry of Women's Affairs and Youth Development 2002).

How then do we account for this obvious dissonance between official policy and scholarship? One plausible reason might be the scarcity of financial resources. A comprehensive analysis of national service in Africa will require a huge fiscal outlay that is clearly beyond what many funding bodies can afford. Second, the phenomenon of national service belongs to that area of domestic politics that traditional political science has continued to neglect, a situation that is only just beginning to receive the necessary redress.

As a result, this paper draws on both country-specific literature and the few existing pancontinental studies of national service. In addition, information on national service in other African countries is accessed via the Internet. Finally, this paper has benefited from McBride, Benítez, Sherraden, and Johnson's 2003 study of civic service worldwide. To begin with, we present at a glance a picture of national service programs in Africa (see Table 3.1).

The idea of national service in postcolonial Africa is best understood within the context of the socioeconomic pressures that beset the newly independent states in the early 1960s. Two such pressures seem to have been replicated across the continent. These were the twin issues of youth unemployment and the emigration of young unskilled people from rural areas to urban settings. African countries have always had a substantial youth population. For example, according to a UNESCO study, by the early 1980s, young women and men under the age of twenty-five constituted up to 60 percent of the total population of Africa. In the immediate postindependence period, therefore, official concern centered on finding a solution to these problems, especially as the urban unemployment situation steadily worsened. This was the case, for example, in Kenya (Gillette 1977). The idea of national service emerged within this context as a way to stem the unhealthy rural-urban drift, impart useful skills in the bourgeoning youth population, and provide temporary employment for the increasing number of high school graduates.

Thus, national service was seen, not as something possessing any intrinsic value, but as a possible solution to identified problems in the youth-rural-urban migration interface. The allied social project of using national service as a tool for national integration amid the fierce articulation of rival ethnic identities appears, in this light, as an afterthought. This is not to deny that there were objective problems in the nascent political space that national service might have definitely helped in obviating. The point is that the idea of national service seems to have been stumbled on and adopted for its sheer utilitarian value as opposed to a clear recognition of its innate potential for enhancing citizenship (Moskos 1988).

This misrecognition of the value of service has been partly responsible for the situation across the continent in which successive regimes have expressed a certain impatience with the perceived inability of national service to deliver the goods, the goods here ranging from national integration and cross-cultural exposure in Botswana to raising the moral tone of young people in Nigeria. In fact, there seems to have been a definite perception that the average university graduate was a member of the privileged elite who needed to pay back by rendering some compulsory service to the country (Molefe and Weeks 2001).[4]

In the case of Nigeria, the cause célèbre was the Civil War (1967–1970), which apparently ruptured the young nation's tender civic bonds and made the task of national reintegration particularly urgent (especially of the Igbo-

41

Table 3.1

National Service in Africa at a Glance

Country	Name of program	Year established	Target	Types of activities	Duration	Age limit	Mandatory/ voluntary
Botswana	TS (*Tirelo Setshaba*)	1980	"O" Level secondary school leavers	Teaching, health service and general development delivery	12 months		Voluntary initially, became mandatory in 1984
Eritrea	National Service Program	1994	Every youth of 18 years and above	Military, followed by civic/development duties	18 months statutorily, but could be indeterminate		Mandatory
Gambia, The	The Gambia National Youth Service Scheme	1996 (with technical assistance from Nigeria)	Single, unemployed youth with at least nine years of schooling and no criminal record	Skills training and community development	22 months	25	Voluntary
Ghana	Ghana National Service Scheme (NSS)	1973	Initially university graduates, later expanded to include youth age 18 and above. Now only graduates.	Public service, teaching, industry. Of late emphasis on rural development	12 months	45	Mandatory
Kenya	National Youth Service (NYS)	1964	"Militant," unemployed and unmarried youth (ages 18–22)	Development, para-military, and police duties	24 months	22	Voluntary

Biafra). A similar situation existed in postapartheid South Africa. Just as Nigeria needed to expose youth to "people in different parts of the country with a view to removing prejudices, eliminating ignorance, and confirming at first hand the many similarities among Nigerians of all ethnic groups," South Africa badly needed to do the same, although this time along racial contours (Federal Ministry of Women's Affairs and Youth Development 2002, 10).

For Eritrea, which became independent in 1993, the motivation was even clearer. The young country needed to put enough men under arms to confront the perceived Ethiopian threat to its sovereignty and national integrity. As Araia has noted, it was obvious that Eritrea as "a small and poor nation, could ill-afford a large standing army and thus the country would have a pool of well-trained reservists who would be activated for exigencies" (2002, 9). Consequently, the national service program was started in 1994, shortly after the soldiers of the war for independence were demobilized.

Similarly, postbellum Kenya needed to act quickly in respect of the thousands of young veterans who had fought the war of independence against the British. Thus, while Kenya had to "relieve youth unemployment, create a pool of trained and disciplined young people to support the army and police force, undertake national development projects and create national cohesion," as Khasiani has noted, it also had to reorient and assimilate the militant youth whose continued resistance could be a disruptive factor as the young nation took its first steps toward political and economic development (Khasiani 2000, 2). Symbolically, therefore, "the Kenya National Youth Service (NYS) was created by an Act of Parliament in 1964 at the insistence of the youth wings of the political parties which had been engaged in the struggle for independence" (Khasiani 2002, 2).

Given the diversity of the social canvas, plus the fact that political and economic developments have unfolded in different African countries at an uneven pace, it is logical to expect that national service in Africa should produce a variety of outcomes, both for the servers and the served.

Inaugurated after a three-year civil war in 1973, the Nigerian NYSC program has remained a reference point for other African countries. The scheme is actually one of the oldest on the continent, preceded only by the service programs in Zambia, which started in 1963, and Kenya, 1964. Officials of the NYSC directorate in Nigeria have provided technical assistance to sister African countries, notably The Gambia. The program celebrated its thirtieth anniversary in May 2003 amid criticism that it has derailed from its founding goals. The following excerpt from the report of the technical committee on the reorganization of the NYSC set up by the Federal Ministry of Women's Affairs and Youth Development summarizes the general criticism.

The Scheme has over the years become associated with many problems, in particular, the explosion in the number of corps participants and the inability of government to adequately fund the Scheme. This has created serious distortions in the Scheme and undermined its efficiency and integrity ... there is also a general public perception ... that the objectives of the Scheme are no longer being met. (Federal Ministry of Women's Affairs and Youth Development 2002, viii)

How serious are these claims and what are the challenges facing the NYSC program given persisting skepticism about its usefulness? Thirty years after its inception, there exists as yet no comprehensive analysis of the effects of national service in Nigeria on both the server and the served. Existing literature has evaluated the scheme's effectiveness in achieving the founding objective of fostering national unity in the face of ethnic diversity and has surveyed the perceptions of ex-participants of its effectiveness (Iyizoba 1982; Agu 1995; Kalu 1987). This analysis attempts to fill the existing void.[5] The following section provides background information on the Nigerian NYSC program.

The Case of Nigeria's National Youth Service Corps Program

The NYSC is a valuable source of manpower, particularly in education and healthcare in rural areas. It has made immense contributions to national development. Above all, it has helped to promote national understanding. Young Nigerians now know their country better. (*Newswatch* 1985)

Many Nigerians are yet unaware of the objectives of the scheme; some employers often see corps members as government subsidized labor market which makes them take advantage of their cheap labor and reject them after the period of service. Today, many corps members feel ashamed to wear their uniforms outside the orientation camp. This is why the uniforms are found worn by roadside beggars, mechanics and lunatics. In any case, there seems to be no more joy, honor and respect for corps members in Nigeria. (*Daily Trust* 2002)

The above excerpts from two Nigerian publications give an idea of the divergence of public and critical opinion on the effects of the NYSC in Nigeria. A cursory review of the history of the scheme shows that this divergence is nothing new. It is on record, for example, that just as a cross-section of the populace applauded the introduction of the scheme in May 1973, opposition to it was also substantial. For example, the National Union of Nigerian Students (NUNS) protested the introduction of the scheme, arguing that participation in the NYSC would delay the entry of young Nigerian university graduates into the labor market, thus unduly punishing parents who had invested in the education of their children.[6]

Thus, the sharp divide over the value of the scheme and whether or not it should be continued has always been part of its history. In the past decade, the problems associated with the scheme have mounted following a series of political events, some of which appear to raise fundamental questions about the continued existence of Nigeria as a single political entity. Arguably the most controversial of such developments remains the introduction and implementation of the Sharia penal law by some northern Nigerian states, a result of which is concern about the physical safety of corps members from secular parts of the country. The introduction of Islamic law worsened religious tensions among the nation's dominant ethnic groups (*Daily Times* 2000)[7] and precipitated "a deluge of requests for preferential postings and redeployments, which frustrate the achievement of the objectives of the Scheme" (Federal Ministry of Women's Affairs and Youth Development 2002, ix; Obayuwana and Sunday 2000, 18; Okocha and Muraina 2000, 3).[8]

Why was there such a fuss about the introduction of the Sharia, especially as its possible effects seem to have been exaggerated? The introduction of the Islamic penal code in some northern states was more symbolic than real, although this does not in any way vitiate its significance. Properly conceptualized, the Sharia law represents a fundamental challenge to the extant political order in Nigeria, posing in a very basic way an alternative religious community as opposed to the secular community that Nigerians had taken for granted (IDEA 2000). The Sharia law therefore seems to signify a basic questioning of the credo of national service, encapsulated in the second stanza of the NYSC anthem, which exhorts corps members to "put the Nation first in all."

It was, of course, not the first time that political dynamics would threaten to capsize the NYSC or at the very least jeopardize its basic objectives. It must be recalled that the program itself was a direct consequence of turbulence in the political sphere and as such likely to be influenced by political fallouts from time to time. More important, the crisis actually draws our attention to two considerations. The first is the salience of the sociopolitical context in coming to terms with the ramifications of national service, whether in Nigeria or the continent at large. In Nigeria, the fortunes of national service are often bound up with the ebbs and flows of politics, a connection that sheds critical light on the phenomenon itself. A second important consideration is that, more often than not, political crises are often helpful in highlighting problems within the scheme. Thus, as a result of the furor generated by the introduction of the Sharia, many of the problems associated with the NYSC in Nigeria came into public glare.

These problems can be divided into those internal to the NYSC, especially organizational structure, and those external to it, especially the interaction between corps members and the host communities. The NYSC program as it exists in Nigeria today is a product of the continuous interaction of these internal and external problems. The technical committee on the reorganization of the NYSC identifies the problems thus:

> Phenomenal growth in the numbers of corps participants[9] and inadequate funding[10] both affect the general state of facilities needed for its effective operation. Also, insecurity resulting from ethnic and religious crises as well as high post-service unemployment has led to a deluge of requests for preferential postings and redeployments, which frustrate the achievement of the objectives of the Scheme. Consequently, there is surplus of *corpers*[11] in some States, exacerbating the incidences of corps rejection, under utilization, acute accommodation problems, and difficulty in meeting other welfare needs of corps members. (Federal Ministry of Women's Affairs and Youth Development 2002, viii, ix, 26)

Some perspective is required to fully understand the ramifications of those political developments for national service, a task made more important because of similarities between the patterns observed in Nigeria and other African countries.

A major theoretical statement on the problem of civic decline in Africa is Peter Ekeh's 1975 study, "Colonialism and the Two Publics in Africa." In it, Ekeh famously advanced the thesis that instead of a single public that, apparently, is the hallmark of "modern" societies everywhere, there are two publics in Africa. The "primordial public" is "moral and operates on the same moral imperatives as the private realm"; the "civic public" is amoral and lacks the generalized moral imperatives operative in the private realm and in the primordial public (91–112).

These two publics of African politics emerged in the context of colonialism and postindependence politics. While the civic realm continues to be seen because that of appropriation as it is identified with the colonial enterprise, the primordial public continues to enjoy the civic allegiance of the populace because of its perceived authenticity. Ekeh uses this theoretical proposition to unlock the taxation conundrum in African communities, in particular the riddle of why many citizens who would normally hold back from paying into the coffers of the state remit enthusiastically into the coffers of their ethnic and hometown associations. Ekeh's thesis has had its fair share of criticism (Trager 2001). Nevertheless Ekeh's argument remains crucial to understanding the crisis of civic loyalty across postcolonial Africa. It helps explain the failure of both the state and national mobilization across the continent.

In an earlier section, it was argued that part of the reason why the call to service worldwide has become so compelling of late is the perceived failure of the welfare state and the associated conviction that service can resurrect the civic energy that is needed to reclaim the spirit of community and enlightened patriotism. It is this desired missing element that Moskos defines as "civic content," or

> the performance of citizen duties that allow individuals to have a sense of the civic whole—a whole that is more important than any single person or category of persons. It is upon some such norm of fulfillment of a civic obligation, upon some concept of serving societal needs outside the marketplace, upon some sense of participation in a public life with other citizens that the idea of national service builds. (Moskos 1988, 2)

In general, Africa's developing countries appear to be in great need of this all-important content. There is some agreement that the postcolonial state on the continent has failed, victim of a rapacious political elite, a hostile international economic environment, endemic public sector corruption, and the corrosive influence of persistent ethnonational mobilization (Ake 1996; DFID 2003). Over the past two decades, this steadily worsening situation has occasioned two types of responses, recalling Hirschman's famous postulation regarding "exit" and "voice."

The exit option takes two forms: rural-urban migration and emigration abroad. Recent studies of urbanization trends have shown that "Africa's urban settlements are growing in both number and size faster than in any other region of the world" (Hirschman 1970, 2; see also Matovu 2002; Ghai 2000). In fact, the urban population of Africa is believed to be growing by 6 percent per annum, twice as fast as that of Latin America or East Asia. For most young people in Africa today, migration to the city is merely the first step in a process that ultimately terminates in any of the major Western capitals (Afolayan 2002, 743–756).

The voice option, on the other hand, involves a series of actions, ranging from political activity geared to reforming the state and holding it accountable, to social projects aimed at extracting territorial concessions from the state through the instrumentality of violence. At times, this kind of approach straddles both the exit and voice options, for in many places the threat of secession has often proved to be nothing but a strategy for gaining improved welfare and greater concessions within extant political boundaries. Thus, while a good number of African countries have had to contend with outright secessionist attempts, the situation in Nigeria arguably embodies the use of exit to gain more voice in the political system (Sesay et al. 2003; Ikelegbe 2001, 1–24).[12]

The sum total of the development challenges and political strife is the civic denudation that has become a defining feature of political life across Africa, a pattern that is compounded by the poverty of social policy especially in regard to youth. Khasiani's summation that "while youth policy does exist in Kenya, it is fragmented, lacks clarity and is not comprehensive" unfortunately holds true for most African countries (2000, 2). What results is a paradoxical situation in which the very target of national service in African countries—young people—appear not only to have lost interest in their countries of birth, but also to be permanently looking over their shoulders for exit opportunities (BBC Africa Service 2003).[13] This is the crucial sociopolitical context of national service and any appraisal of its effects in Africa. If, therefore, as Moskos argues, "a civic-oriented national service program must ultimately rest on some kind of enlightened patriotism" (1988, 7), what are the prospects for African countries in the context of the profound civic apathy sketched above? How do you stimulate patriotism (enlightened or not) amid the evident slide in common commitment to citizens' obligations and the loss of faith in the state as a welfare-enhancing institution?[14]

These dilemmas speak to African polities at large. Part of the wider question that apparent civic withdrawal in the Nigerian context raises, for example, is whether any act of citizenship or dedication to service can be expected of persons whose overwhelming historical experience has been permanent disempowerment and marginalization. Can individuals who have not enjoyed the benefits of citizenship be expected to contribute to the political whole? Can performance of duties be expected in a situation of continued denial of rights?

If the situation in Nigeria is a reliable barometer, then the answers are by no means positive. My own research into the service-citizenship nexus in Nigeria argues for citizenship as being *prior to* the performance of service (Obadare 2004). This view negates dominant views that service is *antecedent to* and necessarily impacts positively on citizenship. Using data from open-ended interviews, questionnaires, and focus group discussions, my research traced the multiple ways in which political forces have shaped the implementation of the NYSC program in Nigeria and the attitudes of corps members. Thus, while it is evident that the national service program in Nigeria has had qualified success in relation to its founding objectives, the study concluded that "the NYSC could effectively enhance patriotism *only if* the state discharges its reciprocal obligation to youths in the country" (Obadare 2004, 52).

Indeed, if the NYSC has failed to promote citizenship values in Nigerian youths toward the construction of a new *civis,* the study argues that this failure can only be attributed to the objective and subjective conditions of the sociopolitical context. From the second half of the 1980s, the Nigerian state has witnessed a relentless savaging of the Nigerian idea, resulting in the inevitable loss of political and social solidarity. This loss is indexed by the upsurge in interethnic and interfaith clashes, which, for its part, has enhanced the failure to build a multi-faith, transethnic national ethos in the country. These overarching changes in Nigeria resonate continentally, and it is within their parameters that one needs to examine the effects of national service in Africa.

National Service in Africa: An Analysis of Effects

> An idea that almost but not quite crystallises itself in the mind . . . is like a thread that wilts before reaching the eye of the needle. After advising and reporting on youth services in Africa for fifteen years I cannot help wondering if they haven't met a similar fate: a great idea that never quite realized its full potential. (Gillette 1977, 95)

Contextualizing Gillette's pessimism is a recent movie, *Agunbaniro*,[15] from Nigeria's fast expanding home-video industry.[16] In the movie, corper Femi, having taken off brilliantly as a moral beacon par excellence, soon meets his waterloo. His sexual liaisons result in the impregnation of a good number of village girls, and he has to escape for dear life with the entire savings of the village cooperative that he helped set up. He eventually finds salvation and curses his erstwhile morass, but the bond of goodwill and trust between the national service corps member and the community has been ruptured irretrievably. Significantly too, corper Femi fails to provide inspiring leadership in a context where much is expected of him. *Agunbaniro* is a subtle commentary on contemporary national service in Nigeria—an indictment, a moral critique, and a grim reflection on the distrust that appears to exist between the servers (youth corps members) and the served (the communities) across the country.

As suggested earlier, the apparently contradictory developments in different African countries (fatigue in Botswana relative to euphoria in South Africa and Namibia) point to a lack of consensus in regard to the perceived effects of national service. Part of the problem, to be sure, is the misplaced hope that national service might provide a panacea for the multiple ills of the different societies. Thus, while national service can and does "instill work habits, provide job training and basic education," and "serve unmet social and environmental needs," it seems to discharge such functions best only in a situation whereby it exists to complement larger social policy addressed to these same problems (Moskos 1988, ix).

This was one of the major conclusions from the Nigerian study. National service cannot exist in relative sociopolitical isolation, and it seems to work best where citizens' perception of their obligations to the state and other citizens is strong. Failing this, the *server* merely wanders through the motions of *service,* while the *served* view the service program with suspicion or outright derision. A clear majority of those interviewed (both serving and former corps members) during the research insisted that the state ought to discharge its obligations to the servers before expecting any service from them. This position clearly contradicts Selbourne's contention that duties ought to take precedence over rights (Obadare 2004).

Notably, given the general situation in many African countries where, as demonstrated earlier, it is hardly possible to speak of citizenship and civic commitment in any substantive sense (Taiwo 2000; Adebanwi 2003; Kazah-Toure 2003), the possible effects of national service are tempered. Since this civic erosion has taken place over a period of time, one observes the quite disturbing pattern in which the real achievements that seemed to follow the introduction of national service have steadily given way to institutional despondency. Botswana offers an excellent illustration.

When the government of Botswana launched the Tirelo Setshaba in 1980, expectations were quite high. The scheme was "designed as an elite program, mainly for those who would go on to tertiary education" (Molefe and Weeks 2001, 106). There was, indeed, strong justification for its introduction: a grim shortage of human resources, particularly teachers, in the remote areas (Molefe and Weeks 2001, 107). More crucially, there was a void in the education system as its tertiary component was yet to be developed. O-level graduates were therefore expected to spend the gap year following twelve years of schooling developing a different array of skills and simultaneously contributing to national development.[17] From an initial cohort of twenty-eight volunteers, the program took in more than 6,000 participants by the close of the 1990s. Naturally, implementation costs also rose. According to Molefe and Weeks, by the late 1990s the program costs were over US$10 million a year.

Finance was therefore one reason why the government decided to lay the scheme to rest; but it may not have been the overriding reason. In reality, by the mid-1990s, trends had emerged which suggested that a section of the public had become dubious about the value of the scheme. It was observed, for example, that the well-off tended to dispatch their children overseas to avoid the mandatory one-year service, while an increasing number of students saw it as a frustrating delay in their journey to tertiary education. As such, rather than being a year of learning as was initially envisaged, Tirelo Setshaba became, in the indelible words of a participant, "a year of forgetting" (Molefe and Weeks 2001, 106).

To compound matters, government, too, had clearly grown weary of the program, arguing that it benefited a small elite minority, about 17 percent of the total youth population, excluding the majority. Molefe and Weeks also make the interesting speculation that globalization and international expectations may have had adverse consequences for the participants in the program, but they do not develop the point any further.

The foregoing scenario should make any evaluation of the effects of national service in Botswana fairly straightforward, or so it seems. The government's decision to commit the scheme to the scrap heap can mean only one thing—it was not having the desired effects. However, the situation was much more complex than that, an indication of how difficult it can be to determine the effects of national service in any country. In fact, contrary to the negative signal given by the decision to terminate the program, a majority of participants evaluated by Molefe and Weeks indicated that they had learned from the teaching and work experience that were integral to service, while nearly 80 percent of former servers said that the program had been *good, very good,* or *excellent.* Participants also agreed that the program went a long way in deepening their knowledge of other groups and their cultures, which was one of its set objectives.

One obvious deduction from the above is that national service can have opposite effects for both server and served. For Botswana, despite the underside of general impatience with the program by participants who saw it as an unnecessary delay, the overall effect for the servers seems to have been truly positive. The judgment in respect of the served as well as the larger public is, however, more mixed. While Tirelo Setshaba generally helped in alleviating the problems of manpower shortage as designed, there were persistent complaints that participants brought with them the ugly face of urban life—alcoholism, overt sexuality, and drugs, thus unwittingly corrupting young people in their host communities. It is interesting to recall that national youth service has attracted similar criticism in Nigeria, as evidenced by *Agunbaniro.* It is possible, therefore, that the government considered that the negative effects of the program outweighed the positive ones and decided to eliminate it, with any lingering doubts erased by the forbidding cost of implementation.

The travails of national service in Botswana ought to impart fundamental lessons about the politics and dynamics of national service in Africa. Tirelo Setshaba was introduced to fill a perceived gap in the education system, and it appeared initially to be an appropriate measure. With the passage of time, however, participants and primary beneficiaries (especially the host rural communities) became dubious about its continued relevance, thus strengthening the argument for its eventual stoppage. With minor variations owing to contextual variations, the same pattern can be observed in, say, Eritrea.

Introduced in 1994 soon after the country's independence, national service in Eritrea is mandatory for every citizen of eighteen years and above. Its founding vision, according to Araia, was, among other things, to introduce postwar Eritrean youth to military discipline and as such close the perceived gap between the Tegadelti (freedom fighters) and the emerging generation

(Araia 2002). As noted earlier, there was also a more urgent rationale in the form of the uncertain military situation involving the newly independent country and Ethiopia, with whom it had fought a protracted and bitter war (Negash and Tronvoll 2000). As a result, national service in Eritrea was a combination of both military training and purely civic duties, including building bridges, harvesting plantations, terracing hills, and participating in illiteracy eradication campaigns (Araia 9). On the whole, this ensured that certain tangible benefits accrued to the served.

The situation with respect to the servers is, however, less inspiring. Drawing on an earlier study by Mayer and Schoepflin, Araia has argued that military service in Eritrea has been a massively disruptive factor in the life course of the young serving population. Mayer and Schoepflin had insisted that states generally intervene drastically in the life course of their citizens when at war, thereby altering their collective life course by drafting a large number of them into military duties (Mayer and Schoepflin 1989). Using Eritrea to illustrate their point, Araia divides changes in the youth life course into economic and attitudinal. This is how he summarizes the economic situation:

> Many families of the mobilized are in a critical economic situation since the young members of the family are not producing for the family for quite a long time . . . For the youth themselves, the war has affected their life course. One newspaper article puts it like this: When youth of other countries are playing with computers, Eritrean youth's fingers are left with pulling the triggers of the Kalashnikov. (Araia 2002, 9)

National military service has also had a massive impact on the attitude of the servers. According to Araia, perhaps as a result of the length of time that is spent, many have been known to evince deep behavioral changes, particularly in terms of risky behavior (unprotected sex, drugs, etc.). These changes, he observes, are clearly linked to the stress that servers are known to undergo in the course of national service.

This is not a flattering picture, but it is consistent with Gillette's pessimism and gives us some idea of the kinds of effects that national service can and has produced in two divergent contexts. We are, therefore, in a position to draw a few tentative conclusions. Contextual variations notwithstanding, national service in Africa seems to have sprung from a common social vision—to retool the youth for the challenges of a rapidly changing world, develop a sense of citizenship in what is clearly the most ebullient segment of the total population, tackle rampant illiteracy, and stimulate rural development. According to Mulaudzi, while most schemes may have emerged to address specific needs, "common to them all was the development of young people so that they can lead positive lives and contribute to the development of their communities" (2000, 135). The degree of success achieved in the pursuit of these objectives has varied from place to place, depending on the prevailing sociopolitical circumstance. In some cases, the takeoff has been trickier than anticipated. In South Africa for instance, Perold notes that because the anti-apartheid struggle involved making the country generally ungovernable, "it has been a challenge to change this attitude in young people towards positive support for reconstruction and development in the new democracy." In any case, the concept of national service remains contested because of its perceived affinity with the ancient regime's "repressive actions and militaristic tendencies" (Perold 2000).

To return to the broader canvas, it would seem as if the effects produced by national service in Africa have not been as anticipated by its founders. With hindsight, it could hardly have been otherwise. As indicated at several points in this analysis, African governments generally seem to have envisioned national service as a panacea for all the problems of economic development, low literacy, massive (youth) unemployment, and national integration. If their undue optimism has not been repaid, the blame cannot certainly be laid at the doorstep of the idea. Of course this is not to ignore the many positive achievements attributable to national service across the continent. As we have learned in the case of Botswana, for example, national service was instrumental in exposing participants to other cultural norms and orientations, a significant factor in African countries where the sword of ethnic misgivings eternally hangs on shared national resources. In Nigeria, many rural dwellers credit the NYSC program for whatever fleeting acquaintance they may have had with some indexes of modernity (Iyizoba 1982).

From the foregoing, national service in Africa appears like a double-edged sword, producing contradictory effects and subtly reinforcing Kateb's worry that "political institutions that embody high moral principles in their procedures and processes too often do not prevent terrible results" (2000, 917). We propose that a helpful way of seeing through this fog is to appreciate national service itself within the context of intermingling national and international political processes. Over the past decade, African societies have been swept by a gale of radical transformations: the rapid economic globalization of the world and its unsettling consequences, the emigration of increasing numbers of (mostly young) people across the globe but mainly from the south to the north, continuing environmental degradation, and the evident helplessness of the state (Nye and Donahue 2000; Held et al. 1999; Castells 1996). All these changes have had mostly deleterious consequences for young people in Africa, where specific youth policy has often been marked by its absence (Durham 2000).

National service and its effects in contemporary Africa ought to be seen within the scope of these crushing pressures. Amid this flux, the main challenge for African states is how to retain youth interest in the project of enlightened patriotism, which is what national service is really about. This challenge is made more formidable by the fact that the state itself, ordinarily the primary focus of allegiance, is increasingly remote in the calculations of young people.

Where the state is both helpless (in dealing with the whirl of changes unfolding globally) and corrupt (as is believed to be the case in Nigeria), national service is hindered from having a range of positive effects because of significant alterations in the perception of servers. With its glorious years of perceived contribution to national integration and cultural tolerance arguably behind it, national service in Nigeria has come to be seen, in the words of an interviewee, as "young people's own share of the national cake" (Akinsan 2003). In fact, the situation in contemporary Nigeria is such that the three main categories of stakeholders in the program (the servers, the served, and the state) have in different ways exhibited what we may call service fatigue—the youth because of disillusionment with the Nigerian political process, the served because of general mistrust of youth corps members (as in Botswana), and the state because of the spiraling cost of implementation (again, like Botswana).

There seems to be some merit in each of these positions. For example, in the case of serving corps members, one notes the tendency to "see service from an economic point of view," thus contributing to "the problem of frequent requests for re-deployment and concessional posting" (Federal Ministry of Women's Affairs and Youth Development 2002, 72). With regard to the state, the expenses of maintaining each corps member have grown over the years, a situation that has led successive governments in Nigeria to adopt a series of clearly counterproductive measures. One example is the decision to reduce the age of enrollees from thirty to twenty-five, unwittingly increasing the possibility that the program might become even more exclusionary. Over the years, due possibly to the same financial constraints, graduates of monotechnics and colleges of education respectively have been barred from enrolling in the scheme. Further evidence that the state finds the cost of continued implementation prohibitive can be seen in the plan to prune down the number of orientation camps for new corps members from thirty-seven to nineteen, the confusing transfer of the scheme from the presidency to one flummoxed ministry after another, the reduction of the usual one month of paramilitary training to three weeks, and the stoppage of honors and awards at the national level. As pressure on the state mounts (both in Nigeria and the rest of the continent) to channel more funds into competing and seemingly more justifiable social welfare programs, it is reasonable to expect that more questions will be asked (and more insistently) about the continued relevance of national service. Should this happen, more countries may follow the Botswana option, a tragedy, given that the case for national service on the continent has never been clearer.

Dire as the financial situation admittedly is, it is a problem that can be innovatively tackled. As the technical committee set up in Nigeria to review the NYSC program has observed, such is its potential in terms of possible contribution to national development that everything must be done to ensure its survival. In the meantime, African governments must resist the temptation to ignore national service simply because they are unable to make it amenable to a narrow political agenda. This is one challenge that is arguably bigger than the paucity of funds.

Policy and Research Directions

Today, national service in Africa stands at a crucial intersection: between sociopolitical conditions that compel it and a resource situation that frustrates its implementation. This is the raw material from which both policy and research must forge a future, with scholarly reflections pointing the way for policy to follow. The examination above suggests some of the issues that warrant further research.

The first is the connection between national service and other youth-focused and/or service-inspired initiatives. In the case of Nigeria, the interface between the NYSC and state initiatives like the Technical Aid Corps and the National Poverty Eradication Program immediately come to mind. While research ought to ponder how to make these initiatives and the notion of national service cohere, mechanisms should be put in place at the level of policy to close the apparent gap between them. Until now, the government has tended to view these outfits as more relevant and politically more rewarding than the NYSC. Further research might unveil their essential interrelatedness.

Second, a careful perusal of national service in Africa shows that, thus far, it is overwhelmingly focused on the literate segment of the population, with a number of national service programs favoring only graduates of tertiary institutions (see Table 3.1). While the advantages inherent in this plan cannot be overemphasized, it unwittingly creates a class divide that does not bode well for the larger project of national integration. Research must begin to address the implications of this lag and to envision national service programs that embrace the literate and the nonliterate alike.

Another possible research area is determining the effects of the length of service on servers, the served, and the state. We have seen how, in the case of Eritrea, the length of service may, in part, take a toll on servers, resulting in unimagined problems.

If service is a useful tool in the struggle to advance "the human enterprise" (Sherraden 2001), research must also begin to exhume its traditional forms in African societies with a view to providing a much-needed descriptive and contextual background to contemporary national service programs, as well as suggesting what the postcolonial state might learn from these earlier forms. Researchers could also explore how the idea of service might be broadened to incorporate senior members of the community and the implications of such incorporation in the context of the civic erosion discussed earlier.

Finally, there is an urgent need for the kind of theoretically driven research that locates national service within the stream of rapid globalization, the different ways through which globalization impacts young people across the African continent, and its connection with the phenomenon of service. Molefe and Weeks's study on Botswana can be regarded as an important milestone. Youth as a social category has begun to enjoy renewed scholarly attention over the past decade, and the integration of service promises to lend greater scope and depth to an increasingly vibrant field (Herault and Adesanmi 1997).

Notes

1. Molefe and Weeks (2001) have noted that at the dawn of independence, many African countries rushed to create paramilitary, Israeli-assisted national services.

2. The emphasis here is on developments in Nigeria, and there is an exclusive focus on national service even though other forms of service, both local and international, exist in a few African countries.

3. In the case of the United States, Robert D. Putnam's 2000 influential study had already apparently confirmed fears about the unraveling of the country's civic bond (see Putnam 2000).

4. Ghana is a good example.

5. The appointment by the Federal Ministry of Women's Affairs and Youth Development of a technical committee on the reorganization of the NYSC is another example of such efforts.

6. The students' reactions were controversial, as it was rightly pointed out that a few years earlier the Conference of Nigerian Students in the Americas, apparently taking a cue from their home-based counterparts, had implored the then federal military government to introduce a national service program similar to Kwame Nkrumah's Young Pioneers in Ghana (see www.utas.edu.au/docs/ahugo/NCYS/second/five.html).

7. Several ethnic-based associations, including the Middle Belt Patriots, the Ohaneze Ndigbo, the Igbo Youth Movement, and the Igboeze Cultural Association, issued press releases asking their "sons and daughters" to reject postings to states where the Sharia was operative.

8. In general, media analyses and reports also reinforced the impression that the introduction of the Sharia was a huge drawback to the achievement of the objectives of the NYSC.

9. This number grew from an initial 2,364 corps member to more than 100,000 per service year (NYSC 2002, viii).

10. In 2001, for example, the federal government was able to meet only 67 percent of the NYSC budgetary requirements (NYSC 2002, 26).

11. This is the popular shorthand for corps members in Nigeria.

12. Since the return to civil rule in 1999, Nigeria has seen a rise in the intensity of ethnonational mobilization.

13. One example is the emerging trend whereby African athletes adopt new citizenships because of perceived material and other benefits. Many Nigerian, Moroccan, and Kenyan athletes have taken this exit option. On a more despairing note, some Nigerians have used such exit opportunities traveling to Western capitals to become prostitutes and sex slaves. See, for example, *Sunday Times Magazine* (2003) and *Sunday Punch* (2003).

14. An opinion poll by the Lagos *Guardian* indicated that a majority of 2,800 respondents from across the six geopolitical zones of the country expressed a loss of faith in government at all levels and "expressed doubts that their lives would record significant improvement from the activities of such governments" (*Guardian* 2003; Agbaje, Okunola, and Alarape 2003).

15. The word *agunbaniro* is the Yoruba word for a corps member. The literal translation is "one who climbs and descends with another," summarizing the founding notion of the corps member as someone expected to participate fully in the social life of the host community without any reservation.

16. For some reason, the home-video industry in the country has begun to focus attention on the phenomenon of national youth service. The main character in *Thunderbolt* (Mainframe Productions 2001) is Ngozi, an attractive female NYSC member who is simultaneously mistrusted by her husband and pressured for sexual favors by the local nouveau riche. Taken together with *Agunbaniro,* the film provides a good idea of, at least, the average public perception of corps members and what they represent.

17. This is what Molefe and Weeks (2001) call a "thirteenth year of education."

References

Adebanwi, W. 2003. The politics of inclusion and exclusion: Interrogating the dilemmas of citizenship in Nigeria. Unpublished mimeo.

Afolayan, M.O. 2002. The impact of the United States diversity lottery visa on elite migrants. In *Nigeria in the Twentieth Century,* ed. T. Falola. Durham. NC: Carolina Academic Press.

Agbaje, A., R.A. Okunola, and A.I. Alarape. 2003. *Perspectives on Positive Leadership in Nigeria: Report of a National Survey October–December 2002.* Lagos, Nigeria: Macmillan.

Agu, U. 1995. *NYSC and Nigerian Unity: A Critical Appraisal.* Enugu, Nigeria: Acena Publishers.

Ake, C. 1996. *Democracy and Development in Africa.* Washington, DC: Brookings Institute.

Akinsan, E. 2003. Personal interview. April 12.

Araia, B.B. 2002. Citizenship, youth situation and activism in postwar Eritrea. Paper prepared for the Social Science Research Council Workshop on Youth Violence, Activism, and Citizenship, Dakar, Senegal, June 7–10.

Barber, B. 1998. A place for us. In *Democracy as Discussion II. The Challenges and Promise of a New Democratic Era: A Handbook,* ed. S. Myers. New London, CT: Toor Cummings Center for International Studies and Liberal Arts.

BBC Africa Service. 2003. August 30.

Brav, J., A. Moore, and M. Sherraden. 2002. *Limitations of Civic Service: Critical Perspectives.* CSD Working Paper 02–12. St. Louis, MO: Washington University, Global Service Institute.

Castells, M. 1996. *The Rise of the Network Society.* Cambridge, MA: Blackwell Publishers.

Chandhoke, N. 1995. *State and Civil Society Explorations in Political Theory.* New Delhi: Sage Publications.

Daily Times (Lagos). 2000. July 12.

Daily Trust (Abuja). 2002. September 14.

Department for International Development (DFID). Nigeria. 2003. *Strategic Program of Engagement with Civil Society.* Abuja: Mimeo.

Durham, D. 2000. Youth and the Social Imagination in Africa: Introduction to Parts 1 and 2. *Anthropological Quarterly* 73 (3): 113–120.

Ekeh, P.P. 1975. Colonialism and the two publics in Africa: A theoretical statement. *Comparative Studies in Society and History* 17 (1): 91–112.

Fukuyama, F. 1992. *The End of History and the Last Man.* New York: Free Press.

Ghai, D. 2000. *Renewing Social and Economic Progress in Africa: Essays in Memory of Philip Ndegwa.* New York: St. Martin's Press.

Gillette, A. 1977. National youth services in the development of rural Africa: Some second thoughts on trying to eat the cake. *Rural Africana* 31 (2): 95–103.

Guardian (Lagos). 2003. August 4.

Held, D., D. Goldblatt, A.G. McGrew, and J. Perraton. 1999. *Global Transformations: Politics, Economics and Culture.* Stanford, CA: Stanford University Press.

Herault, G., and P. Adesanmi, eds. 1997. *Youth, Street Culture and Urban Violence in Africa.* Ibadan: IFRA.

Hirschman, A.O. 1970. *Exit, Voice, and Loyalty.* Cambridge, MA: Harvard University Press.

Huntington, S.P. 1997. *The Clash of Civilizations and the Remaking of World Order.* New York: Simon and Schuster.

Ikelegbe, A. 2001. The perverse manifestation of civil society: Evidence from Nigeria. *Journal of Modern African Studies* 39 (1): 1–24.

International Institute for Democracy and Electoral Assistance (IDEA). 2001. *Democracy in Nigeria: Continuing Dialogue(s) for Nation-Building.* Stockholm: International IDEA.

Iyizoba, W.O. 1982. Nigerian youth service corps: An evaluation of an attempt to foster national unity in the face of ethnic diversity. PhD diss., Rutgers University.

Kalu, C.N. 1987. The perceptions of ex-participants on the effectiveness of the National Youth Service Corps (NYSC) in Nigeria. PhD diss., Ohio University.

Kateb, G. 2000. Is patriotism a mistake? *Social Research* 67 (4): 901–924.

Kazah-Toure, T. 2003. The citizenship question in Nigeria. Paper presented at the 2003 Dalmina School of the Centre for Research and Documentation (CRD) Research Methodology Workshop, Kano, Nigeria, August 18.

Khasiani, S.A. 2000. Kenya: Country profile. Report prepared for the Worldwide Workshop on Youth Involvement as Strategy for Social, Economic, and Democratic Development, San José, Costa Rica, January 4–7, 2000.

Marschall, M. 1998. Rapid growth of the civil sector. In *Democracy as Discussion II The Challenges and Promise of a New Democratic Era: A Handbook,* ed. Sondra Myers. New London, CT: Toor Cummings Center for International Studies and Liberal Arts.

Matovu, G.W.M. 2002. Africa and decentralization: Enter the citizens. *Development Outreach* Winter: 12–22.

Mayer, K.U., and U. Schoepflin. 1989. The state and the life course. *Annual Review of Sociology* 15: 187–209.

McBride, A.M., C. Benítez, M. Sherraden, and L. Johnson. 2003. Civic service worldwide: A preliminary assessment. In *Service Enquiry: Service in the 21st Century,* ed. H. Perold, S. Stroud, and M. Sherraden. St. Louis: Washington University, Global Service Institute.

Ministry of Women's Affairs and Youth Development. 2002. *Report of the Technical Committee on the Re-organization of the National Youth Service Corps (NYSC) Scheme,* vol. 1. Abuja, Nigeria: Federal Ministry of Women's Affairs and Youth Development. Originally published by the National Youth Service Corps.

Molefe, D., and S. Weeks. 2001. National Service—Is It a Thirteenth Year of Education? The Rise and Fall of an Innovation in Botswana. *Africa Today* 48 (2): 105–126.

Moskos, C.C. 1988. *A Call to Civic Service: National Service for Country and Community.* New York: Free Press.

Mulaudzi, J. 2000.Working for the nation: National youth service in South Africa: Will it work, can it work? *Quarterly Journal of the South African National NGO Coalition and INTERFUN Development Update* (July): 131–143.

Nairn, T. 1997. *Faces of Nationalism: Janus Revisited.* Verso: London.

Negash, T., and K. Tronvoll. 2000. *Brothers at War: Making Sense of the Eritrean-Ethiopian War.* Oxford: James Currey.

Newswatch (Lagos). 1985. March 25.

Nye, J.S., and J.D. Donahue, eds. 2000. *Governance in a Globalizing World.* Washington, DC: Brookings Institute.

Obadare, E. 2004. *Statism, Youth and the Civic Imagination: A Critical Study of the National Youth Service Corps (NYSC) Program in Nigeria.* CSD Research Report. St. Louis, MO: Washington University, Center for Social Development.

Obayuwana, A., and E.-A. Sunday. 2000. Sharia's poison to NYSC unity role. *Guardian on Sunday,* July 16.

Okocha, C., and F. Muraina. 2000. Don't accept NYSC postings to Sharia states, Ondo House tells indigenes. *Thisday,* July 12.

Perold, H. 2000. South Africa: Country profile. Report prepared for the Worldwide Workshop on Youth Involvement as Strategy for Social, Economic, and Democratic Development, San José, Costa Rica, January 4–7.

Putnam, R.D. 2000. *Bowling Alone: The Collapse and Revival of American Community.* New York: Simon and Schuster.

Reitzes, M. 1994. Civil society, the public sphere and the state: Reflections on classical and contemporary discourses. *Theoria: A Journal of Studies in the Arts, Humanities and the Social Sciences* 83/84: 87–112.

Rossant, M.J. 1988. Foreword. In *A Call to Civic Service: National Service for Country and Community,* ed. C.C. Moskos. New York: Free Press.

Selbourne, D. 1994. *The Principle of Duty: An Essay on the Foundations of the Civic Order.* London: Sinclair-Stevenson.

Sesay, A., C. Ukeje, O. Aina, and A. Odebiyi, eds. 2003. *Ethnic Militias and the Future of Democracy in Nigeria.* Ile-Ife: Obafemi Awolowo University Press.

Sherraden, M. 2001. *Civic Service: Issues, Outlook, Institution Building.* CSD Perspective. St. Louis, MO: Washington University, Center for Social Development.

Sunday Punch (Lagos). 2003. August 31.

Sunday Times Magazine (London). 2003. August 24.

Taiwo, Olufemi. 2000. Of citizens and citizenship. Paper for the seminar document *Constitutionalism and National Question.* Lagos: Centre for Constitutionalism and Demilitarisation.

Trager, L. 2001. *Yoruba Hometowns: Community, Identity, and Development in Nigeria.* London: Lynne Rienner.

University of Tasmania. 1994. Chapter 5: Highlights of country reports. Notes from the 2nd Global Conference on National Youth Service, Abuju, Nigeria, October 10–14. www.utas.edu.au/docs/ahugo/NCYS/second/five.html.

Toward Universal National Youth Service in Israel

Possible Social Capital Effects

Nicole Fleischer and Reuven Gal

As a society comprised of diverse ethnic and religious sectors that coexist in continuous tension, Israel has undergone fundamental changes since its founding in 1948. From an enlisted, collectivist society that strove for homogeneity, Israeli society has become more individualistic and heterogeneous. From a pioneering society in which the primary rite of passage into full membership was military service, with the Israeli Defense Force (IDF) being the major institution of socialization, Israel now enjoys a developed civil society that values a variety of civilian pathways to membership (Bar-Tura and Fleischer 2004). Nonetheless, there is a sense of anomie and a growing sense of a need for new social institutions that will provide a common civic denominator and contribute to the building of national bonds (Sherraden and Eberly 1984; Moskos 1988).

Moreover, different social institutions are needed to balance citizenship rights versus obligations: two critical sectors of Israeli society—the ultra-Orthodox Jews and the Arab citizens of Israel—are exempted from military duty, thus putting the burden of army duty on the shoulders of some but not all of Israel's citizens. These reasons drive the ongoing public debate in Israel about the need to establish an inclusive social institution that will facilitate the expression of civic responsibility and allow the development of common shared denominators. It is the authors' opinions that a national youth service (NYS) that is open and appeals to all sectors of Israeli society could be such an institution.

After describing the population of Israel, this chapter reviews the history and current status of NYS in Israel. A discussion of the policy issues presently at stake will follow. Subsequently we categorize some of the most typical psychological and interpersonal effects of youth service participation, including results of a recent study. Finally, we raise the concern that the current form of implementation of NYS in Israel, rather than contributing to social cohesion by developing *bridging* or *linking* social capital, might further segregate society by developing *bonding* social capital.

The Population of Israel

Israel is home to a diverse population from many ethnic, religious, cultural, and social backgrounds. Of the 6.4 million people in Israel, 77.8 percent are Jews, 17.3 percent are Arabs, and the remaining 4.9 percent are Druze, Circassians, and others. Israel has a high level of informal segregation patterns because of its current multiethnic, multicultural, multireligious, and multilingual populations. While there is no official policy of separation, sectors within the society are self-segregating, maintaining their deep cultural, religious, ideological, and/or ethnic identities.

Many refer to Israel as a new society with ancient roots. Roughly 80 percent of the population, the Jews of Israel gathered from 105 countries, speaking eighty-two different languages. The majority of the Jews can be described as secular, living a modern Western lifestyle and following varied degrees of tradition and religious practice. Among this group are those who choose to affiliate with one of the liberal religious streams, while others follow a more traditional and observant way of life, regulated by Jewish religious law, while completely participating in the country's national life. They regard the modern Jewish state as the initial stage in preparation for the coming of the Messiah and redemption of the Jewish people in the Land of Israel. Most ultra-Orthodox Jews believe that Jewish sovereignty in Israel can be reestablished only after the coming of the Messiah. Maintaining strict adherence to Jewish religious law, they reside in separate neighborhoods, operate their own schools, adorn themselves in traditional clothing, maintain well-defined roles for men and women, and are bound by a closely controlled lifestyle.

About a fifth of Israel's population is Arabic-speaking and comprises diverse cultural, ethnic, and religious groups. Muslim Arabs, about 1 million people, most of whom are Sunni, reside mainly in small towns and villages. Bedouin Arabs, also Muslim (estimated at 170,000), belong to some thirty tribes. Formerly nomadic shepherds, the Bedouin are currently in transition from a tribal social framework to a permanently settled society. Christian Arabs, about 113,000, are primarily affiliated with the Greek Orthodox or Roman Catholic churches. The Druze, about 106,000 people, living in twenty-two villages in northern Israel, constitute a separate cultural, social, and religious community. While the Druze religion is not accessible to outsiders, one known aspect of its philosophy calls for complete loyalty by its adherents to the government of the country in which they reside. The Circassians comprise some 3,000 people residing in two northern villages. Although they share neither the Arab origin nor the cultural background of the larger Islamic community, they are Sunni Muslims. While maintaining a distinct ethnic identity, the Druze and Circassians participate in Israel's economic and national affairs without assimilating either into Jewish or Muslim society. Thus, Israel is definitely not a melting pot society, but rather a mosaic made up of different population groups coexisting in the framework of a democratic state.

National Youth Service

The prevalent form of civic service in Israel is NYS, or *Sherut Leumi* in Hebrew. NYS allows youth (ages eighteen to twenty-two), who are not conscripted into the IDF, to volunteer for a period of one to two years. Since its establishment in 1971, the NYS has been operated by several nongovernmental organizations (NGOs), which recruit, train, and place about 8,000 volunteers a year. Most the volunteers are Jewish religious women, but every year the number of volunteers from different backgrounds increases. Most of the participants serve a period of one year, while 30 percent continue to serve for an additional year.

Unlike military service that is compulsory for men and women at age eighteen, NYS is voluntary, although only for Israeli citizens who are exempted from army duty. Since military and civic are mutually exclusive, it is imperative to look at the development of the draft to the IDF in order to understand the challenges that NYS presently faces.

The comprehensive draft system to the IDF has been in operation since Israel's independence in 1948. The IDF was intended both to constitute a military system for the defense of the country and, no less important, to serve a socialization function, nurturing the creation of a cohesive civilian society composed of immigrants from 105 countries around the world. The view of the IDF as a people's army flowed from the perception of a homogeneous Jewish society undergoing national renaissance, a people under the Jewish legacy and a threatening contemporary Middle East. National service, and primarily national military service, was seen as a privilege of the Jewish majority and as a rite of passage into full membership in the dominant elite (Bar Tura and Fleischer 2004).

Although conscription is theoretically universal, it is in fact selective. It exempts Muslim and Christian Arab Israelis from service out of consideration for their family, religious, and cultural affiliations with the Arab world (with which Israel has had a long dispute), as well as concern over possible dual loyalties. Since 1957, at the request of their community leaders, IDF service has been mandatory for Druze and Circassian men, while Bedouin men can volunteer. Similarly, sensitive to the Nazi decimation of traditional European Jewish culture and religious study, David Ben Gurion's early statehood government bowed to pressure of ultra-Orthodox Jewish political parties and provided a limited number of long-term deferments for male ultra-Orthodox Yeshiva students and exemptions for all ultra-Orthodox women. By the year 2005, less than half of the annual cohort of eighteen-year-old male and female citizens of Israel will serve in the military, thus increasing the significance of NYS, which is universal and appeals to all citizens of Israel.

The Policy Challenge

NYS in Israel is based on a 1970 law that aimed to provide a nonmilitary service alternative for religious observant Jewish girls. Rather than operating NYS directly, the government has chosen to license and regulate NGOs that were established for the purposes of operating NYS. Operating organizations recruit, train, place, and oversee the service of participating volunteers and maintain ongoing relations with the volunteers' supervisors in their place of work. Volunteer placements may be in either public institutions or in nongovernmental, nonprofit organizations. Placements are for one year and may be renewed for a second year. Each of these six operating NGOs recruits its volunteers according to its specific guidelines and beliefs: in fact, the vast majority of the almost 8,000 NYS participants volunteer through Jewish Orthodox organizations.

In 2002, the Israeli parliament (Knesset) approved a five-year deferment law for Yeshiva students based on recommendations of a committee headed by Justice Zvi Tal. The law (Tal Law) calls for Yeshiva students to choose, after a year of work at age twenty-three, whether to continue their Yeshiva studies, to enlist in the army, or to serve one year in a civic service program. If the Yeshiva students decide to do a year of civic service, they must then serve twenty-one days each year until age forty-one. However, at this writing, these men are continuing to work or are idle, since there is no organizational structure for volunteer national service for them. A special committee established in 2002 by Defense Minister Shaul Mofaz, which operates within the National Security Council, will probably recommend that a National Civic Service Authority be formed to absorb ultra-Orthodox men who complete their "year of decision" and are not absorbed by the IDF. It is conceivable that such an authority could become the foundation for the needed expansion of NYS into a social institution that is open and appeals to all sectors of Israeli society.

Therefore, as it stands, the government has fostered mechanisms to include both Jewish men and women in the NYS while continuing to exclude Arab citizens of Israel. The current intellectual and political leadership of the Arab community in Israel categorically rejects the idea of NYS, whether voluntary or compulsory, for Arab Israeli youth, claiming that equality in civil rights must precede responsibilities. Israeli Arabs express suspicion that such a program would lay the foundation for linking rights and responsibilities and would introduce military service through the back door. Moreover, Israeli Arabs point out that even military service has not granted equal opportunity to non-Jews. Despite the high rates of military service in the IDF among Druze, government allocations to education, housing, and infrastructures in Druze villages remain well below those in similarly sized Jewish towns. Demobilized Druze soldiers often find that the equal burden of their military service does not give them equal opportunity in the job market, and the rate of unemployment in the Druze sector is far higher than in the Jewish sector.

Although men who were exempted from military service were allowed to volunteer for NYS, under the 1970 law of national service they were not eligible for the benefits given to women volunteers. Supported by research on a pilot project designed to allow men to volunteer in NYS (Amit and Fleischer 2004), the Israeli government decided to change the NYS policy in May 2004 so as to allow all men exempted from army duty to volunteer and receive all benefits. Particularly in days when budget cuts threaten the sustainability of the existing frameworks of NYS, research such as this plays an important role in policy (Hammersley 1995). In brief, the major obstacles to expanding NYS for all Israeli citizens are a lack of legitimization of nonmilitary forms of youth service and a lack of awareness by the Israeli public and its decision makers about the potential benefits of NYS and its return on investment.

Possible Effects of Service

As previously mentioned, one of the drives of the ongoing debate about the change of NYS policy is the need to establish an inclusive social institution that will allow the development of shared denominators in Israel's deeply divided society. Social capital is a concept that can help explain the results of the exposure of volunteers to heterogeneous populations across the divides. Although it is a contested concept, how much social capital one has can be defined as the number and strength of social relations that an individual or household can call upon (Putnam 1995). Social capital can be split into three connecting strands: bonding, bridging, and linking (Putnam 2000). Bonding social capital refers to strong ties between family members, neighbors, or friends who share similar characteristics. Bridging social capital refers to weaker ties between people from different religious, national, and cultural groups who nevertheless have similar economic and social status. Linking social capital refers to ties between people who have low socioeconomic status and those in positions of power and influence, such as police, bankers, and public officials. Putnam claims that these forms of social capital can be found in different social institutions: the bonding social capital will be found in organizations such as private clubs and ethnic-based associations, while the linking and bridging social capital might be found in civil rights movements or civic service programs. Thus, in organizations like NYS, where there is exposure to heterogeneous populations, the social capital formed could be of the bridging or linking type.

Due to the lack of research on the impacts of civic service programs in Israel, we at the Carmel Institute for Social Studies (authors' research organization) have relied on anecdotal evidence, observations, personal communication, and research from other NYS programs worldwide. Gal (2001) categorizes some of the most typical psychological and interpersonal outcomes of NYS participation as a sense of citizenship and affiliation, locus of control, social and emotional intelligence, sexual maturity, independent identity, self-confidence and self-efficacy, sustained loyalty, and generosity and sense of giving.

Assessing the cost-effectiveness of NYS is complicated and difficult. Any attempt to arrive at a figure must compare the actual costs of NYS operations against the direct and measurable financial benefits, as well as the multitude of indirect benefits (social, psychological, educational, ideological, etc., as mentioned above) that usually result from such programs. A cost-benefit analysis of the implementation of a future universal NYS in Israel was conducted by the Carmel Institute for Social Studies in cooperation with the Israeli Institute for Economic and Social Research (Nathenson, Gal, and Bar-Tura 2001). Like its international parallels, this study concluded that the direct benefits of a program of voluntary NYS in Israel would balance or slightly outweigh the costs. This research measured the monetary benefits of service as well as the costs it bears on Israel's economy. The conclusion of this analysis was that, over time, the monetary costs and the benefits balance out. A somewhat different analysis (Amir 2001) arrived at different conclusions, but it only explored the monetary aspects of service, not the possible benefits.

A Study of Service

What are the possible benefits? We have a first glimpse from research conducted on Israeli NYS volunteers' motivations for service, sense of self-efficacy, social attitudes, and satisfaction from service (Gal et al. 2003). The goals of this particular study were to examine possible changes in NYS volunteers' perceptions at

Table 4.1

Sample Description

	Phase 1 (percent)	Phase 2 (percent)
Number of respondents (N)	464	440
Number and percent of respondents to	—	87
both questionnaires	—	20
Gender		
Male	—	7.4
Female	—	92.6
Religion		
Christian	—	1.4
Jewish	—	93.5
Muslim	—	2.6
Druze	—	0.2
In process of conversion to Judaism	—	2.2
Level of religious observance		
Secular	30.2	43.8
Traditional	57.7	49
Religious	10.7	6
Orthodox	1.4	1.2
Economic status		
Under national average	14	19.8
On national average	69.2	60.7
Over national average	16.8	19.5
Matriculation		
No matriculation	—	7
Partial matriculation	—	25
Full matriculation	—	68
Area in which parents reside		
North	37.2	25.7
Central	41.4	39.3
South	18	23.6
West Bank and Gaza	3.4	2.5
Stage in service		
Beginning on year 1	78.3	—
End of year 1 (final)	1.4	51.6
End of year 1 (continuing)	19.6	28.5
End of year 2	0.7	20

the end of a year of service. The research focused on attitudes toward tolerance, civic involvement and volunteering, and government and democracy.

The data were collected by distributing two similar questionnaires at two points in time, at the beginning of the year of service and at the end (Phase 1: October 2001 and Phase 2: June 2002) (Table 4.1). The sample included 464 volunteers in the first phase and 440 volunteers in the second phase. At the time of the study, there were 1,700 volunteers in that particular NGO and a total of 8,000 NYS volunteers overall. In order to examine the research questions, a self-administered survey was distributed at regional conventions that were held around the country.

The sample was composed mainly of women (92.6 percent) and Jews (93.5 percent). Regarding the level of religious observance, about half (49 to 58 percent) of the respondents defined themselves as traditional, 30 to 40 percent as secular, 10 percent as religious, and 1 percent as Orthodox. At Phase 1, most of the respondents were at the beginning of their first year of service (78 percent), while in Phase 2 most of the respondents were at the end of their first year of service. The majority (68 percent) had passed their matriculation examinations (necessary to enter universities) and belonged to households with average to slightly above-average income (69.2 percent).

Overall, the findings indicate that most of the volunteers are satisfied or very satisfied with their service experience (65 percent). Their motives for joining NYS were the responsibility to serve the country, to help people, and to gain knowledge and professional experience. Participants reported becoming more tolerant, involved, and connected to the community, while there was no perceptible change in the volunteers' democratic attitudes and sense of self-efficacy.

Motivation for Service

At Phase 1 and Phase 2, respondents were asked what were their principal motives for joining national service. Questions regarding motivation were similar in both phases, but not identical. At Phase 2, a question was added for those respondents who decided to continue for a second year of service. These questions asked the respondents to rank the importance of different motives on a scale from 1 (not important) to 5 (extremely important). Table 4.2 summarizes the means and standard deviations of the distributions.

As can be seen from Table 4.2, the main motives for service were the opportunity to help people, the responsibility as a citizen to serve the country, and the opportunity to gain knowledge and professional experience. Of lesser importance were motivations such as the responsibility to give based on religious belief, the opportunity to collect monetary benefits, and the sense that service is expected. In both questionnaires, respondents ranked their single, most important motive, and the results were similar in both phases: 40 percent of the respondents chose the responsibility to serve the country, 30 percent chose the responsibility to help people, and 20 percent chose the opportunity to gain knowledge and professional experience.

Table 4.2

Perceived Importance of Possible Motivations for Service: Phases 1 and 2
(scale of 1 to 5)

Motivations	Phase 1 mean (standard deviation)	Phase 2 mean (standard deviation)
The responsibility as a citizen to serve the country	4.44 (0.90)	4.35 (0.98)
The opportunity to help people	4.67 (0.94)	4.39 (0.89)
An opportunity to gain knowledge and professional experience	4.36 (0.90)	4.31 (1.01)
An opportunity to collect monetary benefits	3.60 (1.29)	3.60 (1.38)
The responsibility to give, based on religious belief	2.98 (1.30)	2.57 (1.35)
An opportunity to help people in distress	—	*4.34 (0.90)
An opportunity to widen one's horizons	—	*4.33 (0.89)
An opportunity to live independently outside of home	—	*3.11 (1.56)
Because it is expected of me to serve	—	*2.53 (1.44)

*These motivations were only included in the Time 2 survey.

Benefit of Service as Perceived by the Volunteers

Approximately 86 percent of the respondents believed that NYS primarily benefits the hosting organizations, 70 percent claimed that the main benefit goes to society or the community, and 54 percent agreed that they benefited most. As far as the perceived effects on the volunteers, 76 percent thought that service benefited their occupational experience, 67 percent believed that NYS offered them an advantage in the labor market, 66 percent reported that service made them want to pursue higher education, and 46 percent agreed that they may pursue employment in a field similar to the one in which they served.

Table 4.3

Comparison of Attitudes Between Time 1 and Time 2

Attitudes–subjects	Phase 1 mean (standard deviation)	Phase 2 mean (standard deviation)	t-score (standard error)
Attitudes toward community	3.30	3.48	3.76*
	(0.65)	(0.75)	(0.04)
N	439	427	
Volunteering and involvement	3.89	4.46	13.9*
	(0.66)	(0.52)	(0.04)
N	463	433	
Tolerance	3.77	3.88	2.29**
	(0.68)	(0.69)	(0.05)
N	410	377	
Attitudes toward government and democracy	4.14	4.18	1.14
	(0.43)	(0.42)	(0.03)
N	426	386	
Sense of self-efficacy	4.15	4.17	0.05
	(0.51)	(0.56)	(0.04)
N	452	423	

$*p < 0.01; **p < 0.05$

When queried about the perceived impact on community or society, 38 percent of respondents considered any effects attributable to their dedication, 27 percent saw the main benefit as cost savings for the state, and 24 percent thought the main benefit was the improvement of public services.

Social Attitudes of the Volunteers

Four social attitude indexes and one self-efficacy index were created by adding the responses to each question. The values of each index range from 1 (low) to 5 (high). Descriptive analyses and tests of difference between the two time periods were conducted, as was a test of difference for the seventy-one respondents who completed both questionnaires.

Table 4.3 illustrates that all the attitudes in both phases were generally positive (around 4.0). Of the index values obtained at Phase 1, the highest values are in sense of self-efficacy, attitudes toward government and democracy, and volunteering and involvement. At Phase 2, these three indexes stood out as well, but in a different order, with attitudes toward volunteering and involvement ranked first.

Comparisons between Phase 1 and Phase 2 reveal statistically significant differences in attitudes related to tolerance, volunteering, civic involvement, and communities. These reported attitudes are stronger at Phase 2 than at Phase 1. However, there are no statistically significant differences between the time periods regarding attitudes toward democracy and sense of self-efficacy. It should be noted that both of these indexes were high at Phase 1; hence, the possibility of improvement at Phase 2 was limited. This finding could reflect a self-selection bias, since these youth chose to volunteer for national service in the first place. A characteristic of a potential volunteer may be a highly developed democratic attitude and a strong sense of self-efficacy.

Paired sample t-tests were used to assess the degree of difference between those who completed the survey at both time periods ($N = 71$). The year of service may have increased their tolerance. Respondents were asked about their self-perceived changes in attitudes toward the *other,* including people of a different religion, socioeconomic status, ethnic background, and those holding different political opinions. In general, the respondents did not report a significant change in their attitudes toward others after a year of service. However, when those respondents who actually served with people from different backgrounds are compared to those who did not, a significant difference is found ($t = 6.58$, $p < 0.05$). Thus, the findings show that while a higher level of tolerance was reported, in general, by the respondents, only those volunteers who actually worked with people of other backgrounds became aware of the change that occurred in their perceptions.

Discussion

The main limitation of the reported study is the lack of a control or comparison group. Comparison to a matched group of participants who did not participate in a year of service would justify claims of the impacts of NYS on volunteers' attitudes. Hence, a primary research implication for the consideration of the impacts of NYS—information that is vitally needed for policy development—is a more rigorous design. From this point of view, the present research can be viewed as a pilot study that suggests possibilities for further research.

To summarize the main findings: most of the respondents said that the chief motivations for service were connected to their will to serve the country and to help people, while a relatively small percentage of respondents indicated that their motivation was to gain professional knowledge, collect monetary benefits, or exercise religious duties. Comparing these findings with other research about motivation to serve in the Israeli army (Gal and Mayseless 1990) reveals a different pattern: the young conscripts, before being drafted, emphasize personal motives (e.g., personal fulfillment) rather than social motives as is the case with the NYS volunteers. One possible explanation for these differences derives from the difference in frameworks. While military service in Israel is mandatory, national service is voluntary, and therefore, there is a possible positive preselection factor for those choosing to volunteer. Furthermore, there is, likely, a gender factor as well: most of the participants in NYS (as well as in this research) are women. The social motive may be stronger among women than it is with men within the same age group.

Results regarding the respondents' social attitudes indicate that most of the NYS volunteers show positive attitudes for tolerance, volunteering, community involvement, and democracy prior to service. These attitudes were strengthened after one year of service, whereas attitudes toward government and democracy and a sense of self-efficacy showed no change. These findings are congruent with those found in a recent study (Ichilov 2003) that examined the impact of a nationwide, high school service-learning program, *Mechuyavut Yishit* (Personal Commitment), on the participants' attitudes. Ichilov's research, similar to the present research, shows changes in attitudes toward involvement and volunteering following the year of program participation, while no changes are reported in attitudes toward government and democracy. The present study demonstrates that day-to-day exposure and actually working with people from different backgrounds through service may contribute to more tolerant attitudes toward the *other*.

Conclusions

The research reported here and in Gal et al. (2003) was the first of its kind to evaluate the nonmonetary benefits of NYS in Israel as well as the changes and developments that occur among the volunteers. The findings of this research encourage public debate about the need to expand NYS into a social institution that is open and appeals to all sectors of Israeli society. For example, the relatively high levels of satisfaction from service demonstrate the potential attraction and challenge of NYS for those Israeli youth who are not drafted to the military.

Secondly, the findings indicating attitudinal change show the potential embedded in national service to strengthen these attitudes. In view of the fact that Israeli society is comprised of diverse ethnic and religious sectors that coexist in continuous tension, a universal NYS could diminish the polarization and reduce the tensions between these sectors. The possible influence that national service has on strengthening the voluntary orientations of its graduates bears high importance in Israeli society. In times when voluntary frameworks and NGOs play such important roles (in deprived areas or in institutionally neglected fields), there is critical significance to the intensification of these orientations and to the consequent strengthening of the civil society.

Finally, the results just presented suggest that those volunteers who served within mixed groups are more aware of their change in attitude toward others, which could support the claim that forms of civic service can contribute to linking or bridging social capital or, as we previously mentioned, that a universal NYS could significantly diminish the polarization and reduce the tensions between sectors in society.

However, a word of caution is necessary. The current model of implementation of NYS is such that volunteers are drafted through several organizations that recruit their candidates according to their own beliefs and guidelines. Consequently, volunteers in each organization come from specific sectors of society (e.g., religious or secular). Seen from this perspective, rather than contributing to social cohesion by developing bridging or linking social capital, NYS in Israel might contribute to further segregation by developing bonding social capital. Possible policy implications follow from this perspective. Rather than continuing to allow sectarian NGOs to operate youth service, a national framework could operate NYS so as to enable exposure of volunteers to different sectors of society. Moreover, as a way to create bridging and linking social capital, volunteers could work in teams of, say, Arab and Jews, or secular and religious people. The only way of clarifying these uncertainties and bridging between differing points of view is by developing more specific knowledge about the impacts of national service in Israel, by further experimenting and testing forms of implementation of NYS, and by following these experiments with systematic, theoretically driven research.

References

Amir, R. 2001. *Civic Service Arrangement: An Economical Analysis.* Ramat Hasharon, Israel: National Security Council.

Amit, K., and N. Fleischer. 2004. *Male Volunteers in National Youth Service in Israel: The Pilot Project (2002–2003).* Jerusalem: Ministry of Welfare.

Bandura, A. 1977. Self-efficacy: Toward a unifying theory of behavioral change. *Psychological Review* 84: 191–215.

———. 1982. Self-efficacy mechanism in human agency. *American Psychologist* 37: 122–147.

Bar Tura, M., and N. Fleischer. 2004. Civic service in Israel. *Non-Profit and Voluntary Sector Quarterly* 33 (4 Supplement): 51S–63S.

Endler, N.S., and L.J. Summerfeldt. 1995. Intelligence, personality, psychopathology, and adjustment. In *International Handbook of Personality and Intelligence,* ed. D.H. Saklofske, and M. Zeidner. New York: Plenum Press.

Erikson, E.H. 1950. *Childhood and Society.* New York: Norton.

———. 1968. *Identity: Youth and Crisis.* New York: Norton.

Gal, R. 2001. Voluntary youth work as a psycho-social process. Paper presented at the Seminar on Development of Voluntary Youth Work for the Finnish Ministry of Education Youth Division, May 10–11, Helsinki, Finland.

Gal, R., K. Amit, N. Fleischer, and N. Strichman. 2003. *Volunteers of National Youth Service in Israel: A Study on Motivation for Service, Social Attitudes and Satisfaction from Service.* Zichron Ya'akov, Israel: Carmel Institute for Social Studies.

Gal, R., and Mayseless, O. 1990. Attitudes of Israeli youth toward military service and national security during the Intifida. In *The Seventh War,* ed. R. Gal. Tel Aviv, Israel: Hakibbutz Hameuchad (Hebrew).

Gardner, H. 1983. *Frames of Mind: The Theory of Multiple Intelligences.* New York: Basic Books.

Hammersley, M. 1995. *The Politics of Social Research.* London: Sage Publications.

Ichilov, O. 2003. Hafalat talmidim ba kehila ve hahinuh le ezrahut ba demokratia: Haproyekt "Mechuyavut ishit-sherut la zulat" (Assigning students for community service and education for democracy: "Mechuyavut ishit" project, unauthorized title translation). Unpublished manuscript.

Mayseless, O., R. Gal, and E. Fishof. 1989. *Attitudes and Perceptions of High School Students Towards Military and Security Issues.* Zichron Ya'akov, Israel: Israeli Institute for Military Studies.

Moskos, C. 1988. *A Call to Service.* New York: Free Press.

Nathenson, R., R. Gal, and M. Bar-Tura. 2001. *Cost-benefit Analysis: Implementation of National Youth Service in Israel.* Zichron Ya'akov, Israel: Carmel Institute for Social Studies and Israeli Institute for Economic and Social Research.

Putnam, R. 1995. Turning in, turning out: The strange disappearance of social capital in America. *Political Science and Politics* 28: 664–683.

———. 2000. *Bowling Alone: The Collapse and Revival of American Community.* New York: Simon and Schuster.

Rotter, J. 1966. Generalized expectancies for internal versus external control of reinforcement. *Psychological Monographs* 80: 1–28.

———. 1975. Some problems and misconceptions related to the construct of internal versus external control of reinforcement. *Journal of Consulting and Clinical Psychology* 43: 56–57.

Sherraden, M., and D. Eberly. 1984. Individual rights and social responsibilities: Fundamental issues in national service. *Public Law Forum* 4: 241–257.

Sternberg, R.J. 1990. *Metaphors of Mind: Conceptions of the Nature of Intelligence.* New York: Cambridge University Press.

The Effects of National Service in the United States

A Research Synthesis

James L. Perry and Ann Marie Thomson

The most recent national service legislation in the United States—the National and Community Service Trust Act of 1993—is the latest in a fifty-year line of legislative actions that reflects America's commitment to civic service (Perry and Thomson 2004). A by-product of many national service programs in the United States, extending as far back as the Civilian Conservation Corps (CCC) of the 1930s, is program evaluation intended to assess the effects of national service. Evaluation research is salient to a variety of stakeholders, including program designers and managers concerned about the quality of results achieved from their initiatives, servers and service beneficiaries who are directly interested in the meaningfulness and impacts of service, and nonprofit donors concerned about the stewardship of their philanthropy (Perry 2003). The success of national service in the United States is, at least in part, a result of consistent attention to an objective assessment of the ways in which service creates social value.

This chapter synthesizes findings from almost 140 evaluation studies of national service in the United States. We identify similarities, differences, and patterns across this comprehensive group of studies in order to develop contingent generalizations about service, its outcomes, and mediating factors that may enhance the likelihood of the positive outcomes frequently attributed to national service. The analysis also identifies gaps in our cumulative knowledge about national service's effects in the United States that not only inform U.S. policy and research, but may also offer insights for development of an international research agenda on service.

The studies drawn on in this analysis include service programs at both the national and community levels. Increasingly the focus of national service policy in the United States involves the creation of new institutional forms—joint ventures of governmental, nongovernmental, nonprofit, and for-profit organizations. This focus is founded on the belief that community building occurs best when "people, [community–based organizations], and their government work at the grass roots in genuine partnership" (Corporation for National Service 1994, 1).

Conceptual and Operational Definitions of Service

As an ideal, service in the United States has most frequently been viewed as a means for educating citizens about the civic virtues so necessary for democratic citizenship. For America's founders, the development of civic virtue was the responsibility of individuals, not government, whose only role was to elicit rather than to command appropriate actions from virtuous people. Although their political philosophy rested on belief in the necessary relationship between the realization of the ideal of the Republic and citizen virtue, the founders, writes scholar David K. Hart, "took the bolder and riskier path of moral individualism, understanding that virtue had no meaning if it was not achieved through the voluntary efforts of a free people" (Hart 1984, 113).

Service, as an ideal, can best be understood as caught between America's two competing ideologies—classic liberalism and civic republicanism. Classic liberalism—with its emphasis on the individual, limited representative government, private interest, and primacy of the private realm—finds its roots in the moral individualism of America's founders. Civic republicanism's roots, on the other hand, rest in an equally strong belief that without civic obligation to the whole, the ideal of the republic will never be realized. Like the development of U.S. politics, the development of support for national service embodies inner tensions between seemingly conflicting relationships—liberty and obligation, individual rights and public duty, dread of the power of government to create artificial character by mandating civic virtue and yearning for a natural virtuous citizenship rooted in community (Barber 1984; Morone 1990).

These ideologies have tended to fuel the policy debates over national service, clouding our ability to clearly define the concept of service. Historically, however, the ideal of national service has been expressed in concrete ways—as a means to revive the economy devastated by the Great Depression in the early twentieth century, address issues of poverty in the 1960s, provide youth with meaningful educational and work opportunities in natural resource conservation, and build local communities through problem-solving strategies (Perry and Thomson 2004). Over time, a multitude of national service interventions have emerged. Some of these institutions, like the CCC, no longer exist, while others, like the Peace Corps, continue to operate with broad popular support.

The historical evolution of national service suggests increasing popular support for an institutional perspective on service in which the meaning of service lies in its instrumental value. Service is nearly always a means to achieve particular ends, public and private. This view of service champions a strong public sector role in an otherwise private activity, although that role need not be a national government role. Nevertheless, the moral individualism that also defines the psyche of U.S. citizens cannot be dismissed altogether; the meaning of service to those who embrace moral individualism lies primarily in volunteerism, which is necessarily a private, even intimate, individual response to a particular need. Most proponents of this view believe that any intrusion of the public (government) in this essentially private realm should be resisted.

We believe that a conceptual definition of service in the United States, while it must acknowledge the essentially private nature of volunteerism, must also emphasize its essentially public nature rooted in the persistent, rhetorically powerful belief that citizenship demands some kind of self-sacrifice for the sake of the demos. From this perspective, Sherraden and Eberly's definition of national service still stands as one of the best in the service literature. "As a general term," they write, service "refers to a period of service given by the individual to the nation or community [that] embodies two complementary ideas: one, that some service to the larger society is part of individual citizenship responsibility; and two, that society should be structured in ways which provide citizens with opportunities to make meaningful contributions" (1982, 3). The value of this definition lies in its emphasis on the dual nature of service, which is both private (individual citizenship responsibility) and public (structuring society to provide citizens with service opportunities).

For the purposes of our analysis, we begin with this broad conceptual understanding of national service, but we narrow our definition to consider the key attributes of service that help us identify studies (from among a myriad of studies) to include in the analysis. We define service operationally in terms of the following criteria for selection of studies:

- a participant's engagement in service is frequent;
- the commitment to service is long-term, rather than episodic;
- the service is probably remunerated in some way, but at less than market rates;
- the program is formal;
- the program addresses either difficult public problems or needs that have been defined collectively as critical.[1]

These attributes helped us identify a total of 139 studies that exhibit a wide range of sampling methods, sample sizes, data collection techniques, and research designs (Perry and Thomson 2004).

National Service Programs Included in the Analysis

National service programs in the United States are diverse, encompassing a variety of programmatic goals and identities. These diverse programs cluster into five conceptually distinct, but not mutually exclusive types: youth and conservation corps, capacity building, direct service, senior programs, and mutual understanding.

Youth and Conservation Corps

This class of programs is best represented by the CCC (Sherraden 1979), a Depression-era program designed to reduce unemployment and preserve natural resources, and the California Conservation Corps (Wolf, Leiderman, and Voith 1987). They have been defined collectively as "a special class of social programs that promote the development of young people while they do useful work of real value to their communities" (Branch, Leiderman, and Smith 1987, i.). Although the traditional corps model engages youth primarily in physical work projects in rural or wilderness areas, it has also been transplanted to urban settings where corps members may do physical and human service work. Among the prominent urban variants of the conservation corps model are the San Francisco Conservation Corps (Rosenbaum and Leiderman 1986), the City Volunteer Corps (Branch and Freedman 1986), and the Marin Conservation Corps (Lah, Wolf, and Leiderman 1985). Other youth and conservation corps programs include the Youth Conservation Corps (Marans, Driver, and Scott 1972; Scott, Driver, and Marans 1973), Youth Community Service (Gittel 1981), Georgia Peach Corps (Lahey, Brudney, and Newbolt 1995), and City Year (Goldsmith 1993).

Capacity Building

Volunteers in Service to America (VISTA), created in 1964 as part of the Johnson administration's antipoverty initiatives and merged with AmeriCorps in 1994, and the Teacher Corps, a program created in 1965 and discontinued in the early 1980s, are two good examples of capacity-building programs. AmeriCorps*VISTA's mission is to provide full-time volunteers for one year to local public and nonprofit organizations to assist them in alleviating poverty and poverty-related problems. Projects are designed to create a working partnership among the project's sponsoring organization, the community, and the private sector. To sustain these projects, members focus on building community capacity, mobilizing private and public resources, and recruiting community volunteers.

The Teacher Corps pursued an ambitious set of goals that sought to reform teacher development and engage the schools in their communities. The Teacher Corps program had two main components, divided between preservice and in-service activities. During preservice, interns took graduate education courses and observed schools and communities. The in-service component of the program consisted of university study, an internship in poverty schools, and a service experience with poor children and their families (Corwin 1973).

Direct Service

This class of program focuses primarily on getting things done in communities. AmeriCorps*State/National, authorized by the National and Community Service Trust Act of 1993, is an exemplar of this type of service program. It is community-based, designed to respond to local needs and concerns. In addition to community-based programs, AmeriCorps supports a variety of national nonprofits that provide direct service, including Public Allies, Teach for America, and Habitat for Humanity. Direct service programs that preceded AmeriCorps are University Year for ACTION (ACTION 1973) and the Program for Local Service (PLS) (Control Systems Research 1973).

Senior Programs

The shared attribute of programs in this category is the age of participants, but the missions of senior programs are quite diverse. The Foster Grandparent Program, a federally funded program for low-income seniors originating in 1965, provides opportunities for foster grandparents to develop ongoing relationships with children and youth who have exceptional or special needs. The Senior Companion Program also originated in the mid-1960s and enrolls low-income seniors. Its target population is adults with special health, welfare, and social needs. Two senior programs of more recent origin, Experience Corps and Seniors for Schools, connect the talent and skills of older adults with the needs of children in public elementary schools (Freedman and Fried 1999; Project Star 1998, 2000).

Mutual Understanding

Such programs, in a pure form, are rare in the United States. City Year places racial harmony and understanding high among its priorities. Perhaps the purest form of this type of program in the United States is the American Friends Service Committee (AFSC) workcamp.[2] In a 1952 study, Riecken describes an AFSC workcamp program in the United States as "a society in microcosm—a group of assorted individuals who are gradually integrated in the course of a summer into a religiously centered community serving others" (49). Campers were typically college students or teachers who could devote two months to the experience. They received no pay and were required to cover their subsistence costs. The activities of the workcamps were a combination of physical labor and study and reflection about the conditions of the people and area where the camp was located. Among the projects pursued by the camps were installation of a water supply system near Greensburg, Pennsylvania; repairing a schoolhouse in Crawford, Tennessee; and constructing and supervising playgrounds in racially diverse areas of Detroit and Chicago.

Nature of the Evidence on National Service in the United States

Understanding the effects of national service involves processes operating at numerous levels. The issues involved in these processes range from the psychological (e.g., changes in self-image and self-efficacy) to the interpersonal (e.g., working cooperatively with others, tolerance of diverse others) to the organizational, institutional, and societal (e.g., community capacity). Accordingly, the kinds of research relevant to assessing the effects of service run the gamut: studies of the relationship between exposure to service and individual development; research on changes in reading and other education outcomes associated with tutoring and similar interventions; cost-benefit analyses; and studies of changes in community networks related to community service initiatives.

Because the issues of interest lie at the intersections of different disciplines and levels of analysis, there is no single type of research evidence to which we can turn. Instead, we are faced with the task of comparing, contrasting, and synthesizing very different kinds of evidence. Each brand of research has its strengths and its limitations, and each implies what kinds of evidence are most relevant and useful (Perry and Thomson 2004; Perry and Imperial 2001; Grantmaker Forum on Community and National Service 2000).

The quality of the constituent studies determines how much we can glean from our analysis, but there are a number of things we can learn. In their discussion of hypotheses and problems in research synthesis, Hall and her colleagues argue that research synthesis can never be used as a "substitute for primary studies meant to uncover causal relationships," but it can contribute to learning by finding, "summarizing, and describing the already existing results of research [and by adding] analyses that shed new light on variations in the phenomenon under study [such that] the synthesist can sometimes make inferences that go well beyond the original results" (1994, 18–19). We discuss the outcomes of national service in the United States in this spirit.

Outcomes of National Service in the United States

Four types of outcomes associated with national service are summarized in Table 5.1. Beginning with a discussion of the effects of national service on servers, we then consider the effects on beneficiaries, institutions, and communities. It is important to note that when there was doubt whether an outcome was positive or null, we took a conservative approach and coded the outcome as no effect or null.

The synthesis of research about national service outcomes shows a broad range of effects, which are summarized in Table 5.2. These effects impact servers, beneficiaries, institutions, and communities. Positive outcomes exceed null or negative effects by better than a 7:1 ratio. There is one fact about the range of potential outcomes that may go unnoticed but is worth highlighting —almost none of the studies found any significant negative results.

The impact of national service as it has been designed and implemented in the United States affects some outcomes more strongly and consistently than others. National service appears to have particularly salutary effects on server skill development and satisfaction, direct beneficiaries, service quantity and quality, and volunteer leveraging.

The analysis also indicates that national service generates positive effects in other areas. These include civic responsibility, educational opportunity, self-esteem, physical and mental health, indirect beneficiaries, and community strengthening. The magnitude of evidence for these positive outcomes is substantial, but not as compelling as for the other outcomes. One of these outcomes, civic responsibility, appears to be mediated by several factors, among them gender and ethnicity and the civic content of the service.

The evidence for tolerance for diversity and institution creation did not show clear effects associated with national service. The reason for this conclusion varies between the two outcomes. Tolerance for diversity appears to be sensitive to several mediating factors that affect whether outcomes are positive, null, or negative. In the case of institution creation, the volume and quality of the research prevents concluding other than that the findings are equivocal.

A relatively large number of benefit-cost studies complement the inference from the analysis of other outcomes that national service is an efficient and effective problem-solving approach. In all but one of fourteen studies, benefits exceed costs. Conservation corps, which typically tackle a difficult two-pronged task of conservation work and youth development, yield ratios slightly above 1. Ratios for AmeriCorps*State/National average about 1.7:1, and for other types of programs, around 1.3:1.

Extracting generalizations about national service outcomes is challeng-

Table 5.1

Outcome Definitions

Outcomes	Definition
Servers	
Skill development	The extent to which the civic service experience leads to improvements in server's job or life skills.
Civic responsibility	The extent to which service enhances the server's understanding of community issues and problems, commitment to civic duty, and/or willingness to participate in advocacy or political processes.
Educational opportunity	The extent to which civic service opens opportunities for further education in the period following service.
Self-esteem	The extent to which the server's sense of personal worth improved as a result of the service experience.
Tolerance for diversity	The extent to which servers' tolerance of people different from them or appreciation of diversity changed as a result of service.
Satisfaction from serving	The server's global effect toward the service experience.
Health	The physical and mental well-being of the server.
Beneficiaries	
Impacts on direct beneficiary	The extent to which service brought about the intended changes in the target of the service.
Impacts on indirect beneficiary	The extent to which service affects relevant third parties who are not the direct targets of the service.
Institutions	
Expand service	The extent to which providers are able to increase the number of units of a good or service.
Improve quality of services	The extent to which providers are able to improve the quality of existing services.
Create new institutions	Whether new organizations or organizational units resulted from the service program.
Communities	
Community strengthening	The extent to which social capital, service networks, or other multi-organizational arrangements are enhanced.
Benefit-cost ratio	The ratio of benefits to costs reported for the program.
Volunteer leveraging	The extent to which civic service participants are able to involve other volunteers.

Source: Perry and Thomson (2003).

Table 5.2

Summary of National Service Outcomes

Outcome	Positive	No effect	Negative
Servers			
Skill development	33	5	—
Civic responsibility	14	5	—
Educational opportunity	11	—	1
Self-esteem	10	2	—
Tolerance for diversity	4	5	—
Satisfaction from serving	33	—	—
Health	5	1	—
Beneficiaries			
Impacts on direct beneficiary	30	—	—
Impacts on indirect beneficiary	6	1	—
Institutions			
Expand service	23	—	—
Improve quality of services	24	—	—
Create new institutions	6	4	—
Communities			
Community strengthening	11	5	—
Benefit-cost ratio[a]	13	—	1
Volunteer leveraging	16	—	—

Source: Perry and Thomson (2004).
[a]Benefit-cost ratios greater than 1 are reported in the positive column; ratios less than 1 in the negative column.

ing, but we succeeded in synthesizing important details about the effects of national service. In the interests of service scholarship, it is important to interpret these positive outcomes with caution. The body of research on national service is marked by a number of flaws (Perry and Thomson 2004; Perry and Imperial 2001; Grantmaker Forum on Community and National Service 2000). Nevertheless, contingent generalizations about national and community service based on these findings can be used as guideposts for new primary research.

Discussion and Implications of Findings

Our analysis provides a broad picture of the relationship between service and outcome that allows us to reflect on potential cause-effect relationships. More importantly, our research offers insight into the mediating factors that influence this relationship and underscore its complexity. We summarize these relationships in the form of four propositions.[3]

Proposition 1: The documented outcomes of national service are positive over time and across units of analysis. Research on domestic national service in the United States, all of it produced in the last half of the twentieth century, shows consistently positive results during each of the last five decades. Eighty-five percent of the results for servers are positive. The proportion rises to 97 percent in the case of service recipients and 93 percent for institutions. Research findings on community outcomes approach 90 percent positive. These results were produced even as the level of scrutiny paid to national service increased throughout the 1990s.

From the outset, the Corporation for National and Community Service (CNCS), an umbrella agency created by Congress in 1993 to house all federal domestic service programs, was intended to be a model for government reinvention (Lenkowsky and Perry 2000). Creating CNCS placed the issue of national service program results front and center. Eli Segal, the first chief executive officer for the CNCS, chose to emphasize accomplishments above member development, which magnified the importance of measuring and monitoring results. In addition, because the CNCS launched new programs like AmeriCorps (Perry et al. 1999) and introduced new provisions such as an education award for national service, evaluation became more prominent as a means to understand and measure the consequences of new initiatives.

Although the research findings are largely positive, they are not compelling for all outcomes. In the case of two outcomes, tolerance for diversity and institution building, the mix of research findings produces more ambiguous results. The mediating factors of program design and program management play a key role in determining the nature of these outcomes. It is unlikely, for example, that tolerance for diversity will occur without deliberate implementation tactics such as an organizational culture that values diversity or the design of a program that explicitly incorporates diversity into national service activities.

As for institution creation, although the studies reviewed do not shed a great deal of light regarding mediating factors, some evidence suggests that the tangible and immediate impacts of programs specifically designed to provide direct service may lead to more institution creation than reform-oriented programs designed with more ambiguous, long-term goals focused on institutional change. Clearly, the findings suggest that for each of these two outcomes, high-quality primary studies are needed.

Proposition 2: The effects of service on individual outcomes are mediated by server characteristics. Although many factors influence the relationship between service and outcome depicted in the preceding proposition, differences in server attributes represent one of the most likely and prominent of the factors. Individuals bring different motivations, experiences, abilities, and other attributes to their service. Variations in these individual attributes can reasonably be expected to influence how service affects key outcomes.

Several findings from the analysis serve to illustrate the general point of the proposition. The lower the members' skills at entry, the less likely service will succeed in changing participants' skills. Even if, in the long run, service has transformational effects on some individuals, there is a question of what it can achieve in the short run, particularly when members are seriously deficient in a range of skills. Service may not be the best or right intervention for individuals who lack basic job skills, social skills, and other developmental benchmarks that are critical for labor market competency.

The analysis suggests that the relationship between service and skill development is more nuanced than the preceding discussion reflects. One of the nuances involves the type of skills national service programs seek to develop through service. Service is more influential on generalized life skills than on technical or certification skills. The differential effects seem plausible in that general life skills must be practiced and acquired in social settings. Technical skills involve more esoteric knowledge that may not be readily acquired in a service context alone. Furthermore, the analysis seems to suggest that the greater the intensity of service (long-term or frequent) the greater the likelihood of positive generalized life skill development.

In contrast to the relationship between service intensity and skill development, the relationship between service intensity and civic responsibility is equivocal. Service intensity does not appear to be a requisite for instilling civic responsibility. Low-intensity service is as effective as high-intensity service for producing improvements in civic responsibility. The dynamics underlying this generalization are not entirely clear, but several are defensible given the research. One dynamic is that less intense service opportunities are associated with programs whose primary goal is development of civic responsibility. This is certainly true of many summer programs for youth, such as the Youth Volunteer Corps of America (Ford 1994), that are reported in the research. More intense service experiences, like the CCC or AmeriCorps, are likely to have other primary goals.

Another interesting finding suggested by the analysis is the mediating effects of other server attributes—gender and ethnicity—on the development of civic responsibility. One high-quality study in the analysis did demonstrate a significant increase in civic responsibility among African-American males with no significant changes for the sample as a whole. Overall, however, the research to date does not provide sufficient information about the mediating factors likely to enhance the development of strong civic commitments.

Proposition 3: The type and number of service goals are consequential for service outcomes. A long-term debate in national service revolves around the question, "Who benefits?" (Moskos 1988). Some suggest that the server is the primary beneficiary; others claim that society should be the beneficiary. This analysis suggests that the two goals can comfortably coexist, but that society should receive the higher priority. In addition to placing public benefit ahead of personal benefit, the evolution from service as a server benefit to service as a public problem-solving strategy has been effective in improving the sustainability of service, resulting in greater legitimacy and, not surprisingly, an increase in service opportunities.

The inference that member skills at entry mediate relationships between service and outcome is confounded by the fact that service programs addressing the neediest youth in American society typically pursue multiple goals. For example, many conservation corps seeks to train unskilled youth, preserve the environment, and instill participants with a service ethic. This broadness of scope is not surprising given that the preamble to the 1993 National and Community Service Trust Act identifies no less than eight expansive goals for national service programs, equally demanding and often conflicting.

In his book *The Bill*, Steven Waldman describes the AmeriCorps program as the "public policy equivalent of a Swiss Army knife [in] one affordable package" (1995, 20). This Swiss Army knife characteristic necessarily creates administrative complexity that poses a significant threat to the likelihood of successful national service outcomes. Our analysis suggests that national service can achieve many goals, but few are achieved by serendipity. The CCC is an example of a complex program that worked because responsibilities were clearly allocated among cooperating departments (Sherraden 1979).

Proposition 4: Implementation tactics can mitigate the mediating influences of server characteristics. Besides the mitigating effects of management and design on programs with multiple goals, our analysis suggests additional variables that intervene and may mitigate the adverse effects of server attributes on relationships between service and outcome, not least of which is volunteer training. The volunteer literature strongly underscores the critical role training plays in successful service outcomes. But training, though necessary, is not sufficient to assure successful achievement of service goals. The training must be both effective and efficient. This analysis and the volunteer literature suggest that on-the-job training may be more effective and less costly than formal academic training for service. Capacity of program staff to accurately identify training needs is equally important for successful service outcomes.

This capacity is closely linked with leadership that demonstrates a clear vision for how best to use corps member resources to achieve service goals.

Supplemented by this vision, clear goals for member development, and experienced team and crew leaders, effective and efficient training can greatly mitigate low member skills at entry and the adverse effects of low income and educational attainment among participants in national service programs.

Gaps in Knowledge About National and Community Service

Although the four propositions above provide the first guideposts for developing a research agenda, they are not sufficient for that purpose. Identification of gaps in cumulative knowledge about national service outcomes add the second important piece of information needed to successfully achieve that goal. Our analysis identified explicit and implicit research needs that represent what we believe are the limits and modifiers of the four propositions. Null findings related to the relationship between service and outcome across some of the studies suggest the need for further refinement in research methods and design to better understand the factors that mediate this relationship.

As the preceding discussion of potential causal relationships reflects, one surprise finding is the mediating relationships that emerged. Attendant to the mediators identified in the analysis is the need for research about them; we do not readily understand these mediators within the context of the relationship between service and outcome. Individual attributes, such as the member's skill at entry, age, gender, ethnicity, educational attainment, and socioeconomic status emerge from the analysis as important mediating factors.

The analysis was less successful in finding mediators that explain variations across programs, such as specific service attributes critical for producing strong civic commitments; the mediating effects of quality of service program and individual service experience on the development of self-esteem; or the factors that influence the creation of new service institutions, especially mediators that affect participants' willingness to accept and implement reform. This gap merits attention in future research.

The analysis also exposed many areas where research is underdeveloped. At the individual level of analysis, underdeveloped areas of research on the impacts of service on servers and beneficiaries (direct and indirect) range from ignorance about which skills are most substantially affected by service to lack of reliable and consistent measures of satisfaction from service. We also have a relatively narrow and limited view of service as a problem-solving strategy.

At the institutional level of analysis, the primary gap in research lies with the institution-creation outcome. Clearly, the complexity of this outcome makes it difficult for researchers to define this construct conceptually and operationally. This difficulty, in turn, makes it even harder to identify valid measures.

The key areas ripe for research lie in identifying and examining mediating variables that enhance or decrease the likelihood of this outcome occurring. Which service attributes, for example, affect the likelihood of institutionalization of service in local communities? How do service programs that take a direct-service orientation differ from those that make institutional reform a primary goal? How do programs with different orientations compare across variables such as institution creation, community strengthening, or benefit-cost ratios? Research at this institutional level will generate hypotheses and help to inform research on community-level outcomes.

Like institution-level outcomes, community outcomes are equally amorphous and difficult to define conceptually and operationally. Clear logic models underlying the relationship between service and community strengthening need to be developed to improve our conceptual understanding of how service changes communities. Despite the value of cost-benefit studies for improving our knowledge of the impacts of service on communities, struggling with the more difficult issues implicit in research on community building cannot be avoided if we want to gain a deeper understanding of service and its impacts.

Given that attitudinal outcomes are more easily conceptualized and measured than institution- and community-level outcomes, it is not surprising that most of the service-related research has been done at the individual level of analysis, especially examining what Perry and Katula call "the psychology of service" (2001, 360). This gap in the current body of research needs to be filled. Examining implementation tactics as mediating factors in the relationship between service and outcome provides one way to fill that gap.

Implementation themes such as program management, member recruitment and retention, leadership, and program visibility each represent areas ripe for research, and the policy implementation literature provides a rich field from which to draw insights and hypotheses concerning mediating effects.

Each of these themes needs to be examined individually and in various combinations using logic models that specify a theory of change. Which implementation tactics work synergistically to enhance certain outcomes more than others? Why? What are the implications of these synergies for the design of national service programs? Do funding strategies differ in national service contexts compared to other policy settings? How is financial sustainability realized given the unique political and programmatic barriers characteristic of national service programs? How does leadership change when practiced in a shared-power setting across sectors and within local communities?

Overall, the field of national service in the United States represents a relatively new area for research. As a new field, it has benefited from having developed a large best practices literature, but the focus now needs to shift to the underdeveloped area of behavioral research. Greater emphasis needs to be placed on rigorous research designs and longitudinal studies examining the relationship between service and outcome through the mediating factors identified in this analysis.

Aside from less than optimal research designs that characterize many national service studies, another vexing weakness in the research is the validity and reliability of measures. This limitation of the research is multi-pronged. Part of it stems from the lack of clarity about core constructs in service research. Concepts like service, community building, public work, and civic responsibility are often either poorly defined or not defined at all.

Even when key constructs are adequately defined, they may not be adequately or consistently measured. The reliabilities of measures are frequently unknown. Self-esteem, for example, is frequently measured using only a single survey item. Compounding these problems is lack of standardization of concepts and measures; civic responsibility, for example, may be defined in widely different ways by different researchers despite carrying the same concept name across studies.

Scholar Harry Boyte argues that "from the perspective of civic education, the weakness of community service lies in a conceptual limitation . . . [namely, that service] lacks a vocabulary that draws attention to the public world that extends beyond personal lives and local communities" (1991, 766). Boyte is concerned that most service programs focus on the private nature of service by emphasizing personal growth at the expense of learning political skills such as public judgment, negotiation, and public accountability. He believes that the personal language of many service programs seldom signals the reality of effective citizen action. Community service, from Boyte's perspective, needs a "conceptual framework that distinguishes between personal life and the public world," one that places service explicitly in the public realm by bringing diverse groups of people to "work together effectively to address public problems," what Boyte calls "problem-solving politics" (766–767).

Finally, besides conceptual clarity, the analysis identifies the need to reconsider the nature of the questions being asked about the relationship between service and outcome. Much of the research investigates issues with low probabilities of disconfirmation. Did service increase? Did quality improve? We need to ask more substantively challenging questions, some of which have already been identified in the previous discussion.

Outcome questions should also involve consideration of benefit-cost ratios—that is, benefits in relation to investments. Comparing effects of national service programs (particularly those supported by public dollars and stipended participants) on solving public problems to the effects of individual voluntarism (expressed through the nonprofit sector), for example, is one empirical question in need of examination. A sample of social initiatives of the type showcased in recent analyses of social entrepreneurship (Garr 1995; Sagawa and Segal 2000; Shore 1999) could be compared to a sample of national service programs. Comparisons could be made on a number of dimensions, among them costs, efficiency, and impacts on beneficiaries. In addition to comparing discrete indicators of inputs, outputs, intermediate outcomes, and impacts, an examination of the environment of conduct would be important. We suspect that successful public and private initiatives share a great deal in common.

Developing a Global Research Agenda on National Service

Many challenging questions emerge from this analysis of national service effects in the United States, questions that demand greater attention to conceptual and operational definitions, identification of change models that include mediating factors, and rigorous research designs, preferably longitudinal and comparative in nature. These may be important areas for a global research agenda on national service as well.

Of these questions, however, we believe that the most important issue (because it is foundational) that emerges from our analysis is the need to focus on the meaning and measurement of service. Measurement error frequently occurs in the social sciences because observed data are often *assumed* to represent an underlying concept; without careful attention to the details of clearly defining the concept under study and assessing the validity of indicators used to measure it, the empirical tenability of a theory is often at risk. Lack of attention to the meaning and measurement of the concept of service in service-related research represents a serious gap that greatly limits our capacity to adequately tease out relationships between service and outcome in the United States (Grantmaker Forum on Community and National Service 2000).

At the global research level, the problem becomes even more complex because focusing on the meaning and measurement of service necessarily requires answering the vexing question of whether service is a universal or unique concept. If it is unique, what are the key factors that help to explain this uniqueness (e.g., cultural, social, or political factors)? Does service have a different meaning (with implications for measurement), for example, in democracies than it has in other political forms such as theocracies, socialist or totalitarian regimes, and countries transitioning to democracy? If the concept does vary under different conditions, then how are we to make meaningful cause-and-effect statements beyond single studies? Identifying what those different conditions are and examining the extent to which patterns exist as conditions vary will help, but overall, developing a global research agenda on service is a daunting task. The nature of the research questions will also change depending on whether service is a universal or a unique construct; these questions will, in turn, also impact the development of a global research agenda. Despite these challenges, however, if we are to make meaningful cause-effect statements about service and its outcomes (nationally or internationally), we cannot afford to neglect this specification.

Another facet of the meaning and measurement issue is what "counts" as national service. Our current operational definitions contain biases that merit consideration and resolution prior to embarking on global research efforts. Although we operationally defined national service as involving significant, intense commitments for minimal monetary reward, few, if any, studies associate the work of religious and faith-based communities with national service. From nation to nation, the service of priests, ministers, nuns, rabbis, and other clerical and religious personnel from a variety of religious denominations may be a nontrivial component of national service, but it is seldom classified or measured as such. A similar issue arises in the context of service associated with restitution for criminal or socially proscribed behaviors. Yet another form of national service that may be undercounted is international or transnational service (McBride, Benítez, and Sherraden 2003) because it is performed by foreign nationals who do not have citizenship in the country in which they are working. Each of these potential biases in the way we count national service suggests a research challenge that lies ahead as we develop a research agenda for global service.

Another area closely related to meaning and measurement that illustrates how the research questions may change depending on the universality or uniqueness of the concept of service is this: to what extent are national and community service similar or different? In democracies rooted in federalism, an inherent tension often exists between achieving community service goals and those articulated by the national government. Anecdotal evidence from AmeriCorps*State/National service programs suggests that this tension frequently leads to confusion in the implementation of national service programs through local community-based organizations (Thomson and Perry 1998; Thomson 1999; Perry et al. 1999). In this case, lack of attention to differences in perspectives on the meaning and measurement of service across the different levels of society undermines the implementation of service programs (and hence the outcomes) in the United States. Is this tension unique to democratic and federalist systems of governance or do we find a similar tension between community and national understandings of the nature and purpose of service in other societies with widely different political forms?

We have concluded this chapter with reflections about ways to develop a global research agenda on service. Analysis of the effects of national service in the United States demonstrates a number of critical issues have not yet been adequately addressed in establishing a U.S.-based research agenda. Nevertheless, we believe that service is a sufficiently universal phenomenon that findings from research on national service outcomes in the United States offer insight that can inform a global research agenda.

Notes

1. The key dimensions are closely related to dimensions identified by other scholars such as Charles Moskos, who defines national service as "the full-time undertaking of public duties by young people—whether as citizen soldiers or civilian servers—who are paid subsistence wages" (1988, 1), and Richard Danzig and Peter Szanton, who conclude that "national service is a federally supported program in which, for a period of time, participants sacrifice some degree of personal advancement, income, or freedom to serve a public interest" (1986, 10). The key dimensions are also closely related to Sherraden's definition of civic service as "an organized period of substantial engagement and contribution to the local, national, or world community, recognized and valued by society, with minimal monetary compensation to the participant" (2001, 2).

2. The AFSC is, according to the Global Service Institute's definition, an international service program because the scope of service activity spans two or more nations and is often performed outside of one's nation of origin. We have included Riecken's 1952 study in our synthesis, however, because the program involves Americans working in American communities. That service programs can be both international and national in scope raises the more fundamental question about what makes national service distinctly *national?* This question is a definitional question and one that needs to be debated and discussed, but is beyond the scope of this article. We agree with the Global Service Institute's perspective (McBride, Benítez, and Sherraden 2003), however, that this question represents an important area for continued scholarship if we are to successfully develop a global research agenda on civic service.

3. For additional propositions and a more detailed discussion, see Perry and Thomson (2004), Chapter Seven.

References

ACTION. 1973. *University Year for Action: An Evaluation.* Washington, DC: ACTION.
Barber, B.R. 1984. *Strong Democracy: Participatory Politics for a New Age.* Berkeley: University of California Press.
Boyte, H.C. 1991. Community service and civic education. *Phi Delta Kappan* 72: 765–767.
Branch, A., and M. Freedman. 1986. *YouthCorps Case Studies: The New York City Volunteer Corps.* Philadelphia: Public/Private Ventures.
Branch, A., S. Leiderman, and T.J. Smith. 1987. *Youth Conservation and Service Corps: Findings from a National Assessment.* Philadelphia: Public/Private Ventures.
Control Systems Research Inc. 1973. *The Program for Local Service: Summary Findings.* Seattle, WA: Control Systems Research.

Corporation for National Service. 1994. *Principles for High Quality National Service Programs*. Washington, DC: Corporation for National Service.

Corwin, R.G. 1973. *Reform and Organizational Survival: The Teacher Corps as an Instrument of Educational Change*. New York: Wiley.

Danzig, R., and P. Szanton. 1986. *National Service: What Would It Mean?* Lexington, MA: Lexington Books, D.C. Heath.

Ford, L. 1994. *Youth Volunteer Corps of America: Final Evaluation Report*. Charleston, SC: College of Charleston.

Freedman, M., and L. Fried. 1999. *Launching Experience Corps: Findings from a Two-Year Pilot Project Mobilizing Older Americans to Help Inner-City Elementary Schools*. Oakland, CA: Civic Ventures.

Garr, R. 1995. *Reinvesting in America*. Reading, MA: Addison-Wesley.

Gittel, M. 1981. *Final Evaluation Report on Syracuse Youth Community Service: Executive Summary*. New York: Graduate School and University Center of the City University of New York.

Goldsmith, S. 1993. *A City Year: On the Streets and in the Neighborhoods with Twelve Young Community Service Volunteers*. New York: New Press.

Grantmaker Forum on Community and National Service. 2000. *The State of Service-Related Research*. Berkeley, CA: Grantmaker Forum on Community and National Service.

Hall, J.A., L. Tickle-Degnen, R. Rosenthal, and F. Mosteller. 1994. Hypotheses and problems in research synthesis. In *The Handbook of Research Synthesis,* ed. H. Cooper, and L.V. Hedges. New York: Russell Sage Foundation.

Hart, D.K. 1984. The virtuous citizen, the honorable bureaucrat, and "public" administration. *Public Administration Review* 47: 111–120.

Lah, D., W. Wolf, and S. Leiderman. 1985. *YouthCorps Case Studies: The Marin Conservation Corps*. Philadelphia: Public/Private Ventures.

Lahey, M.A., J.L. Brudney, and W.H. Newbolt. 1995. Implementing the goals of the Corporation for National and Community Service: Lessons learned in the state of Georgia. Paper presented at the Independent Sector Spring Research Forum, Alexandria, Virginia, March 23–24.

Lenkowsky, L., and J.L. Perry. 2000. Reinventing government: The case of national service. *Public Administration Review* 60 (4): 298–306.

Marans, R.W., B.L. Driver, and J.C. Scott. 1972. *Youth and the Environment: An Evaluation of the 1971 Youth Conservation Corps*. Ann Arbor, MI: Institute for Social Research.

McBride, A.M., C. Benítez, and M. Sherraden. 2003. *The Forms and Nature of Civic Service: A Global Assessment* (CSD Report). St. Louis: Washington University in St. Louis, Center for Social Development.

Morone, J.A. 1990. *The Democratic Wish: Popular Participation and the Limits of American Government*. New Haven, CT: Yale University Press.

Moskos, C.C. 1988. *A Call to Civic Service: National Service for Country and Community*. New York: Free Press.

Perry, J.L. 2003. Civic service in North America. *Nonprofit and Voluntary Sector Quarterly,* 167S–183S.

Perry, J.L., and M.T. Imperial. 2001. A decade of service-related research: A map of the field. *Nonprofit and Voluntary Sector Quarterly* 30: 462–479.

Perry, J.L., and M.C. Katula. 2001. Does service affect citizenship? *Administration and Society* 33 (3): 360–365.

Perry, J.L. and A.M. Thomson. 2004. *Civic Service: What Difference Does It Make?* Armonk, New York: M.E. Sharpe.

Perry, J.L., A.M. Thomson, M. Tschirhart, D. Mesch, and G. Lee. 1999. Inside a Swiss army knife: An assessment of AmeriCorps. *Journal of Public Administration Research and Theory* 9: 225–250.

Project Star. 1998. *Seniors for Schools: Content Analysis of 1997–98 Project Evaluation Reports.* San Mateo, CA: Project Star.

Project Star. 2000. *Seniors for Schools Evaluation Results: 1998–1999 School Year.* San Mateo, CA: Project Star.

Riecken, H.W. 1952. *The Volunteer Work Camp: A Psychological Evaluation.* Cambridge, MA: Addison-Wesley.

Rosenbaum, S., and S. Leiderman. 1986. *Youth Corps Case Studies: The San Francisco Conservation Corps.* Philadelphia: Public/Private Ventures.

Sagawa, S., and E. Segal. 2000. *Common Interest, Common Good: Creating Value Through Business and Social Sector Partnerships.* Boston: Harvard Business School Press.

Scott, J.C., B.L. Driver, and R.W. Marans. 1973. *Toward Environmental Understanding: An Evaluation of the 1972 Youth Conservation Corps.* Ann Arbor, MI: Institute for Social Research.

Sherraden, M.W. 1979. The civilian conservation corps: Effectiveness of the camps. PhD diss., University of Michigan.

Sherraden, M.W. 2001. Civic service: Issues, outlook, institution building. Paper presented at the Biennial Conference of the Inter-University Seminar on Armed Forces and Society, Baltimore, October 19–21.

Sherraden, M.W., and D.J. Eberly, eds. 1982. *National Service: Social, Economic, and Military Impacts.* New York: Pergamon Press.

Shore, W. 1999. *The Cathedral Within: Transforming Your Life by Giving Something Back.* New York: Random House.

Thomson, A.M. 1999. *AmeriCorps Organizational Networks on the Ground: Six Case Studies of Indiana AmeriCorps Programs.* Washington, DC: Corporation for National and Community Service.

Thomson, A.M., and J.L. Perry. 1998. Can Americorps build communities? *Nonprofit and Voluntary Sector Quarterly* 27: 399–420.

Waldman, S. 1995. *The Bill: How the Adventures of Clinton's National Service Bill Reveal What Is Corrupt, Comic, Cynical—and Noble—About Washington.* New York: Viking.

Wolf, W.C., S. Leiderman, and R. Voith. 1987. *The California Conservation Corps: An Analysis of Short-Term Impacts On Participants.* Philadelphia: Public/Private Ventures.

III

CIVIC SERVICE ACROSS THE LIFE COURSE

_____ 6

Civic Service Among Youth in Chile, Denmark, England, and the United States

A Psychological Perspective

Judith Torney-Purta, Jo-Ann Amadeo, and Wendy Klandl Richardson

There is wide agreement that civic service is valuable for society. It is also assumed that volunteering has benefits for citizens in general and young people in particular (Morton and Saltmarsh 1997). Cross-national research in this area has been difficult to conduct, in part, because of different concepts that are common in different areas of the world. For example, *service-learning* is a term often used by North American researchers (but sometimes questioned by those in other regions), while the term *solidarity* is commonly used by European researchers (but not always understood by North Americans).

This chapter reports analysis from a cross-national study relevant to civic service, defined as "an organized period of substantial engagement and contribution to the local, national, or world community, recognized and valued by society, with minimal monetary compensation to the participant" (Sherraden 2001, 2). We also use Niemi's (2000) distinction that civic or volunteer service refers to work done in the community that is not directly linked to an academic course or part of a formal school or college curriculum (even if it is arranged by an educational institution). In contrast, service-learning typically refers to activities incorporated into a course or formal curriculum where the volunteer experience is usually preceded by conceptually oriented information about politics or social problems and followed by classroom discussions and written reflections (Eyler 2002b). Being prompted to think and write about the experience is what distinguishes service-learning from youth volunteer programs. Many programs, however, fall between a fully developed service-learning program and civic volunteering.

In the last decade there has been a resurgence of interest in the United States in civic service and service-learning with the development of programs designed to link experiences in the real world with academic learning (Stukas, Clary, and Snyder 1999). Surveys on related topics have been undertaken with large samples. In 1992, as part of a follow-up to the National Education Longitudinal Study of 1988 (National Center for Education Statistics 1988), high school seniors were asked about community service performed during the previous two years. Forty-four percent of the cohort had been involved in a relevant activity. Females, students from higher socioeconomic status families, those with higher reading proficiency, and those in private or in urban schools were more likely to perform community service than other students (National Center for Education Statistics 1995). The National Education Household Surveys of 1996 and 1999 (National Center for Education Statistics 1996, 1999) estimated that just over half of U.S. high school students participated in some kind of community service activity during the previous school year (Kleiner and Chapman 1999).

There have been attempts to define the dimensions of high-quality programs, but the role of self-selection is problematic. Johnson et al. (1998) found that estimates of a service program's effects on high school students' self-esteem and grade point average were reduced when student characteristics were taken into account. There are also differing perspectives about outcomes. Stukas, Clary, and Snyder indicate that coordinators often view service programs as ways "to enhance personal growth of students, particularly their self-esteem and social responsibility" (1999, 2). Instructors, in contrast, often incorporate service-learning to motivate students to learn content. Program goals differ based on the age of the student participant as well as the nature of the work and the community and the duration or intensity of the activity.

In spite of these difficulties, Billig (2000), after an extensive literature review, has argued that some program characteristics enhance the possibilities for positive impact: attributing responsibility to students, student autonomy, student choice, direct contact with the service recipient over a reasonable time, high-quality activities, and well-prepared teachers. On methodological issues, Billig has argued for more complex models for service-learning and called for research to evaluate the effectiveness of service programs (Billig and Furco 2002).

A Selective Review of Research on Outcomes of Civic Service

Research has focused primarily on benefits to the students' psychological development, social development, and academic learning. A brief, selective review of research will give a sense of its variety.

Perry and Katula (2001) conducted a review of 219 empirical studies examining the relationship between service programs and citizenship. Although the studies surveyed small samples and utilized different methodologies, participation in these programs seemed to influence achievement as well as future volunteering and giving. The researchers did not find much evidence connecting service and volunteer programs to civic or political participation or to sense of efficacy (Perry and Thomson 2003).

Based on surveys and the records of 1,000 middle and high school students from seventeen Learn and Serve programs in nine states, Melchior (1997) found positive impacts of service-learning on civic attitudes (including measures of acceptance of cultural diversity, leadership, and personal and social responsibility), school engagement, school grades, and students' educational aspirations. On the other hand, he found no statistically significant impacts on students' communication skills or work orientation. The data were collected only from Learn and Serve programs identified as well established and fully implemented, and all were linked to school curricula.

In another study of a substantial sample, Simon and Wang (2002) examined the impact of service on AmeriCorps volunteers in four U.S. states during a two-year period. Using preservice and postservice measures, the researchers found the greatest positive increase in volunteers' valuing of family, security, and freedom. Simon and Wang did not find a change in optimism, civic attitudes, or social trust. The volunteers did not become more confident in public institutions and reported that the service experience had little impact on their beliefs regarding politics and society. In fact, they became more likely to distrust government and officials.

Increases in understanding of injustice were cited by Primavera (1999), who assigned college students in a psychology class to volunteer in a Head Start family-based literacy program. The effects may have been enhanced by experiences in the volunteer setting linked with topics in the class. Markus, Howard, and King (1993) randomly assigned students to traditional and service sections of a political science course. One of their most interesting findings was the significantly greater degree to which students in the service section reported that they had performed up to their potential in the course and that they had developed awareness of societal problems. Giles and Eyler (1994) reported that among college students involved in community service, self-efficacy rose significantly, and the students aspired to leadership roles in order to have an impact on the political system. Finally, Roker, Player, and Coleman (1999), using data from a study of 1,160 adolescents, found that they were most interested in direct participation that aligned them with community service organizations and in single-issue political groups such as Amnesty International and Greenpeace.

Few empirical studies provide evidence to support the connection between these civic service programs and political participation such as voting or writing to elected officials. Niemi concludes that much community participation is "decidedly nonpolitical, possibly even anti-political, in the sense that it conveys to participants that the way to get things done is by direct, personal action by non-government groups rather than by any governmental programs" (2000, 17). Although such experience could influence a sense of membership in a political community, a number of scholars question whether that happens in most programs.

Cross-national research on civic service by youth is notable for its rarity. Cutler (2002a, 2002b) reviewed young people's involvement in public decisions affecting their lives in a series of monographs, including one on the United Kingdom and one on the United States. A few convention papers describe national service in Scandinavia, but focus more on conscription and conscientious objection service than on volunteering. In fact, the conclusion of one author is that in Denmark it is high local and national taxes used to purchase professional assistance, rather than citizens offering voluntary or mandatory service, that is the basis of the welfare system (Sorensen 2000). Torpe (2003, 340) also reviews evidence about the relative inactivity of Danish youth, calling them a generation that wants to participate in enjoyable activities but does not want to officially join the organization that manages the activities. Among Danish adults, however, organizational involvement is associated with involvement in local politics and internal political efficacy but not with political tolerance.

In contrast to this Nordic view, Yates and Youniss (1999) in their collection of chapters noted that countries such as Italy and Taiwan have difficulty in establishing the necessary level of trust for service activity by youth because of historic problems of corruption. In Italy students often wished to belong to organizations but were not especially interested in the volunteer purposes of the groups. In Taiwan, the stress on high academic achievement tended to drastically reduce the time young people were willing to spend in volunteer activity. Reports of studies in Eastern Europe and Japan have found environmental organizations to be more popular than civic service groups (Yates and Youniss 1999).

In Chile much of the research on participation has been conducted on groups of adult women and not on young people (Torney-Purta and Amadeo 2004).

According to Pilotti (2004), however, organizations of civil society have been established for youth with the hope that these will make up for deficiencies in other areas of civic education in Latin America. Tapia (Chapter 7) describes the research on service-learning in this region.

This review raises several questions about civic service, which will be explored in this chapter:

- Can concepts from psychological theories provide helpful framing for outcomes of civic service?
- Is civic service an experience that is valuable in early adolescence?
- Are experiences in the community (linked with or separate from school experiences) associated with attitudes about political engagement?
- Can the study of social problems in schools have the same types of influence on students' learning as volunteer programs in the community?
- Are the benefits of civic service similar cross-nationally?

These questions expand previous research, which has been largely atheoretical, concentrated on older adolescents and young adults, focused on personal outcomes such as grades or self-esteem, imprecise in examining the relationship between in-school study and community experience, and conducted primarily with data from the United States.

The Psychological Perspective on Civic Service

Psychological theory has been of relatively minor importance in service research, although it has a great deal to contribute. Penner (2002, 463), a social psychologist, has examined volunteerism, emphasizing the long-term nature of these altruistic behaviors that benefit strangers in the context of an organization. In his studies of adults, dispositional factors within the individual can be distinguished from organizational variables related to the decision to volunteer. At the individual level, religiosity and other-oriented empathy are important factors prompting initial volunteering. Penner has posited the development of a sense of identity as a volunteer leading to sustained volunteer activity. Pancer and Pratt (1999) also studied the distinction between factors prompting the original decision to volunteer and factors sustaining a commitment.

Looking at adolescents, Flanagan (2004) has tried to build a coherent approach to the study of civic engagement. She refers to research on identity, social trust, and tolerance but does not deal in depth with theories. After looking at some work that applied cognitive and moral development theories to service-learning (Delve, Mintz, and Stewart 1990; Boss 1994), Eyler (2002a), one of the leaders in research on service-learning, has called for more rigorous research designs that elaborate theoretical frameworks and use them to operationalize better measures of programs and outcomes.

In line with these suggestions, this chapter begins with an examination of four psychological theories and their conceptual frameworks: a stage-developmental personality theory (Erikson), social cognitive theory (Bandura), sociocultural theories (relating to communities of practice), and theories of sociopolitical development and empowerment (from community psychology). The theories are concretized in concepts relevant to civic service for adolescents.

Major concepts identified from these theories will then be operationalized using data from the International Association for the Evaluation of Educational Achievement (IEA) Civic Education Study in which 140,000 fourteen- to nineteen-year-olds in twenty-nine countries were tested and surveyed. The data from the United States, England, Chile, and Denmark relating to civic service (volunteering) and outcomes related to these concepts will be examined for the sample of fourteen-year-olds. In each country a substantial proportion of the nationally representative sample of students reported that they had engaged in some form of volunteering to benefit their community, thus providing groups of reasonable size for comparison purposes.

An Introduction to Four Theories and Five Concepts Relevant to Civic Service

The theories chosen for discussion in this chapter converge around a small number of concepts: trust, efficacy, identity, prosocial attitudes, and a sense of community (see Table 6.1).

Erikson's Stages of Development

Erikson's theory is the most developmentally oriented of the approaches. It is a stage theory delineating periods from infancy to old age. Progression to a more advanced stage builds on the resolution of a previous stage. Each stage presents a conflict or tension exemplified in a continuum of opposites influenced by both biological factors (e.g., the helplessness of the infant) and social factors (e.g., the societal expectation that parents will provide a caring atmosphere for the young child). In infancy these factors interact to establish generalized trust (rather than mistrust), the first psychosocial conflict the individual confronts. Most infants establish a generally trusting relationship with parents who provide the background for later relationships of trust. Although trust is considered in political science and sociology, its roots in the early years are seldom explored. Of interest in this chapter is the

Table 6.1

Emphasis on Concepts Related to Civic Service in Four Psychological Theories

Concepts	Psychosocial developmental stage theory (Erikson)	Social cognitive theory (Bandura)	Socio-cultural theory (Wenger, Lave)	Empowerment/ sociopolitical theory (Watts et al.; Zimmerman)
Trust/social cohesion	X			
Efficacy/industry/agency empowerment	X	X		X
Political/civic identity/meaningful practice	X		X	(X)
Prosocial attitudes/generativity; responsibility for others	X	(X)	(X)	
Sense of community/negotiation tolerance		(X)	X	X

Note: X means that the concept receives major emphasis in the theory; (X) means that the concept is implied or indirectly addressed in the theory.

extent to which trust in political institutions is associated with the experience of service-learning.

The second and third stages of Erikson's theory deal with the child's growing autonomy and initiative, while the fourth deals with the sense of industry (counterposed to the sense of inferiority and confronted when the child enters school). The concept of industry captures the idea that individuals set goals for themselves and realize to one degree or another that they are able to meet those goals. A sense of industry is actually quite close to the self-efficacy delineated in other theories, such as Bandura's.

Logan (1985), a psychologist, speaks of the way in which achieving a sense of industry assists in resolving the crisis of identity at adolescence. Confirming a sense of industry by seeing the results of one's own productive work is a rare experience for adolescents in contemporary society. Logan believes that barriers between age groups drive young people toward consumerism rather than cooperative work that challenges their abilities as the basis of identity. Thus, shared productive work in the community can assist in personal development when students obtain feedback on their actions and see the positive results of their industry-motivated activities (Logan 1985; Youniss and Yates 1997).

In Erikson's theory the concept of identity (characteristic of the adolescent period) has a critically important place. The basic question answered during this fifth stage is "Who am I?"—as a friend, a worker, a member of a profession, or a citizen. The achievement of a sense of identity by the adolescent requires exploring different possible niches and roles. Recent research has indicated that this exploration takes place along related but independent dimensions, such as occupational identity and political identity. Although the political aspect of identity has received less attention than other aspects, Erikson had something like this in mind when he speculated that individuals feel inner connectedness to a group's ideals and a collective future (Erikson 1958, 109). As Youniss and Yates put it, "as youth focus inwardly to find self-sameness (continuity with the past), they must also look outward to form relationships with society's traditions" (1997, 22). Erikson (1968) also believed that society was responsible for providing clear statements and symbols of its traditions, including ideologies based on economic, religious, political, and ethnic group memberships.

To summarize, three principles ground Erikson's understanding of identity:

1. Identity is based on industry as the individual designs action to meet self-chosen goals.
2. Identity advances through joint verification when individuals look to those they trust for feedback and understanding.

3. Individuals can move beyond self- or group-interest to treat differences between individuals and groups in morally just ways (Youniss and Yates 1997, 25).

Erikson's ideas explain the effects of community service in several ways.

> When youth are given opportunities to use their skills to redress problems, they can experience themselves as having agency and as being responsible for society's well-being. . . . When participation is encouraged by respected adults, youth begin to reflect on political and moral ideologies. . . . It is this process of reflection, which takes place publicly with peers and adults as well as privately, that allows youth to construct identities that are integrated with ideological stances and political-moral outlooks. (Youniss and Yates, 1997, 36)

In this process some beliefs and observations are validated, while others are challenged.

Although researchers from various traditions have used the term *civic identity* (Conover and Searing 2000) and have examined political identity in relation to other dimensions of identity (Goossens 2001), the multifaceted concept of identity as defined by Erikson or Youniss has not been studied. The IEA data set allows exploration of identity along with industry (and in relation to other psychological concepts).

Finally, in Erikson's schema of developmental stages, generativity is an issue usually dealt with in later adulthood when responsibility is taken for the next generation. Some recent work by McAdams and de St. Aubin (1998) suggests that a focus on generativity is not confined to adulthood. Altruistic feelings of responsibility for others can be a feature of adolescence. The psychological process that underlies the development of these feelings is the decentration of focus from the self to others, and this begins to take place in middle childhood. Thus the precursors of prosocial attitudes and a sense of responsibility for the welfare of the community may be laid down in early adolescence and may be furthered by community service experiences.

To summarize, Erikson's theory is useful in framing four issues—trust, industry, identity, and prosocial attitudes—that are indicated in Table 6.1.

Bandura's Social Cognitive Theory

Unlike Erikson, Bandura does not conceptualize learning and development as occurring in stages, though he often discusses children's socialization. This theory addresses aggression, prosocial behavior, self-regulation, the role of models, and the sense of self-efficacy.

In Bandura's theory, self-efficacy forms the foundation of humans' capabilities for exercising control over all aspects of their lives (Bandura 2001). As individuals regulate their behavior, they engage in self-observation and evaluate their performance in terms of general abilities or, at other times, in terms of specific standards or goals. A number of studies have linked self-efficacy to behavioral and academic outcomes. Self-efficacy beliefs "vary across domains of activities, situational circumstances, and functional roles" (Bandura 1997, 485).

Bandura asserts that self-efficacy appraisals are based on four types of experience. First, actual performance is perhaps the most influential source of self-efficacy beliefs. Simply put, if a person succeeds at a task, self-efficacy increases. Second, self-efficacy is influenced by observing others. After seeing peers succeed at a task, the belief in one's own success increases. A third source of self-efficacy is verbal persuasion from others. Finally, physiological cues associated with fatigue or tension may signal to an individual that a task is too difficult (Crain 2000).

A positive sense of self-efficacy is important throughout the lifespan as it motivates people to try new activities and to engage energetically in tasks. Bandura writes, "Unless people believe they can produce desired results and forestall detrimental ones by their actions, they have little incentive to act or persevere in the face of difficulties" (2001, 12). Four core features are important in developing a sense of agency: intentionality (formulating alternative plans for action), forethought (developing expectations of the effects of different actions), self-reactiveness (choosing goals and evaluating performance in those terms), and self-reflectiveness (thinking about a broad set of life goals) (Bandura 2001). These are all germane to the process of reflection that is central in many conceptualizations of effective service-learning.

While personal self-efficacy is vital, many things can be accomplished only in concert with others. Bandura (2001), therefore, extends the conception of human agency to collective agency. A key ingredient of a sense of collective efficacy is the belief that social reforms can be achieved by "a critical mass of activists rather than requiring universal participation" (Bandura 1997, 498). Collective efficacy is acquired in similar ways and serves functions similar to those served by personal efficacy beliefs. The idea of collective efficacy has, however, received less elaboration than the personal efficacy construct.

Bandura also discusses political efficacy, which is "the belief that one can produce effects through political action" (1997, 483). He sees belief systems anchoring the models of the world that people use in planning how to achieve desired societal goals. Discussions of this theory have rarely dealt with political efficacy, but Bandura notes, "Children's beliefs about their capabilities to influence governmental functioning may also be partially generalized from

their experiences in trying to influence adults in educational and other institutional settings in which they must deal" (1997, 491). Thus young people's
abilities to influence adults in civic service groups or in schools may enhance
their sense of political efficacy. Efficacy or agency (in both its individual and
its community-based or collective form) is the major concept from this theory
included in Table 6.1.

In contrast to this psychological perspective, in the political science literature internal efficacy and external efficacy are distinguished. Individuals who
believe that they understand and know how to make a difference in the polity
have a high sense of internal political efficacy. External efficacy, in contrast,
is a belief in the responsiveness of social or political institutions to attempts
made to influence them. In most respects, internal efficacy is like self-efficacy.
In contrast, external efficacy may be either self-oriented efficacy beliefs (the
government's, school's, or college's functioning is responsive to individual
action) or collective-oriented efficacy beliefs (the government's, school's,
or college's functioning is responsive to action on the part of groups). One
measure to be examined from the IEA study deals with actions in relation to
the school as the institution to which adolescents are most closely related.
The items were built on a measure designed by political scientists to focus
on collective political efficacy in solving community problems (Yeich and
Levine 1994).

In summary, young people's participation in civic service may influence
their beliefs about personal self-efficacy and also their beliefs about collective
and political efficacy (especially if they are performing tasks where they can
see change). There are two ways in which social cognitive theory extends our
thinking about civic service. Those community or volunteer settings in which
adolescents partner with adults and discuss shared reasoning and beliefs may
be important to developing a sense of efficacy or agency. Further, the term
reflection in civic service has been inadequately defined. This assessment of
Bandura's views of efficacy prompts an examination of the role of adults in
coaching or facilitating the reflection process (Wilkenfeld and Torney-Purta
2004). Reflection is an internal process of thinking through the implications
of actions in service-learning (self-reflectiveness), but benefits from the young
people having opportunities to discuss and elaborate their thinking with adults.
When adults serve this function they serve as more than role models; they also
share their ideas with adolescents (and coach them through difficulties).

Sociocultural Theory

The idea of using adults as coaches or of young people serving as apprentices
in important life settings is elaborated more fully in sociocultural theories,

such as the situated cognition view of Lave and Wenger (1991). This set of theories is now deeply embedded in psychology, but has roots in anthropology and sociology.

Sociocultural theories use the term *legitimate peripheral participation* to describe observation or partial participation in a setting by individuals who are young, relative newcomers or apprentices. Lave and her associates conducted extensive studies of apprentices in tailor shops in Liberia. Along with sewing skills, the apprentices also acquired knowledge of the kinds of garments worn by different social classes and appropriate ways of dealing with persons of different genders and statuses. Through experience that was either intentionally or unintentionally shaped and scaffolded by older group members, novice members gradually moved away from peripheral participation to more central involvement in a community of practice of tailoring.

Although this theory expands ideas about sites of learning beyond the school, several authors have also described school-based learning in these terms. Lampert (2001), in her decade-long study of mathematics classrooms as communities of practice, showed how students moved from peripheral to more central participation in the practices of mathematics. These communities of practice were negotiated around a content focus that teachers and students shared, which was also influenced by forces outside their control (for example, standards and tests, what is perceived necessary for economic success). Teachers attempted to make their classrooms into sites of productive social interaction around the topic of mathematics in which students learned both from teachers and from their peers as members of the community.

These ideas about legitimate peripheral participation can also be applied to citizenship and political socialization. This notion of moving from peripheral to more central participation in various levels of community shaped the ideas about citizenship in the IEA Civic Education Study. The adult-oriented nature of some aspects of citizenship (voting, giving money to candidates) means that adolescents are limited in their practice and must observe or participate in a peripheral way.

Sociocultural theory can also be applied to adolescents or young adults volunteering in a homeless shelter. Like the tailoring apprentices, volunteers have the opportunity not only to learn how to make sandwiches, but to observe the distribution of wealth in society and to grasp the meaning of poverty, including different ways in which people seek to maintain their self-respect. For this to happen effectively, adults must be available to coach or scaffold learning. Another problem is that the young person may not have sufficient time in the setting to move from being an observer to being a more central participant.

In recent formulations of sociocultural theory, Wenger (2001, 1998) has defined communities of practice as focused around a common concern or motivated by passion about an issue. Interaction with others in the community of practice and the search for knowledge to solve problems are essential. The concerns might be about economic well-being or social justice. The passion might be for a political ideology or an issue such as the environment.

In communities of practice, individuals negotiate identities, acquire knowledge and skills that are meaningful as defined by the group, and are engaged in practice. The term *community* can be thought of as helping to define the other elements. Learning as belonging is what Wenger emphasizes (1998, 208). Communities of practice may range from neighborhoods to classrooms to cliques of peers to ethnic group associations to workplaces to the nation. These groups define valued and competent participation for community members. One aim of civic service is that young people feel that they are members of a community of practice consisting of other citizens and of public or private leaders. Definitions of worthwhile goals and practices are continually co-constructed by members through negotiation. Prosocial attitudes and negotiation appear in Table 6.1 among the contributions of sociocultural theory.

Practice, or learning by doing, is also central to this model (Wenger 1998, 14). This usually consists of a joint enterprise or activity, ranging from processing insurance claims (the subject of one of Wenger's books) to cleaning up a polluted stream. Ideas about community and practice are seldom discussed separately, and this chapter will consider them together.

Membership in a community of practice helps its members develop and negotiate "personal identities." Learning as becoming and taking on an identity is what Wenger emphasizes (1998, 14). Identities are personal histories or trajectories that link the individual's experience in families with experiences in other communities of practice. Different communities provide templates for identities, such as a helpful neighbor, an academically successful student, a fashion leader, an environmentalist, an activist for social justice, or a responsible citizen. The development of identity is situated or shaped by communities' definitions and is often conflicted. For example, the identity of *cool person* in the peer group may work against development of the identity of *person concerned about social justice* in a volunteer setting. Sociocultural theory provides richness to the ideas about identity (see Table 6.1).

In sociocultural theories, meaningfulness is shaped through everyday participation in the practice of discussion within the communities to which the individual belongs. Learning as experience is what Wenger emphasizes (1998, 137). Educational institutions try to make a variety of concepts, including citizenship, meaningful to students. The aim of many civic service programs is to make ideas relating to social justice meaningful for young people as they see how experience in the community either validates or conflicts with learning from textbooks. Wenger notes that meaning can be developed on either an individual or a social basis and that it can be either tacit or explicit. Civic service is likely to promote meaningful knowledge in a tacit way and on a social basis. Classroom-based learning about the community is more likely to be explicit and individual in character.

In summary, sociocultural theory is relevant for understanding civic service in its emphasis on identities, meaningful practice, and negotiation in communities (see Table 6.1).

Empowerment Theory and Sociopolitical Development Theory

The final set of theories is recently developed and narrower in scope than those previously considered. Empowerment theory (Zimmerman 2000) and sociopolitical development theory expand on concepts of social change and activism in community psychology. Rather than a focus on a particular developmental stage or on groups such as schools and youth organizations, the focus is on understanding cultural forces, including power, inequality, injustice, and oppression, as they shape status in society. Psychological empowerment connects personal competence with action in the public domain (Zimmerman and Rappaport 1988). People with a sense of empowerment and a critical understanding of the social environment become participants in organized activities to achieve a common goal.

Zimmerman and Rappaport (1988) performed three studies, one with college students (using scenarios of community problems) and two with adult community members (studying their actual involvement in action). Across these studies, political efficacy, self-efficacy, the sense of civic duty (belief that one ought to participate as part of a responsibility to others), and perceived competence (possession of relevant skills and abilities) were predictors of willingness to take public action.

Empowerment theorists believe in the importance of a critical awareness of the social context of a community issue. That awareness includes, first, recognition of the interests of those with power in the situation and how they are connected to the source and solution of the issue; second, the ability to distinguish when conflict is likely to be useful and when counterproductive; and third, the ability to identify resources needed to achieve given goals (Zimmerman 2000, 50).

Watts, Griffith, and Abdul-Adil (1999) in their sociopolitical development theory build on empowerment theory by concentrating on a group that lacks political power: African-American males. They posit five stages: acritical, adaptive, precritical, critical, and liberation. They also suggest coaching strategies designed to move the individual from stage to stage (most of which

Figure 6.1   **Illustration of Two Alternative "Trajectories" Resulting From a Potentially Empowering Experience**

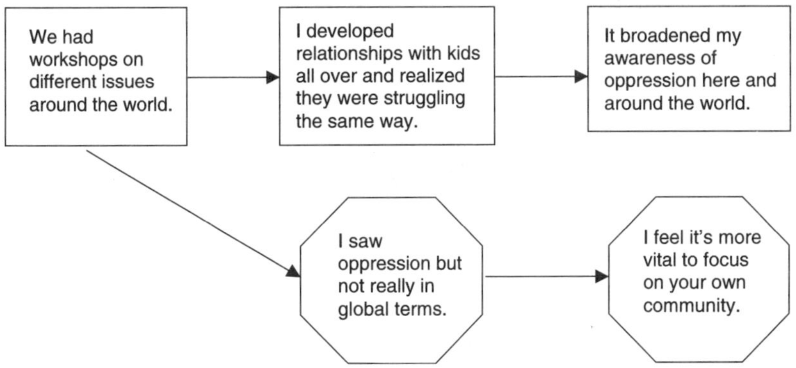

Source: Based on material in Watts, Williams, and Jagers (2003).

involve encouraging critical thinking about oppression, cognitive reframing, recognition of moral challenges, and discussion of community solidarity).

Watts, Williams, and Jagers (2003) build on this theory with an empirical analysis of retrospective interviews with African-American activists, chosen for study because they illustrate a sense of self, incorporating both cultural and sociopolitical dimensions. In addition to considering context generally (as in sociocultural theory), these authors are interested in significant life events that shape development (especially those connected with a particular program or organization) as well as in sociopolitical insight and self (empathy, spirituality). They looked at venues of upbringing experience: (family, schools, communities), the period of late adolescence and early adulthood (especially higher educational organizations), and the postcollege years (often a business or industrial setting where the individual is employed). Their approach is based on the notion that events and effects cumulate across the life period. The interviews are presented in trajectories of sociopolitical development, which are contrasted with alternative versions of events that could have resulted if the respondent had drawn a different set of conclusions from a given experience (see example in Figure 6.1). Persons who are further along than others in sociopolitical development are more aware of social inequality and its sources and are more likely to be empowered or activist in their orientation.

Watts and his collaborators have intersected developmental and sociocultural or ecological factors in their model. This set of theories from community psychology is most relevant to the concepts of efficacy and agency, to identity (especially as an activist), and to community (see Table 6.1).

Theoretical Concepts Common to the Four Theories

Concepts related to efficacy (industry) and concepts related to the sense of identity receive extensive consideration in all these theories. For Erikson, particular periods are especially important (the early school years for efficacy and adolescence for identity). The most thorough explication of self- and collective efficacy is found in Bandura's theory. The community and the role of power and negotiation are especially highlighted in sociocultural theory and in empowerment and sociopolitical development theory. Trust and pro-social attitudes are covered explicitly only by Erikson, but are implicit in other theories.

It appears that the experience of a sense of efficacy (incorporating a sense of autonomy) is vital in civic service. However, there is a long-standing argument in this field about whether overemphasizing students' sense of personal political efficacy may suggest that the average person acting alone can have an unrealistic amount of influence on politics (Hess and Torney 1967, 2006). Sociopolitical development theory introduces a new dimension by discussing injustice and the empowerment of groups that have been marginalized, topics that are not central in Erikson's and Bandura's theories.

There is considerable debate about how narrow a definition of political or civic identity should be adopted. In line with sociocognitive theory's views about the sense of identity as part of meaningful action (Wenger 1998) and the views of political scientists such as Conover and Searing (2000), civic identity will be viewed as broader than political party identification. We will concentrate on the extent to which young people hold norms that support conventional political activity and the extent to which they envision themselves performing political activity in the future. An examination of these theories suggests how experiences of civic service may influence students' trust, efficacy, sense of community, civic or political identity, and altruism. The next sections will operationalize these concepts using data from the IEA Civic Education Study.

The Origin and Methodology of the IEA Civic Education Study

The IEA, a consortium of educational research institutes in nearly sixty countries, focused its large-scale data collections on literacy, mathematics, and science during the 1980s. In the early 1990s, spurred by recent massive changes in political and social structures, some member countries asked for a study of civic education, including measures of young people's attitudes and behaviors. Their aim was to study schools in the context of other institutions and to take advantage of the IEA organization's resources, which included a wide network of research institutes in different countries and a wealth of technical and methodological expertise in cross-national comparative education research. The first phase of the IEA Civic Education Study, from 1994 to 1998, consisted of structured national case studies used as the basis for a consensus process to develop content specifications for a test of civic knowledge (with right and wrong answers) and also a survey of political attitudes and civic behavior items. These data also provided context for interpreting the more quantitative data collected in 1999–2000. For analysis of the data collected during the first phase, see Torney-Purta, Schwille, and Amadeo (1999) and Steiner-Khamsi, Torney-Purta, and Schwille (2002).

The second phase of the IEA Civic Education Study began in 1997. An international steering committee, together with national research coordinators, constructed items and prepiloted and then piloted an instrument (test and survey) that would be suitable for young and older adolescents and would take about two class periods to complete. The attitude survey included a number of scales drawn from political scientists' surveys of adults and was substantially the same for the two age groups. Thirteen scales based on item response theory (IRT) were developed for the knowledge items and for sets of attitudes items (with means set to 10 for attitudes). IRT scaling allows estimation of missing and do not know responses, and the inclusion of anchor items at both age levels makes it possible to compare older and younger respondents on the same metric. Nationally representative samples of students in the modal grade for fourteen-year-olds (a total of about 90,000 students from twenty-eight countries) were tested in 1999; students ranging in age from sixteen to nineteen (a total of about 50,000 students from sixteen countries) were tested in 2000. For a description of scaling and analysis, see Torney-Purta et al. (2001) and Amadeo et al. (2002).

Patterns of Volunteering and Learning About the Community in Different Countries

The IEA instrument asked adolescent respondents about several types of participation in community organizations and in school. The two items discussed in this chapter ask whether students belong to a voluntary organization that benefits the community (yes or no) and whether students believe that in school they learn about how to solve problems in the community (rated on a scale from 1, strongly disagree, to 4, strongly agree).

Table 6.2 indicates the percentage of students reporting that they participate in an organization that conducts volunteer activities to benefit the community. Students in the United States were by far the most likely to report belonging to

Table 6.2

Percentage Participating in Groups Conducting Voluntary Activities to Benefit the Community (fourteen-year-olds)

Above median		Below median	
United States	50	Latvia	12
Colombia	34	Switzerland	12
Hong Kong	34	Russia	11
Australia	33	Slovenia	11
Chile	33	Romania	10
Denmark	32	Portugal	9
Greece	29	Bulgaria	8
England	25	Estonia	8
Hungary	23	Italy	8
Norway	18	Sweden	8
Cyprus	22	Lithuania	7
Czech Republic	22	Finland	6
Belgium (French)	17	Slovak Republic	6
Germany	16	Poland	5

a volunteer organization (with 50 percent of students reporting this activity). High levels of volunteering (20 to 35 percent) were also reported by fourteen-year-olds in the other English-speaking countries, the two Latin American countries, the one Asian country in the study, one of the four Nordic countries (Denmark), and two of the eleven postcommunist countries (Hungary and the Czech Republic).

The analysis in this chapter focuses on four countries. The United States and England were chosen because of current interest in civic service in both countries and high levels of volunteering. These countries share a common political heritage, but differ from each other in the extent to which preparation for citizenship has been an explicit part of the curriculum. In England the average age of students tested was 14.7; 3,043 students were tested from 128 schools. In the United States the average age of students tested was also 14.7; 2,811 students were tested from 124 schools. Two other countries were chosen where the proportion of students who reported volunteering in activities to benefit the community was also large. Chile and Denmark fit this criterion and had participated in the testing of both fourteen-year-olds and upper-secondary students. In Chile the average ages of students tested were 14.3 and 17.9; 5,688 students from 180 schools were tested and formed the sample of the younger population; 5,777 students from 180 schools were tested and formed the sample of the older population. In Denmark the average ages of students tested were 14.8 and 19.4; 3,208 students from 178 schools were tested and formed the sample of the younger population; 2,761 students from 141 schools were tested and formed the sample of the older population. The

Figure 6.2   **Plot Illustrating Correlation Between Adolescent Volunteering and Adult Volunteering**

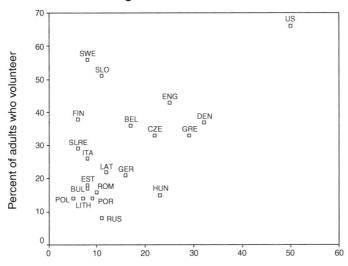

Percent of students who volunteer in community

Sources: Data from Hodgkinson and Weitzman (1997); IEA Civic Education Study, see Torney-Purta et al. (2001).

Notes: Correlation ($r = .54$, $p < .05$); data unavailable for adults who volunteer in AUS, CHL, COL, CYP, HK, NOR, SWI.

older Danish students were the oldest sample in the study (average age 19.4). They were thus the closest to adulthood (and in fact the age of many college students in the United States).

However, before examining within-country relationships of volunteer activities in these four countries, we will examine two relationships at the country level using all twenty-eight countries. Figure 6.2 shows a scatter plot of countries relating the extent to which adolescents in a country volunteer (the percentage from Table 6.2) and the extent to which adults in the country volunteer (data collected by Hodgkinson and Weitzman 1997). The correlation is .54 (significant at the .05 level).

The strong association between volunteer rates at these two ages reflects the large percent of both adults and young people who volunteer in the United States and the low percentage of both adults and young people who volunteer in the postcommunist countries. The correspondence between rates of volunteering by adults and by adolescents is not perfect. In Sweden, Finland, and Slovenia, a large percentage of adults but a relatively small percentage of young people volunteer. The value of behavioral modeling by adults was alluded to in the discussion of Bandura's theory and generally receives support from

Figure 6.3   **Plot Illustrating Correlation Between Adolescent Volunteering and Attitudes Toward Government Responsibilities**

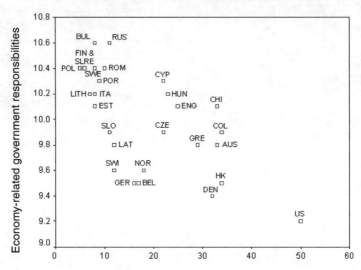

Percent of students who volunteer in community

Sources: Data from IEA Civic Education Study, see Torney-Purta et al. (2001).
Note: Correlation ($r = -.64$, $p < .01$).

this analysis. Keeter et al. (2002) also found that students who volunteered came from families in which adults had volunteered.

Figure 6.3 shows a scatter plot of countries relating the extent to which adolescents in a country are volunteers and the scores of these adolescents on a scale measuring the belief that the government has a responsibility to provide for economic and social welfare needs of the population. This analysis was suggested by research noting that citizens in the Nordic countries attribute responsibility for redressing social and economic inequality to the government, which collects high taxes to pay for these services. The correlation is significant but negative, $-.64$ ($p < .01$). The more that students in a country believe that the government should assume these responsibilities, the less likely they are to volunteer. Again, this relationship is anchored by the United States, where students are especially unlikely to want the government to take these responsibilities and also very likely to volunteer, and by the postcommunist countries, where the opposite is true. Sweden and Finland appear to be social welfare democracies, where the government is given these responsibilities and students do not volunteer. Interestingly Denmark is more like the United States in its pattern than like the other Nordic countries. Although adolescents in Chile and

England have relatively high volunteer rates, they also are relatively likely to believe that the government has responsibilities for social welfare.

There are also many countries where community problems and ways to solve them are an important part of the school's curriculum. Students were asked how frequently they studied about community issues, and when these percentages are examined, the four countries analyzed are sixth in rank (Chile), twelfth (United States), thirteenth (England), and nineteenth (Denmark). In other words, many students in these four countries have the opportunity for both volunteer experience and curriculum-based learning.

Gender and educational experience are among the demographic characteristics of interest. In all four countries females were more likely than males to volunteer (39 percent of females vs. 33 percent of males in Chile volunteer; 34 percent of females vs. 29 percent of males in Denmark; 27 percent of females vs. 22 percent of males in England; 59 percent of females vs. 40 percent of males in the United States). The gender differences are quite pronounced in the United States.

It is conventional wisdom that students who expect to attend higher education are more likely to volunteer than those who expect to leave school after secondary school graduation. This relationship was the most pronounced in the United States, where the correlation between belonging to a volunteer organization and expected years of further education was .206. This correlation was .124 in England and considerably smaller and only marginally significant in Chile and Denmark. This pattern of country differences held for correlations between home literacy resources and belonging to volunteer organizations, though these correlations were not as large as those for expected education.

In summary, examination of the scatter plots between countries and of gender and education differences shows that in the United States volunteering is more likely for females and may be used by some students as a way to enhance an application for higher education. The United States is the country with the most clearly developed adult volunteer culture and the country where there is the least expectation on the part of fourteen-year-olds that the government will undertake responsibilities for social welfare that might otherwise be addressed by civic or voluntary service. A comparison of students who have neither volunteer nor curriculum-based experience with community problems and those with both (as well as those with one or the other) will be presented in the remainder of the chapter.

Comparing Students Who Volunteer With Those Who Learn About the Community in School

The review of theories in previous sections of this chapter identified five concepts and potential outcomes of civic service experience: trust, efficacy and industry, identity, prosocial attitudes (generativity), and sense of community.

The Measures and Analysis

From the IEA Civic Education Study's data we operationalized measures of these concepts and then examined the extent to which experiences in civic service (volunteering and learning about the community in school) relate to these measures in the four countries chosen. Measures relating to these concepts are available for both fourteen-year-olds and seventeen- to nineteen-year-olds and are detailed in the Appendix to this chapter.

The four groups to be compared on these scales represent different combinations of classroom learning and volunteer experience. The analysis within each of the four countries divided students into these groups:

Group 1. Students who reported no classroom experience in learning about community problems and no volunteer experience in the community (labeled Neither);

Group 2. Students who did learn about community problems in class, but had no volunteer experience (labeled Learn/school);

Group 3. Students with volunteer experience, but no classroom learning about community problems (labeled Volunteer); and

Group 4. Students with both classroom learning and volunteer experience (labeled Both). This group can be thought of as similar to a service-learning group, though the survey data do not indicate the extent to which the classroom learning and service were explicitly linked.

The four groups were compared on the trust, efficacy, identity, pro-social/responsibility, and sense of community measures. One-way analyses of variance were used within country with the .001 level of significance. An earlier analysis examined an analysis of covariance, covarying expected education, and the results were substantially the same.

In the presentation that follows, only results from fourteen-year-olds are presented in the figures. All four countries tested students at this level, and the students are of comparable age. The United States and England did not test the older group. An examination of the group differences in trust, efficacy, identity, prosocial, and community measures for seventeen- to nineteen-year-olds in Chile and Denmark showed results that were very similar to those for fourteen-year-olds.

The first part of each section will deal with country differences in overall averages, followed by a comparison between the four groups differing in volunteer and school-related community experiences.

Results for Political Trust

There were differences among countries in the average level of *trust in government-related institutions* (discussed in detail in Torney-Purta et al.

Figure 6.4   **Mean Trust in Government by Country and Type of Participation**
(fourteen-year-olds)

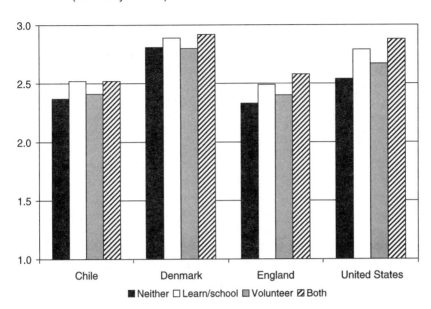

Notes: Significant differences among groups $p < .001$ within all countries.
Both = Volunteer and learn about community problems in school (service-learning).
Volunteer = Volunteer but do not learn about community problems in school.
Learn/school = Learn about community problems in school but do not volunteer.
Neither = Neither volunteer nor learn about community problems in school.

2001). Adolescents in Denmark were the most trusting of those in all twenty-eight countries; adolescents in the United States also rated highly, while those in Chile and England were somewhat less trusting (compare sets of bars in Figure 6.4).

When the four groups differing in experience are compared within country on *trust in government,* students who both participated in volunteer activities and also learned about community problems in school were the most trusting group in England and the United States and were approximately equal to the learn-in-school group in Chile and Denmark. The combination of schooling and volunteering appears to foster trust in institutions, but studying in school about the community without volunteering has a quite similar effect. The profile of differences among groups was the sharpest in the United States, with the highest trust in those with both types of experience, followed by those who only learn about the community in school, followed by those who only volunteer, followed by those with neither type of experience. In the other three countries, adolescents who only volunteered and those who had neither type of experience were similar in having lower levels of trust than those who learned about the community in school.

In summary, there is evidence that learning in schools about solving community problems either by itself or combined with volunteer activity (in an experience like service-learning) is associated with higher trust in government institutions.

Results for Political Efficacy

For *internal efficacy* (a belief that one has the ability to understand the way government works), there were differences among countries, with higher efficacy levels in the United States and Chile than in England and Denmark (Figure 6.5).

Comparing the four participation groups on *sense of internal efficacy,* students who both participated in volunteer activities and learned about community problems in school were the highest group except in Chile (where those with only school-based exposure to the community were approximately the same as those with both types of experience). In the United States and Chile, the group that only studied community problems in school was higher in efficacy than the group that only volunteered (Figure 6.5). This difference was observed to a small extent in Denmark. In contrast, in England the group that volunteered without studying in school had higher efficacy than the group that studied in school without volunteering. Those who had neither the volunteer nor the school experience were the least efficacious in three of the four countries (not in Chile).

Comparing the four groups on *sense of collective efficacy at school,* students who both participated in volunteer activities and learned about community problems in school were the highest group (Figure 6.6). Those who had neither volunteer experience nor school discussion felt the least efficacious in the context of their schools in all four countries.

Reinforcing volunteer experience with study about the community in school appears to be related to higher efficacy of two types (one more explicitly political than the other). Studying about the community in school without volunteering is also related to efficacy. Volunteer experience without associated school learning appears valuable primarily in England.

Results for Political Identity

Political identity was conceptualized more broadly than party identification to include other kinds of conventional citizenship. For *average support for*

Figure 6.5   **Mean Sense of Internal Political Efficacy by Country and Type of Participation** (fourteen-year-olds)

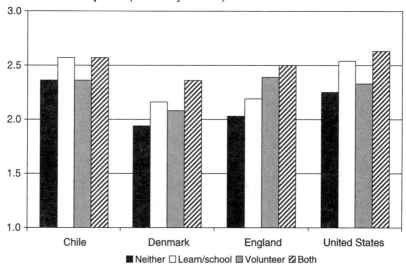

■ Neither □ Learn/school ▨ Volunteer ▨ Both

Notes: Significant differences among groups $p < .001$ within all countries.
Both = Volunteer and learn about community problems in school (service-learning).
Volunteer = Volunteer but do not learn about community problems in school.
Learn/school = Learn about community problems in school but do not volunteer.
Neither = Neither volunteer nor learn about community problems in school.

norms of conventional citizenship by adults, there were differences among countries. Chile and the United States were high, while Denmark and England were relatively low (Figure 6.7).

Comparing the four participation groups on *support for norms of conventional citizenship by adults,* those students who both participated in volunteer activities and learned about community problems in school were the highest group or were tied for the highest group with those who experienced the community only through study in school (Figure 6.7). Although the combination of the two types of experiences appears to foster norms of conventional citizen participation in all four countries, studying in school about the community without volunteering appears to have a similar effect. Across countries, those that had neither volunteer nor school exposure were the least likely to hold these norms. The differences between groups were largest in the United States.

There is one more identity-related measure concerned with the extent to which students envision themselves as future participants in conventional political activities. For the *likelihood of informed voting,* Figure 6.8 shows a pattern very similar to that for support of citizenship norms in Figure 6.7.

Figure 6.6   **Mean Sense of School Efficacy by Country and Type of Participation** (fourteen-year-olds)

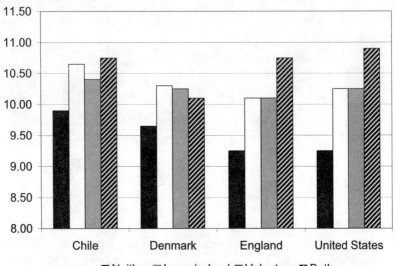

■ Neither □ Learn/school ■ Volunteer ▨ Both

Notes: Significant differences among groups $p < .001$ within all countries.
Both = Volunteer and learn about community problems in school (service-learning).
Volunteer = Volunteer but do not learn about community problems in school.
Learn/school = Learn about community problems in school but do not volunteer.
Neither = Neither volunteer nor learn about community problems in school.
This is an IRT scale with mean set to 10.

Students with both volunteer experience and in-school community study were the most likely to think they would vote in all countries (Figure 6.8). In Chile and the United States, those who only learned in school about the community were more likely to think they would vote than those who only volunteered. In England, the volunteer-only group was higher than the school-only group. Those with neither in-school nor volunteer experience were the least likely to see themselves as voters in all four countries (the smallest difference in Chile).

Results for Prosocial Attitudes

As in the previous section, there are scores for both norms the respondents hold about participation in groups that have prosocial aims and expectations of actual participation. There are substantial country differences in the extent to which students subscribe to *norms of social movement participation.* Again the United States and Chile were high, while Denmark and England were low (for further discussion see Torney-Purta et al. 2001).

Figure 6.7   **Mean Support for Norms of Conventional Citizens Participation by Country and Type of Participation** (fourteen-year-olds)

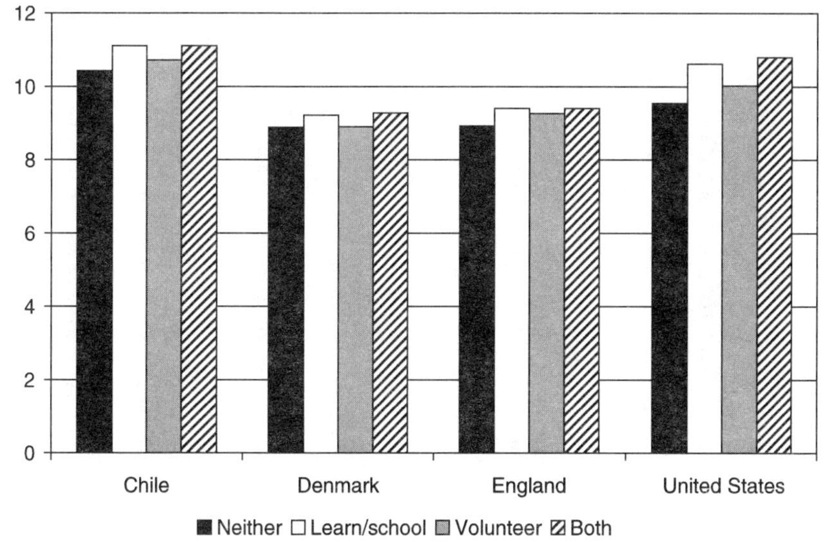

■ Neither □ Learn/school ▨ Volunteer ▨ Both

Notes: Significant differences among groups *p* < .001 within all countries.
Both = Volunteer and learn about community problems in school (service-learning).
Volunteer = Volunteer but do not learn about community problems in school.
Learn/school = Learn about community problems in school but do not volunteer.
Neither = Neither volunteer nor learn about community problems in school.
This is an IRT scale with mean set to 10.

The group differences for *norms of social movement participation* are similar to the norms for conventional political activity (Figure 6.9). In all four countries, members of the group with both volunteer and school-related experiences were most likely to hold these norms relating to prosocial attitudes of social responsibility. In Chile, the group with school experience alone was very similar to the group with both kinds of experience, while in the United States and England, the group with school experience was lower than the group with both experiences, but higher than the groups with only volunteer experience or neither type of experience. The differences in Denmark were small.

When adolescents were asked whether they would be likely to participate in community and charity activities, the differences for the four participation groups in the United States were quite similar to the results for norms (Figure 6.10). Those with both types of experience were most likely to participate, volunteer-only and school-only students had moderate participation, and those with neither experience were the least likely to expect to participate. Across countries, the pattern is that students with neither school

Figure 6.8   **Mean Likelihood of Informed Voting by Country and Type of Participation** (fourteen-year-olds)

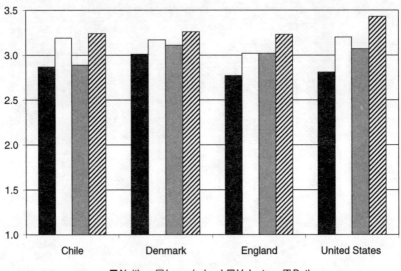

■ Neither □ Learn/school ▨ Volunteer ▨ Both

Notes: Significant differences among groups $p < .001$ within all countries.
Both = Volunteer and learn about community problems in school (service-learning).
Volunteer = Volunteer but do not learn about community problems in school.
Learn/school = Learn about community problems in school but do not volunteer.
Neither = Neither volunteer nor learn about community problems in school.

nor volunteer experiences as adolescents are the least likely to think they will participate in community or charity activities as adults. In Denmark those with only volunteer experience were similar to those with neither type of experience.

Results for Sense of Community

Differences between countries in *ethnic tolerance* were modest. Differences among the four participation groups were also relatively modest, especially in Chile and Denmark. In the United States and England, the highest tolerance was found in the group with both school and volunteer experience. Students with either school-related or volunteer experience were more tolerant than those with neither type of experience in these two countries. These relatively modest differences may result from the variety of experience with diverse groups that students have in volunteer programs.

Figure 6.9 **Mean Support for Norms of Citizens' Participation in Social Movements by Country and Type of Participation** (fourteen-year-olds)

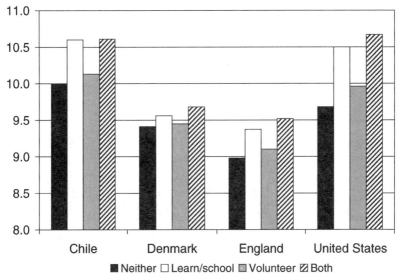

■ Neither □ Learn/school ▨ Volunteer ▨ Both

Notes: Significant differences among groups $p < .001$ within all countries.
Both = Volunteer and learn about community problems in school (service-learning).
Volunteer = Volunteer but do not learn about community problems in school.
Learn/school = Learn about community problems in school but do not volunteer.
Neither = Neither volunteer nor learn about community problems in school.
This is an IRT scale with mean set to 10.

Discussion

We introduced this chapter with the observation that numerous scholars and educators have called attention to the societal value of civic service. This is true in the United States, but also in Latin America and many other regions of the world.

However, attempts to study the impact of civic service have been scattered and have not been carefully related to psychological theories. This chapter has made a first step in identifying relevant concepts drawn from four theories and examining relevant empirical data collected as part of the IEA Civic Education Study.

Across the twenty-eight countries participating in the IEA study, young people tend to become volunteers in countries where large proportions of adults are volunteers. Volunteering is also more widespread in countries where young people do not believe that it is primarily the government's responsibility to provide services for the poor or elderly.

Figure 6.10   **Mean Likelihood of Community/Charity Activities by Country and Type of Participation** (fourteen-year-olds)

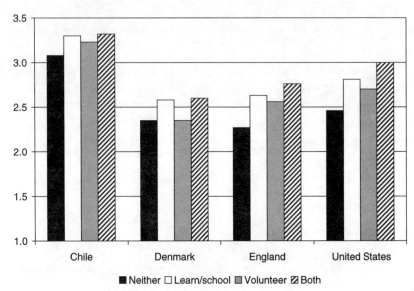

■ Neither □ Learn/school ▤ Volunteer ▨ Both

Notes: Significant differences among groups $p < .001$ within all countries.
Both = Volunteer and learn about community problems in school (service-learning).
Volunteer = Volunteer but do not learn about community problems in school.
Learn/school = Learn about community problems in school but do not volunteer.
Neither = Neither volunteer nor learn about community problems in school.

An analysis of the correlates of civic service experience within four countries shows that participation in voluntary organizations benefiting others in the community and study about community problems in school seem to work together to create an experience that relates to measurable aspects of young people's civic attitudes and engagement (trust, efficacy, identity, prosocial attitudes, and tolerance). This is true to the greatest extent in the United States, to a considerable extent in Chile and England, and to a modest extent in Denmark. These differences may reflect the explicit links between civic education efforts in school and those in the voluntary sector within these countries. Erikson (1958) believes that identity development should be considered within the historical and cultural environment in which it occurs. A stronger historical emphasis on service may have ramifications in both collective and individual identity. Adolescents may also reflect the importance for collective efficacy of a critical mass of adults active in support of an issue, as Bandura suggests.

Schools have an important role to play in this area, and separating academic study from community participation is ill advised (Torney-Purta 2002). In these four countries, students who had experience discussing community problems in school were about as likely to have strong civic identities, to be trusting, and to feel efficacious as those who had both school-based and volunteer experience. The school-learning plus-volunteering and the school-learning-only groups both developed the characteristics that theorists such as Erikson and Bandura advance as vital goals of human development. Students who lacked both types of experience had lower scores on the concepts identified in the four theories. Those who had volunteer experience without learning about the community in school lay somewhere in between. In England, volunteering (even in the absence of school-based learning about the community) seems to be related to some norms and types of expected participation, however. This may be because the voluntary sector has a long and strong history there, while civic education efforts in school have only recently been strengthened.

This empirical analysis is a contribution to our understanding of this area and suggests the need for more explicit links between schools and organizations in the voluntary sector. However, the four theories covered in this chapter provide an even richer source of perspectives, coming as they do from developmental, social-cognitive, cultural, and community psychology.

Erikson's theory envisions a political identity that is more complex than one limited to political party identification. In addition to broadening the meaning of identity, this theory recognizes the importance of young people's trust and sense of agency or efficacy, originating in middle childhood (Torney-Purta, Barber, and Richardson 2004). Both Erikson and the sociocultural theorists emphasize meaning or sense of purpose as fostered by groups in the community. The empowerment theories focus on diminished economic and social power and on particular events as decision points in the trajectories of individuals' lives. Bandura's theory contributes a rich view of several dimensions of efficacy and suggests concrete positive steps (for example, setting proximal goals, providing feedback during periods of reflection, building on past successes, ensuring that positive models are available, and linking self-efficacy with collective efficacy). Not only are the empirical results presented here strengthened by linking them to these theories, but the theories also aid in understanding previously reported findings in the service-learning field (for example, the importance of individuals having a choice of meaningful projects and the value of reflection linking academic study with voluntary service).

When the empirical results reported here are considered together with the perspectives provided by these theorists, they underline the vital role of adults, both inside and outside formal institutions such as the family and the school. Some adults shy away from interacting with adolescents, who are viewed as being interested only in their peer networks. Working together to effect change can help both young people and adults develop a sense of identity as well as meaning or purpose, agency, and self- or collective efficacy. These processes are also important to the development and functioning of communities of practice (Wenger 1998). Adolescents who feel powerless in a society may become empowered by working side by side with adults (Zimmerman 2000). While it is true that young people need to establish their identities on their own terms, they also can benefit from the collective identity that comes from working across generational lines on a common cause. The models of apprenticeship and coaching seem especially promising.

With respect to the issue of the appropriate timing of civic service experiences, many advantages can already be observed in fourteen-year-olds. The two countries that gave the IEA test and survey to older students (ages seventeen to nearly twenty) had results at that level similar to those for fourteen-year-olds. This suggests that these findings have some generalizability to older groups (for example, at the college or university level).

Directions for Future Research

The data from the IEA Civic Education Study can shed light on many aspects of students' civic service and future civic involvement. The availability of well-validated measures from this study, along with compendiums of instruments in the area of civic education, could assist in strengthening measurement in this area (IEA 2004; National Center for Learning and Citizenship 2004).

There are also several lines for future inquiry going beyond the analysis reported here. Future research should build on the exchange of information and research across nations. For example, in England volunteer programs without school-based learning seem to be especially effective; what can other countries learn from the design of these programs? Other research questions raised by these analyses might best be addressed by a combination of quantitative methods with more qualitative or ethnographic studies. For example:

- How does the development of trust early in children's lives influence their future involvement in their communities and their prosocial attitudes? To what extent do young people follow their parents' civic-related behavior or strike out on their own?
- How does the development of individual identity intersect with adolescents' collective identity as members of a school, a community, or a nation? Does civic service enhance the development of collective and/or political efficacy, and if so, in what ways?

- Do young people who interact with adults in a civic service environment have a greater sense of empowerment and self-efficacy than young people who have fewer opportunities to associate with adults?

In short, this expanded set of concepts derived from psychological theories has considerable potential as the basis for more rigorous and cumulative research about civic service.

Appendix. Measures From the IEA Study Operationalizing the Five Concepts

For trust:

- A scale averaging the responses to three items asking about the extent of trust in the national and local government, with high scores indicating more *trust in the government.*

For efficacy/agency:

- A scale averaging the responses to three items about respondents' assessments of their ability to participate in the political realm, with high scores indicating more *internal effica*cy regarding their understanding about and ability to discuss the government.
- An Item Response Theory (IRT) scale (used in the original IEA report with the title Confidence in Participation at School). This is a weighted average of four items, with high scores indicating more *collective efficacy within the school* as an institution (e.g., "students acting together can have more influence on what happens in this school than students acting alone [by themselves]").

For identity:

- An IRT scale (used in the original IEA report), which is a weighted average of six items, with high scores indicating *support for the norms of conventional citizenship by adults* (e.g., it is important for "the good adult citizen to vote; to join a political party; to engage in political discussion").
- A scale averaging the responses to two items about the expectation that as an adult the respondent is likely "to vote" and "to get information about candidates before voting." High scores indicate *a political identity including electoral participation.*

For prosocial attitudes/responsibility:

- An IRT scale (used in the original IEA report), which is a weighted average of four items, with high scores indicating *support for the norms of citizenship in relation to action in social movement groups by adults* (e.g., it is important for "the good adult citizen to participate in activities to benefit people in the community; . . . to take part in activities promoting human rights").
- A scale averaging the responses to two items about the expectation that as an adult the respondent is likely "to volunteer time to help people in the community" and "to collect money for a social cause or charity." High scores indicate *a political identity including community and charity activities participation.*

For sense of community, negotiation, tolerance:

- A scale averaging the responses to four items about the rights of members of ethnic groups, such as "all ethnic [racial or national groups] should have an equal chance to get a good education in this country." A high score indicates *high ethnic tolerance.*

Note

The international mean of each IEA-developed IRT scale is 10 with a standard deviation of 2; the possible range for individual scores is approximately 4 to 16 (for details see Torney-Purta et al. 2001). The mean for each of the other scales varies according to the level of agreement, as does the standard deviation. The possible range is 1 to 4, since each item was answered on a four-point scale (in most cases from strongly disagree to strongly agree, but on some scales from not important to very important or on a scale of frequency).

References

Amadeo, J., J. Torney-Purta, R. Lehmann, V. Husfeldt, and R. Nikolova. 2002. *Civic Knowledge and Engagement: An IEA Study of Upper Secondary Students in Sixteen Countries.* Amsterdam: International Association for the Evaluation of Educational Achievement. www.wam.umd.edu/~ica.

Bandura, A. 1997. *Self-Efficacy: The Exercise of Control.* New York: W.H. Freeman.

———. 2001. Social cognitive theory: An agentic perspective. *Annual Review of Psychology* 52 (1): 1–26.

Billig, S.H. 2000. Research on K–12 school-based service-learning: The evidence builds. *Phi Delta Kappan* 81 (May): 658.

Billig, S.H., and A. Furco. 2002. *Service-Learning Through a Multidisciplinary Lens.* Greenwich, CT: Information Age Publishing.

Boss, J. 1994. The effect of community service work on the moral development of college ethics students. *Journal of Moral Education* 23 (2): 183–198.

Conover, P.J., and D.D. Searing. 2000. A political socialization perspective. In *Rediscovering the Democratic Purposes of Education,* ed. L.M. McDonnell, P.M. Timpane, and R. Benjamin. Lawrence: University Press of Kansas.

Crain, W. 2000. *Theories of Development: Concepts and Applications.* Upper Saddle River, NJ: Prentice Hall.

Cutler, D. 2002a. *Taking the Initiative: Promoting Young People's Involvement in Public Decision Making in the UK.* London: Carnegie Young People Initiative.

———. 2002b. *Taking the Initiative: Promoting Young People's Involvement in Public Decision Making in the USA.* London: Carnegie Young People Initiative.

Delve, C.I., S.D. Mintz, and G.M. Stewart. 1990. Promoting values development through community service: A design. *New Directions for Student Services* 50: 7–29.

Erikson, E. 1958. *Identity and the Life Cycle.* New York: International Universities Press.

———. 1968. *Identity: Youth and Crisis.* London: Faber and Faber.

Eyler, J. 2002a. Reflection: Linking service and learning—linking students and communities. *Journal of Social Issues* 58 (3): 517–534.

———. 2002b. Stretching to meet the challenge: Improving the quality of research to improve the quality of service-learning. In *Service-Learning Through a Multidisciplinary Lens,* ed. S.H. Billig, and A. Furco. Greenwich, CT: Information Age Publishing, Inc.

Flanagan, C.A. 2004. Volunteerism, leadership, political socialization, and civic engagement. In *Handbook of Adolescent Psychology,* ed R. Lerner, and L. Steinberg. New York: Wiley.

Giles, D.E., and J. Eyler. 1994. The impact of a college community service laboratory on students' personal, social, and cognitive outcomes. *Journal of Adolescence* 17(4): 327–339.

Goossens, L. 2001. Global versus domain-specific statuses in identity research: A comparison of two self-report measures. *Journal of Adolescence* 24: 681–689.

Hess, R., and J. Torney. 1967. *The Development of Political Attitudes in Children.* Chicago: Aldine Press.

Hodgkinson, V., and M. Weitzman. 1997. *Volunteering and Giving.* Washington, DC: Independent Sector.

International Association for the Evaluation of Educational Achievement (IEA). 2004. Civic Education Study. www.wam.umd.edu/~iea.

Johnson, J.E., T. Beebe, J.T. Mortimer, and M. Snyder. 1998. Volunteerism in adolescence: a process perspective. *Journal of Research on Adolescence* 8 (3): 309–332.

Keeter, S., C. Zukin, M. Andolina, and C. Jenkins. 2002. *The Civic and Political Health of the Nation: A Generational Portrait.* College Park, MD: CIRCLE.

Kleiner, B., and C. Chapman. 1999. *Youth Service-Learning and Community Service Among 6th-Through 12th-Grade Students in the United States: 1996 and 1999.* Washington, DC: United States Department of Education, National Center for Education Statistics.

Lampert, M. 2001. *Teaching Problems and the Problems of Teaching.* New Haven: Yale University Press.

Lave, J., and E. Wenger. 1991. *Situated Learning: Legitimate Peripheral Participation*. Cambridge: Cambridge University Press.

Logan, R.D. 1985. Youth volunteerism and instrumentality: A commentary, rationale, and proposal. *Journal of Voluntary Action Research* 14 (4): 45–50.

Markus, G.B., J.P.F. Howard, and D.C. King. 1993. Integrating community service and classroom instruction enhances learning: Results from an experiment. *Educational Evaluation and Policy Analysis* 15 (4): 410–419.

McAdams, D.P., and E. de St. Aubin, eds. 1998. *Generativity and Adult Development: How and Why We Care for the Next Generation*. Evanston, IL: Northwestern University.

Melchior, A. 1997. *National Evaluation of Learn and Serve America School and Community Based Programs: Interim Report*. Waltham, MA: Brandeis University, Center for Human Resources and Abt Associates.

Morton, K., and J. Saltmarsh. 1997. Addams, Day, and Dewey: The emergence of community service in American culture. *Michigan Journal of Community Service Learning* 4: 137–149.

National Center for Education Statistics. 1988. National Education Longitudinal Study (NELS). Washington, DC: Institute for Education Studies, United States Department of Education, National Center for Education Statistics. www.nces.ed.gov.

———. 1995. Community Service Performed by High School Seniors (NCES 95–743). Washington, DC: Institute for Education Studies, United States Department of Education, National Center for Education Statistics. www.nces.ed.gov.

———. 1996. National Household Education Surveys Program (NHES). Washington, DC: Institute for Education Studies, United States Department of Education, National Center for Education Statistics. www.nces.ed.gov.

———. 1999. National Household Education Surveys Program (NHES). Washington, DC: Institute for Education Studies, United States Department of Education, National Center for Education Statistics. www.nces.ed.gov.

National Center for Learning and Citizenship. 2004. www.ecs.org/qna.

Niemi, R.G. 2000. Trends in political science as they relate to pre-college curriculum and teaching. Paper presented at the Social Science Education Consortium annual meeting, Woods Hole, Massachusetts, June 22.

Pancer, S.M., and M.W. Pratt. 1999. Social and family determinants of community service involvement in Canadian youth. In *Roots of Civic Identity: International Perspectives on Community Service and Activism in Youth*, ed. M. Yates, and J. Youniss. Cambridge: Cambridge University Press.

Penner, L.A. 2002. Dispositional and organizational influences on sustained volunteerism: An interactionist perspective. *Journal of Social Issues*, 58 (3): 447–467.

Perry, J.L., and M.C. Katula. 2001. Does service affect citizenship? *Administration and Society* 33 (3): 330–365.

Perry, J.L., and A.M. Thomson. 2003. *Civic Service: What Differences Does It Make?* Armonk, NY: M.E. Sharpe.

Pilotti, F. 2004. The promotion of democracy through civic education: An introduction to a project sponsored by the Organization of American States. In *Strengthening Democracy in Latin America Through Civic Education: An Empirical Analysis of the Views of Students and Teachers*, ed. J. Torney-Purta, and J. Amadeo. Washington, DC: Organization of American States, Unit for Social Development and Education.

Primavera, J. 1999. The unintended consequences of volunteerism: Positive outcomes for those who serve. In *Educating Students to Make a Difference: Community-*

Based Service Learning, ed. J.R. Ferrari, and J.G. Chapman. Binghampton, NY: Haworth Press.

Roker, D., K. Player, and J. Coleman. 1999. Exploring adolescent altruism: British young people's involvement in voluntary work and campaigning. In *Roots of Civic Identity: International Perspectives on Community Service and Activism in Youth*, ed. M. Yates, and J. Youniss. Cambridge: Cambridge University Press.

Sherraden, M. 2001. *Youth Service as Strong Policy* (CSD Working Paper 01–12). St. Louis: Washington University in St. Louis, Center for Social Development.

Simon, C.A., and C. Wang. 2002. The impact of Americorps service on volunteer participants: Results from a two-year study in four western states. *Administration and Society* 34 (5): 522–540.

Sorensen, H. 2000. National service arrangements in Denmark. Paper presented at Fifth Global Conference on National Youth Service, Jerusalem, Israel, June 11–15.

Steiner-Khamsi, G., J. Torney-Purta, and J. Schwille, eds. 2002. *New Paradigms and Recurring Paradoxes in Education for Citizenship: An International Comparison*. Vol. 5. Oxford: Elsevier Science.

Stukas, A.A., Jr., E.G. Clary, and M. Snyder. 1999. Service learning: Who benefits and why. *Social Policy Report* 13 (4): 1–23.

Torney-Purta, J. 2002. The school's role in civic engagement: A study of adolescents in twenty-eight countries. *Applied Developmental Science* 6 (4): 203–212.

Torney-Purta, J., and J. Amadeo. 2004. *Strengthening Democracy in Latin America Through Civic Education: An Empirical Analysis of the Views of Students and Teachers*. Washington, DC: Organization of American States, Unit for Social Development and Education (UDSE).

Torney-Purta, J., C.H. Barber, and W.K. Richardson. 2004. Trust in government-related institutions and political engagement among adolescents in six countries. *Acta Politica* 39 (4): 380–406.

Torney-Purta, J., R. Lehmann, H. Oswald, and W. Schulz. 2001. *Citizenship and Education in Twenty-eight Countries: Civic Knowledge and Engagement at Age Fourteen*. Amsterdam: International Association for the Evaluation of Educational Achievement. www.wam.umd.edu/~jtpurta/.

Torney-Purta, J., J. Schwille, and J. Amadeo, eds. 1999. *Civic Education Across Countries: Twenty-four National Case Studies from the IEA Civic Education Project*. Amsterdam: International Association for the Evaluation of Educational Achievement.

Torpe, L. 2003. Democracy and associations in Denmark: Changing relationships between individuals and associations? *Nonprofit and Voluntary Sector Quarterly*, 32 (3): 329–343.

Watts, R.J., D.M. Griffith, and J. Abdul-Adil. 1999. Sociopolitical development as an antidote for oppression: Theory and action. *American Journal of Community Psychology* 27 (2): 255–271.

Watts, R.J., N.C. Williams, and R.J. Jagers. 2003. Sociopolitical development. *American Journal of Community Psychology* 31 (1/2): 185–193.

Wenger, E. 1998. *Communities of Practice: Learning, Meaning and Identity*. Cambridge: Cambridge University Press.

———. 2001. *Cultivating Communities of Practice*. Boston: Harvard Business School Press.

Wilkenfeld, B., and J. Torney-Purta. 2004. Developmental outcomes associated with service-learning in undergraduate students. Unpublished manuscript.

Yates, M., and J. Youniss, eds. 1999. *Roots of Civic Identity: International Perspectives on Community Service and Activism in Youth.* Cambridge: Cambridge University Press.

Yeich, S., and R. Levine. 1994. Political efficacy: Enhancing the construct and its relationship to mobilization of people. *Journal of Community Psychology* 22 (3): 259–271.

Youniss, J., and M. Yates. 1997. *Community Service and Social Responsibility in Youth.* Chicago: University of Chicago Press.

Zimmerman, M. 2000. Empowerment theory. In *Handbook of Community Psychology*, ed. J. Rappaport, and E. Seidman. New York: Kluwer Academic/Plenum Publishers.

Zimmerman, M.A., and J. Rappaport. 1988. Citizen participation, perceived control, and psychological empowerment. *American Journal of Community Psychology* 16 (5): 725–750.

7

The Potential Effects of Service-Learning and Community Service in Educational Settings in Latin America

María Nieves Tapia

Schools and universities around the world have structured and supported students' community service for decades or even centuries. Some combine meaningful tasks in the community with classroom instruction, as service is combined with learning; but only some of these schools and universities call what they are doing service-learning. In Great Britain, some call it "active learning in the community" (Britton 2000), while in Germany the reference is to "action projects" or "civic projects" (MCyE 1998). In Latin America and the Caribbean, schools call it *proyectos educativos solidarios* or *voluntariado educativo solidario* and universities call it *trabajo comunal universitario* or *prácticas solidarias*. No matter what it is called, service-learning can be found in very different cultural contexts, including Latin America.

The first section of this chapter offers service-learning definitions, explores service dimensions in educational settings, and distinguishes between different types of service programs. An overview of the history of service-learning in Latin America and the United States is provided. The second section describes service programs in educational settings in Latin America and the Caribbean, focusing on school-based and university-based community service (service as the primary goal) and service-learning programs (service and learning as dual primary goals). The third section outlines questions for future research to explore the possible effects of service-learning in the region.

Definition of Service-Learning and Service-Learning Concepts

Defining Service-Learning

The difficulties for Spanish-speaking researchers to translate accurately such expressions as civic service and *solidaridad* are outlined elsewhere (Tapia 2002, 2003). Service-learning is an equally complex expression, and its meaning is debated even among English-speaking scholars (Kendall 1990; Furco 2002; Cairn and Kielsmeier 1995; Sigmon 1996). Service-learning as a pedagogical device was named in the mid- to late 1960s when William Ramsay, Robert Sigmon, and Michael Hart used the term to describe a project in the United States that linked students and faculty with tributary area development organizations around the Oak Ridge Associated Universities. The expression was adopted by the first service-learning conference gathered in 1969 in the United States (Eberly 2002; Titlebaum et al. 2004). The term has migrated worldwide. In 1990 Jane Kendall reported as many as 147 definitions, and the number has likely grown since then.

This chapter does not attempt to resolve the conceptual diversity, an effort that may not be necessary in any case. Instead, the chapter takes a practical approach. To ground consideration of service-learning, two definitions guide the analysis. First, according to the U.S. National and Community Service Trust Act of 1993:

> Service-learning is a method whereby students learn and develop through active participation in thoughtfully organized service that:
>
> • Is conducted in and meets the needs of communities;
> • Is coordinated with an elementary school, secondary school, institution of higher education, or community service program and the community;
> • Helps foster civic responsibility;
> • Is integrated into and enhances the academic curriculum of the students, or the education components of the community service program in which the participants are enrolled;
> • And provides structured time for students or participants to reflect on the service experience.

(National Youth Leadership Council and University of Minnesota 1993, 1)

Second, the Argentina Ministry of Education definition considers *aprendizaje-servicio* (service-learning) to be those *proyectos educativos solidarios*

Figure 7.1   **Service-Learning Quadrants**

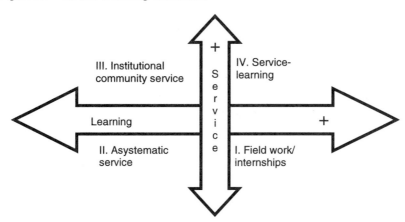

Source: Adapted from Service-Learning 2000 Center (1996).

(solidarity-oriented educational projects) developed by students, aimed to address a real demand of the community, and oriented in an explicit and planned way to enhance the quality of academic learning (Programa Nacional Escuela y Comunidad 2001). When translating service-learning into Spanish, some authors use the phrase *aprendizaje en servicio* or *servicio aprendizaje*, which stresses the learning over the service. The preferred term is *aprendizaje-servicio,* which stresses both service and learning (Tapia 2000).

Service-Learning, Civic Service, and the Quadrants of Service

Service-learning may be considered a form of civic service (Tapia 2002; Sherraden 2001, 2). However, not every service project organized by a school or university is defined as service-learning. It may be helpful to classify different kinds of educationally based service projects and programs as captured in Stanford University's service-learning quadrants.

The vertical and horizontal axes refer to the level of service and learning in a project or program. Quality in the case of service is associated with beneficiaries' satisfaction with the service provided; measurable impact on quality of life, including immediate needs and longer-term development concerns; and collaboration with nongovernmental organizations (NGOs), community organizations, and government institutions. In the case of learning, quality is associated with impact on academic learning and personal growth, strength of institutional policies adopting service-learning, and students' participation in the design and development of the projects (Tapia 2000).

The four quadrants of service and learning have varying levels of these quality dimensions. Quadrant I includes projects primarily oriented to learning but providing de facto service. Field work and internships may be included in this category. Quadrant II includes activities with low levels of community service and little to no connection to classroom learning. Actions are organized by a group of students or teachers with no connection to institutional planning. Generally, nonprogram-based service activities, such as occasional campaigns or reactions to immediate needs in the community, fall into this category. Quadrant III includes community service marked by high service but little or no connection to a curriculum. Quadrant IV includes service-learning, implying both high-quality service and learning. Service-learning projects are oriented to achieve educational and social goals, even if they may stress these goals in different ways (Sigmon 1996).

It would be fair to say that applying these quadrants to any given service project or program will reveal gray zones. The boundaries between community service and service-learning may change over the history of a project, as might the balance between social interest and learning goals. That is why Furco has proposed a neutral, more balanced expression of community service-learning (2002, 14). In South American Spanish we have faced a similar question between *proyectos solidarios* (community service) and *aprendizaje-servicio* (service-learning). As the equivalent of Furco's community service-learning, *proyectos educativos solidarios* can be used to refer to the wide universe of service projects organized in educational settings, including unsystematic service, community service, and service-learning.

The History of Service Learning in the United States and Central and South America

The history of service-learning has followed very different patterns in the United States and South America. A first difference pertains to their diverse theoretical influences. The origins of service-learning in the United States can be traced to the beginning of the twentieth century and the influence of John Dewey on pedagogy. In the 1920s, Dewey organized what is considered one of the first service-learning experiences in an educational setting, at Antioch College in Yellow Springs (Eberly 1968). Dewey's experiential education approach is still one of the major theoretical influences in the U.S. service-learning field, and authors focusing on service-learning theory still refer to him (Conrad and Hedin 1982; Giles and Eyler 1994).

The oldest service-learning practices in Central and South America can be found in Mexico with the 1910 requirement that service be performed by university undergraduates and graduates.[1] Acción Social, the current mandatory requirement of service in Mexican universities, was instated in 1945 as a way for those privileged enough to access higher education to contribute to the country's development (Gortari Pedroza 2004). The Latin American educational system was strongly influenced by French eighteenth-century encyclopedism and positivism, making rational knowledge far more important than empirical experience. In this context, students' community service activities were by definition optional and extracurricular, leaving little space for service-learning in a strict sense.

For cultural reasons more than educational policies, solidarity activities have always been a normal part of students' lives in Central and South America (Tapia 2000), but they began to be especially considered for their educational value in the second half of the twentieth century. Freire (1973, 1992, 1997) and constructivism stressed the need for a stronger relationship between education and the social context and encouraged the development of *proyectos de investigación-acción* (research and social action projects) in the 1970s (PaSoJOVEN 2004). Prosociality and psychological resiliency studies have been significant as a theoretical influence in regional developments (Roche Olivar 1998; Melilo and Suarez Ojeda 2001; MECyT 2004).

A second difference between the United States and Central and South America pertains to the definition of service-learning practice. Since the 1960s, the service-learning concept has been widely used in the United States, where most teachers define their practices either as community service or as service-learning (NCES 1999; Billig 2004). In Central and South America, teachers refer to their projects in many different ways: *proyectos educativos solidarios, voluntariado educativo, acción social, trabajo comunal,* and *prácticas curriculares en comunidad*. Only some teachers call their practices *aprendizaje-servicio* (Tapia 2002), as demonstrated in a collection of case studies over the last few years in Argentina (Tapia and Mallea 2003), Brazil (Cruz 2004), and Chile (Eroles 2004).

The lack of common definition perhaps makes it harder in South America to identify and study service-learning practices, and it also makes the service-learning movement more elusive—even though it may be an empirical reality. In the United States, the service-learning movement has been promoted basically by schools and NGOs. Colleges and universities took leadership in the 1960s and secondary (and some primary) schools followed. Organizations like the National Service Secretariat (founded by Donald Eberly in 1968), the National Youth Leadership Council (founded and directed by James Kielsmeier since 1982), the Campus Compact (1985), and many others were key actors, introducing service-learning in the public arena. Service-learning federal policies in the United States arrived later with the 1993 National and Community Service Trust Act, almost seventy years after Dewey and thirty years after the first service-learning conference. This law established Learn and

Serve America as the first federal resource for service-learning practitioners. Two years later the U.S. secretary of education signed a joint declaration of principles with Learn and Serve America, explicitly backing service-learning methodology (Cairn and Kielsmeier 1995).

In some South American countries, policies and political support are coming sooner than they did in the United States. In Argentina, the oldest documented service-learning projects began between 1978 and 1982 (Tapia, González, and Elicegui 2004), and the first research on service-learning experiences was conducted by the Federal Ministry of Education in 1997. The ministry organized the first service-learning conference (I Seminario Internacional de Escuela y Comunidad) in 1997. With only a fifteen-month interruption during the political crisis in 2002 and 2003, four different administrations have supported service-learning as a national policy (Tapia and Mallea 2003). In Chile, service-learning was introduced in 2000 by the Ministry of Education as a tool to improve educational quality in the poorest schools of the country and rapidly expanded to schools and universities after that (Ministry of Education, Chile 2005). In Costa Rica, it was the secretary of education who established a service requirement in secondary schools. In Colombia, the Ministry of Education is now exploring service-learning as part of its citizenship skills program.

These government interventions do not mean that NGOs and practitioners do not play a key role in promoting service-learning in the region. Opción Colombia, Adopta un Herman@, Faça Parte, Universidade Solidaria (UniSol), Centro del Voluntariado del Uruguay (CVU), Centro Boliviano de Filantropia (CEBOFIL), Alianza ONG, and Latin American Center for Service-learning (CLAYSS) are only some of the NGOs leading the emerging service-learning movement in the region.[2]

A comparative study on service-learning as it is practiced in the United States and in Central and South America as well as the Caribbean is still to be developed, and any generalization in this matter should be tempered. In Central and South America there are no regional studies on average duration of the service projects, but primary and secondary schools' mandatory service requirements range from thirty to ninety hours of service per year. In Argentina, Uruguay, Chile, and Brazil, service-learning is not mandatory and duration of the projects is counted in months, not in hours. According to recent research, the average duration of primary and secondary service-learning projects in Argentina is fifteen months (Tapia, González, and Elicegui 2004). Considering that students serve a minimum of four hours a month, the average service-learning project duration may be about sixty hours, three times the U.S. average, which may provide a more sustainable service to Argentina's communities (Tapia, Gonzalez, and Elicegui 2004).[3] Another difference still to be investigated pertains to the social and economic status of the students providing service. In most of the U.S. service-learning projects, students offer service to people with greater needs than they have. Among the sixteen 2002 Leader Schools selected by Learn and Serve America, only one was attended by students with troubled personal and school histories (Learn and Serve America 2002). On the other hand, twenty of the forty Argentinean schools awarded with the Premio Presidencial Escuelas Solidarias in 2000–2001 were attended by students with unsatisfied basic needs, who were serving people as poor as themselves. It may be that Central and South American service-learning projects are more likely to be inclusive of poor students as service providers and not just as recipients. Projects focus on the students' empowerment, recognizing their potential to solve problems affecting them and their families. Service-learning represents a powerful tool for citizenship education among populations formerly passive and entangled in clientelistic relations with governments (Tapia and Mallea 2003).

Education-Based Community Service and Service-Learning in Central and South America

In this second section, education-based community service and service-learning in Central and South America are reviewed. According to the service quadrants already presented, under community service we will describe programs focused on service and then programs intended to achieve both social and educational goals. In each case, examples in primary and secondary schools and in higher education are provided. There are mandatory and voluntary programs at educational levels.

Mandatory service and voluntary service are contested approaches to serving. Advocates of mandatory service generally consider it a way to universalize the civic and social commitment of youth, representing the idea of mandatory national service and conscription. If learning language or mathematics is not optional in school, they say, then learning citizenship skills should not be optional either. On the other side, those who see service as a personal, voluntary, and ethical decision consider the idea of forcing someone to be good as misguided and potentially even a denial of basic human rights. Little research has been done in Latin America or any other part of the world to back one position or the other. Recent studies in U.S. universities suggest that mandatory service requirements may produce less positive impacts with possibly some lasting resistance against community service (Furco 2004b). In the Dominican Republic, educational officers report that the mandatory requirement of sixty hours of service in high school has become simply a bureaucratic procedure for most students.[4] On the other hand, countries like

Mexico and Costa Rica claim impressive social impacts from mandatory service provided by their students in vulnerable communities (Gortari Pedroza 2004; Meoño and Mongecorrales 2002).

In Mexico, Costa Rica, Colombia, and the Dominican Republic, mandatory and almost universal service programs for secondary or higher education students have been in place for decades without great resistance. Perhaps endorsement of mandatory service has to do with urgent social needs, but also with the fact that in most of the region more than half of the population has not completed secondary studies and only 10 to 12 percent of the population has completed tertiary or university studies (UNESCO 2001). Mandatory service by secondary and university students is therefore seen as a way for privileged minorities to give something back to society, especially in countries where universities are funded by the state. In other countries, like Argentina, Brazil, Bolivia, Chile, and Uruguay, there is no national tradition of mandatory service for students, and service-learning programs may be mandatory or voluntary according to the decision of each educational institution.

It is worth noting that any descriptive criterion is only an attempt to present in an ordered way a very complex reality. In fact, different types of service may coexist in the same educational setting. For example, Costa Rica University has a mandatory service requirement for graduation but also offers a voluntary service program. In Universidad Autónoma de México (UNAM), students may fulfill their requirement of 480 hours of service in three different ways: *Servicio Social de residencia,* an internship program; *Brigadas de fin de semana o períodos vacacionale,* service during weekends or vacations; or *Servicio Social Titulación,* a classic service-learning program.[5] Something similar happens in schools. Carlos Pellegrini School, a prestigious high school in Buenos Aires, has both a mandatory and a voluntary service program. In schools all around the region, informal community service activities coexist with formal service-learning projects.

Community Service

Higher Education

Latin American universities and tertiary institutions (teachers colleges and technical colleges) have a long tradition of community service. Even if focused on service goals, community service programs usually have an informal but strong educational component, in the sense that students typically improve their skills while they serve and enhance their social and civic consciousness. The vast majority of community service programs are developed on a voluntary basis, with some major exceptions.

Mandatory. Mexico's Servicio Social is a mandatory requirement of service in higher education, which can be considered community service. The vast majority of the service activities are developed in isolation from the curriculum or with very weak links with it, according to the Mexican Secretary of Education (SEP 2001, 192). After a long history, Servicio Social is being evaluated and revised (Gortari Pedroza 2004). The 1910 Mexican constitution established in Article 5 that Servicio Social should be mandatory for every professional. The requirement was part of a vision of the university as a tool for national development (Gortari Pedroza 2004). The service requirement was first implemented in UNAM Medical School with medical students living and practicing for six months in rural and isolated areas. Articles 4 and 5 of the Mexican constitution were regimented in 1945 by a federal law establishing a mandatory, paid, temporary Servicio Social for university students and university graduates less than sixty years old. Each university regulated the requirement, which in the beginning was fulfilled almost exclusively by medical students.

Interestingly enough, it was the 1968 students' protest movement that pushed to extend and diversify the service opportunities provided by Servicio Social. During the 1970s and the 1980s there was a massive expansion of the service system. The number of students engaging in Servicio Social went from 224,000 to 757,000 (Gortari Pedroza 2004). Economic crises since the 1980s reduced the budget available for Servicio Social, and there are growing concerns about the lack of uniformity in implementation across the nation. The ANUIES is currently working with the Secretary of Education to evaluate and redesign Servicio Social. Regardless, the numbers are impressive (Sanchez Soler 2003, 103). All around Mexico, students are providing housing, health, and education to thousands of their fellow citizens, helping isolated villages and contributing to local and national development.

Voluntary. Voluntary community service is the oldest and most widespread form of service in higher education, but also the most difficult to study because of the vast range of activities and programs. In most of the region, these activities are organized basically through three different institutional channels: (1) *extensión* departments, where the higher education institution organizes and funds service opportunities for students; (2) students' unions (*centros de estudiantes*), where service is organized by students through unions or associations, with or without support or funding from university authorities; and (3) NGOs offering service opportunities, where students attending different higher education institutions participate in service opportunities organized by an NGO.

1. Extensión Departments. Most Latin American universities were built on three pillars: teaching, research, and extension. Traditionally, the term *extension* has been used for extracurricular activities involving service given by faculty or students to other institutions or the public. The expression itself reveals a still prevalent notion that the university is essentially different from the community, with service as a tool to extend the university beyond the campus borders. In this context, student community service is seen as part of university outreach and, by definition, as something essentially different from academic activity. Today the extension concept embraces a wide and diverse range of activities, including cultural and recreational programs, advisory and technology sales to corporations, health care, and legal advice. Some extension services are free; others are an important source of income for the university. University faculty and staff provide some of these services; others are offered by students or staff as volunteers. Students' community service may be more or less significant in university life depending on institutional policies.

A characteristic example of extension may be Simón Bolívar University in Caracas, Venezuela. The extension department there has been organizing different activities to serve the local community for the last fifteen years. Currently it provides training, technical assistance, and free legal advice to local NGOs, training for microenterprises, and other educational services to needy communities near the campus. University students, faculty, and employees work together in this voluntary program. Universidad de Costa Rica, along with the mandatory service-learning program, involves students, faculty, and retired professors in projects addressing the environment, health, and education (Meoño and Mongecorrales 2002). Catholic and evangelical universities in the region also provide community service. University missions are organized with a mix of social and practical activities in rural or needed areas. Year-round missions are also growing in almost all the large cities in the region.

Voluntary community service, without any religious component, has been growing in most of the Catholic universities since the 1970s. For example, Universidad Católica de Occidente in Santa Ana, El Salvador, has six special departments for community-oriented projects: Unidad de Proyección Social, Instituto de La Familia, Oficina de Asesoría Legal Católica, Instituto de Asistencia Empresarial, Instituto de Desarrollo Educativo, and Instituto de Desarrollo Rural. Among the wide range of activities, students and faculty operate a literacy program, provide free legal and technical advice for needy families and local NGOs, and repair and rebuild public and private buildings, including almost 400 houses for homeless families to date.

2. Student Unions. Since the beginning of the twentieth century and even before, student unions have been major political forces in Latin America. Even if the political commitment of youth is diminishing in most Latin American countries, student unions are still a strong part of university life, and community service is one of their most traditional activities. Summer service camps, literacy campaigns, and health services are some of the most frequent activities. Unions' community service activities are sometimes linked to political activism, but in recent years service projects tend to be nonpartisan activities. Powerful national federations of students are able to run nationwide service programs, like the literacy program Nunca es Tarde (It's Never too Late) developed by Federación Universitaria Argentina through its regional sections in alliance with NGOs and public and private funding.

3. NGO-Sponsored Service. Local and national NGOs offer specific community service opportunities to higher education students. For example, in Brazil, UniSol, an NGO founded in 1995 and funded by private and public companies, gathered 1,500 students and 150 professors from 148 universities to serve in 149 of the poorest communities of the country in 2001. Even if it is organized basically as a community service program, students are selected to work in projects related to their field of study, promoting informal preprofessional training.

Basic Education

Community service occurs in schools throughout Latin America. Frequently, the service is provided to the community around the school or even inside the school to fellow students. As in any other kind of community service, priority goals have to do with fulfilling community needs. Nevertheless, when community service is organized in educational settings and performed by young students, it may have informal educational effects. Even if there is no local research on the educational impacts of community service, a strong hypothesis is that community service, even if isolated from the curriculum, may have a strong impact on students' attitudes toward social problems, constituting a motivation for lifelong civic participation.

Mandatory. Several countries in the region require students in their last year at secondary school to fulfill hours of community service as a requirement for graduation. These include Colombia, Costa Rica, Honduras, Santo Domingo, and Venezuela. Another mandatory community service program for secondary students in the region is enforced through the IBO. Table 7.1 presents a comparative view of mandatory service requirements in secondary schools in Latin America and the Caribbean.

Table 7.1

Mandatory Service by Secondary Students in Latin America and the Caribbean

	International baccalaureate organization	Colombia	Costa Rica	Honduras	Santo Domingo	Venezuela
Mandatory requirement						
Established	1982	NA	1995	NA	1988	1980
Hours of service	At least one project in two years	90	30	90	60	60
Service performed during	Two last years of studies		Last year of secondary school			
Activity	Creativity, action, and service			Community service		
Supervised by	International baccalaureate organization regional office	Ministry of education	Secretary of education, orientation department	Ministry of education	Ministry of education, orientation department	Ministry of education, culture and sports

The IBO was founded in 1968 in Geneva, Switzerland, as a nonprofit educational foundation. Its original purpose was to facilitate the international mobility of students preparing for university by providing schools with a curriculum and diploma recognized by universities around the world. The IBO Diploma Program is a comprehensive, two-year, international curriculum, available in English, French, and Spanish. As part of the requirements for graduation, students have to perform CAS activities, including artistic projects, sports, and community service. IBO established a regional office in Latin America in 1982 and now has 186 affiliated schools. Service activities developed under the CAS umbrella in Latin American schools may be generally defined as community service. In 2002 an IBO regional conference in Latin America promoted service-learning as an effective way to fulfill the diploma goal.

Colombian students in the last two years of secondary school are required to perform ninety hours of service in the security forces. Civilian defense and traffic patrol are the most common activities. In 1980, the Venezuelan Law of Education (Reglamento de la Ley Orgánica de Educación, art. 27) established a mandatory service requirement to be met by all secondary students before graduation. The Ministry of Education was to regulate the practice, but according to sources, directives have been missing, and schools tend to seek the assistance of NGOs or organize their own ways to fulfill the requirement. In some schools, service is fulfilled by painting a classroom, while in other schools students offer peer tutoring or travel to serve rural communities (Blanco 2002). In the 1980s Honduras established a mandatory service requirement totaling ninety hours for secondary students, which they must meet in order to graduate. No reliable data have been found on the effective enforcement of the requirement, but informal sources suggest that the Honduran Ministry of Education is interested in renewing the requirement.[6]

In the Dominican Republic, the secretary of education established a sixty-hour service requirement for secondary school graduation. Service was originally linked with two important national issues: literacy and reforestation. Planting trees is still one of the most popular activities, but schools and students have also been allowed to choose other service activities. Fulfillment of the requirement is widespread, but there are huge differences in the quality of the projects and the effective enforcement of the total number of service hours. Since 2003, the Dominican Republic's secretary of education has promoted the transition of mandatory community service into service-learning projects, with the support of an alliance of NGOs and international agencies known as Sirve Quisqueya.

Since 1995, Costa Rica's Ministry of Education has established the Servicio Comunal Estudiantil (Student Community Service) program, which provides community service and explicitly teaches community values to secondary students. Each student in Costa Rica must deliver thirty hours of community service through individual or group projects. Projects must be approved by the School Student Communal Service committee and supervised by teachers (Meoño and Mongecorrales 2002).

Even if there is no formal research on mandatory service in Latin American schools, anecdotal evidence suggests that teacher training and initiative are keys in transforming mandatory community service from a formal requirement into effective service programs. The impacts of service on students and communities vary depending on the quality of school planning and leadership, students' motivations, and local support.

Voluntary. Voluntary community service in schools is probably more widespread, though it may be even less studied in the region. There are neither systematic studies nor any kind of national statistics. As it happens with most of the young volunteers, students performing community service are almost invisible to the media and the academy (Tapia 2004, 21). Community service activities are part of normal school life in the region. Many schools have kept their service projects going even in times of military governments, when community service may be considered subversive and students' unions may be outlawed. An expression of solidarity deeply rooted in Latin American people, community service is generally oriented to the community around the school, especially in the case of primary schools.[7] Hospitals and homes for the aged usually host students. At community centers, students organize recreational activities, peer-tutoring, and soup kitchens. Many NGOs sign agreements with schools to benefit from students' voluntary work.

Service-Learning

As already mentioned, service-learning practices are more widespread in the region than the service-learning label. In the following section, service programs that may be considered service-learning are discussed. Criteria used to identify service-learning are active student engagement and meaningful service with academic learning and a structured curriculum. Basic education (primary and secondary schools) and higher education are discussed, distinguishing program examples as either mandatory or voluntary.

Basic Education

It is difficult to say, in the present state of service-learning research, whether primary and secondary schools practice service-learning more than higher education institutions. However, it is clear that, at least in the Southern Cone

(Argentina, Brazil, Chile, Uruguay), secondary schools lead the service-learning movement with high-quality projects (MECyT 2004). Across Central and South American schools, however, service-learning is practiced by every type of learning institution. In fact, service-learning can be found even in preschools and special education schools for children with disabilities. A repeated motto among service-learning practitioners is: "Nobody is too young or too poor not to have something to give."

Mandatory. There is no mandatory service-learning requirement at the national level in any country in Central or South America. Nevertheless, four examples illustrate mandatory service-learning. Some schools may organize service-learning projects for students to fulfill a national learning requirement. In Venezuela and the Dominican Republic, as well as in some IBO schools in Mexico and Argentina, students perform service-learning projects connected to a specific topic in the curriculum. Some schools also require service-learning practices of all students based on institutional policy. Schools may establish particular requirements for graduation or promotion or mandatory extracurricular activities. In Argentina, the 1990s educational reform recommended research and social intervention projects for students concentrating their studies in the humanities, the social sciences, and the natural sciences (MCyE 1997). Another example is service-learning projects that require participation by all students during regular school time. Since they involve every student, they are mandatory, even if they are not required by national or institutional regulations. In Colonia, Uruguay, for example, a sixth-grade teacher organized an environmental education program. Students identified environmental problems on the beach in front of the school and found solutions using contents and skills developed in class. The city and private donors funded the cleaning of the beach, based on the students' recommendations. Service-learning through internships may also be considered mandatory. For example, in Chile, technical students fulfill their fourteen-day mandatory internship by building houses in the rural communities around the school. The experience allows students to get in touch with the communities' traditions and with their common roots (Tapia 2002; Escuela Solidaria Premio Bicentario 2004; Ministry of Education, Chile 2005).

Voluntary. A majority of the documented service-learning experiences in the region may be defined as voluntary because the students perform their service after school hours and during the weekends. The school-based curriculum part of the project may be common to all the students in a given grade, but only those who choose to volunteer complete the service part of it. Teachers, however, are commonly involved, even though they may not be paid for it. They go with the students in their off time. In fact, teachers' commitment has been a key factor in the expansion of service-learning in Latin America. Over the last ten years, voluntary service-learning has also been promoted by national educational policies in several countries through National Ministries of Education (Argentina, Chile), alliances between NGOs and educational authorities (Brazil, Uruguay, Dominican Republic), or NGO leadership (Bolivia).

In Argentina, the Ministry of Education has promoted service-learning since 1997. The administration provides a national award for the best service-learning projects each year. Schools present service-learning projects developed during the year, and the best receive funding to strengthen their practices. Awards are personally delivered by the president, increasing public visibility and recognition. The number of submissions for the award grew from 3,000 in 2000 to 5,500 in 2003, demonstrating teachers' and students' commitment to service-learning even during Argentina's most recent economic and political crisis (2001–2002).

Chile's Ministry of Education has promoted service-learning since 2000. Liceo para Todos is a program that uses service-learning as a tool to fight school dropout and to improve educational quality. The program promotes peer tutoring as an effective service-learning method in more than 200 secondary schools. In 2001 and 2002, 120 schools in Chile were awarded funding to develop quality service-learning projects dealing with specific community problems (Ministry of Education, Chile 2005).

In Brazil, Faça Parte and other NGOs are building nationwide alliances to promote service-learning. Joven Voluntario-Escola Solidaria is a program that was launched during 2001 and has expanded nationwide. Faça Parte uses the concept of *voluntariado educativo* because it found negative resonances in the English term *service,* but the methodology it promotes is fully consonant with the service-learning pedagogy (Sberga 2003). Faça Parte has brought national recognition to schools doing community service and service-learning.

In Uruguay, secondary, private schools were the traditional sponsors of service-learning, but in recent years it is emerging in public, primary, and technical schools. The Aprendiendo Juntos (Learning Together) program is implemented by CVU, funded by the Kellogg Foundation, and backed by the national educational authorities. The program offers teacher training, technical assistance, and economic support for service-learning project development. In the first two years it supported thirty projects in thirty primary schools, with 1,700 pupils and 400 teachers participating (CVU 2004). In Bolivia, CEBOFIL promotes service-learning in public and private schools, offering teacher training and helping schools establish their own youth volunteer centers.

Higher Education

Most of the service-learning projects at the higher education level are generally associated with innovative professors who establish a service requirement as part of a course in order to engage their students in meaningful professional practices. As service-learning is only beginning to be known in higher education, there are a variety of references to its practice, including *pasantías en comunidad, prácticas en terreno, práctica social curricular,* and *prácticas educativas solidarias.* As a direct consequence of the low level of recognition, there are no systematic records on university-based service-learning programs or courses. Using the limited available information, below is a description of the range of programs, again with the mandatory versus voluntary distinction.

Mandatory. A few universities in Central and South America have adopted general service-learning requirements, but most of the mandatory service-learning practices are established for specific courses or careers and not for all the students at a university. Among the pioneers is Costa Rica University's Trabajo Comunal Universitario (TCU), which was established in 1975. TCU's goals include, the following:

> Contribute to Costa Rican society's development process. . . . Give back the benefits provided by University education with service aimed to favor community development [service goals]. . . . Develop students' social sensibility through interaction with national problems. . . . Enrich and feed back to academic life to make it more adequate for society's needs [learning goals]. (Costa Rica University 1975)

While Mexico's Servicio Social may be fulfilled through individual projects focused on a single discipline, such as health, Costa Rica's projects are performed by multidisciplinary teams of students pursuing different careers. Faculty members are heavily involved. During 2003, TCU offered more than eighty different multidisciplinary projects to fulfill the mandatory requirement of 150 to 300 hours of service. In 2004, service-learning programs include developing an oral traditions databank, assisting NGOs in the southern region of the country, and producing educational materials for primary and secondary schools.

Over the last ten years, a growing number of higher education institutions around the region have introduced different kinds of mandatory service-learning requirements, which are normally associated with completion of professional training. Students complete their learning in nonacademic settings. Economic or business students may assist NGOs to improve their accountability and fund-raising systems, while architecture and engineering students give assistance to public housing projects. In this kind of service-learning, students are evaluated on their personal performance, but impacts are generally measured in terms of the beneficiaries. The impacts of these projects on students' learning, life projects, and citizenship are unknown.

In 2004, the Medical School at Tucumán University in Argentina was awarded the first prize in the Presidential Award for Service-Learning Practices in Higher Education. The program requires medical students in the last six months of their studies to work in health care centers in the poorest areas of the city, visiting homes to identify children suffering severe malnutrition and treating them until they are recovered. The impact of the project on the recipients is demonstrable. In two years, 385 children recovered from near starvation.

Voluntary. Voluntary service-learning projects in higher education may be developed by a small or large group of students or they may be organized by governments. In Ecuador, 800 students from the teachers colleges took part in the Monsignor Leonidas Proano National Literacy Campaign over a four-month period. In Argentina, more than 1,000 higher education students tutor 11,000 at-risk high school students as part of the Aprender Enseñando program, promoted by the National Ministry of Education. Large-scale voluntary service-learning programs are also offered by NGOs. In Chile, Fundación para la Superación de la Pobreza is running, among other service programs, Adopta un Herman@ (Adopt a brother/sister): university students develop their social and professional skills by tutoring secondary students, who then are also encouraged to organize their own service-learning projects. Adopta operates in six of the twelve provinces in Chile, in forty universities and teachers colleges.

Opción Colombia, an NGO founded in 1991 by a group of students and professors, is now active in twenty-six universities in Colombia and is currently expanding to five other countries in the region through Opción Latinoamérica. Opción Colombia is oriented both to public service and students' learning. Through the semester of service, one of six main programs, the organization sends volunteer students to work in rural areas for six months. Students offer their knowledge and skills to local community organizations, and they receive academic credit for service.

Building the Knowledge Base on Service-Learning: Consideration of Key Questions

The universe of service opportunities and programs is only beginning to be documented in Central and South America. Information is still fragmentary, and there is an urgent need for more descriptive research as well as comparative impact research on service-learning practices at different educational levels. Informational needs are so great that it is difficult to prioritize, but a number of key questions emerge.

More than half of all Latin America children and youth live in poverty (Kliksberg 2003). Twenty percent of all children in the region do not attend primary school, and even if attendance in secondary schools has increased in recent years, 46 percent of all youth are not in school (UNESCO 2001). In this context, a fundamental question for service researchers is whether service-learning helps schools to include and retain the most disadvantaged children and youth. Even if we do not have conclusive evidence, we do have documentation that service-learning occurs in schools in the region that are attended by very vulnerable students. Some service-learning impacts have been identified in relation to the most critical variables: school attendance, prevention of school failure, and institutional climate.

The Chilean Ministry of Education has assessed the first three years of service-learning projects in 200 of the most vulnerable schools in the country. Results demonstrate consistent impacts in school attendance with a reduction of school dropout and academic failure.[8] Especially successful, according to the first evaluations, are the peer-tutoring activities, with positive impacts on both volunteers and beneficiaries (Eroles 2004). A case study in eight Argentinean schools with disadvantaged youth also found improvements in school attendance, dropout rates, and performance on national educational tests (Gonzalez and Elicegui 2004, 188–206). The research design and methods do not allow for the control of other potential influences on these changes (e.g., faculty, administration, curriculum changes, outreach, funding), but service-learning may be one of the variables creating the positive effects.

Does service-learning improve the quality of education? In the Latin American countries where school attendance has grown significantly, the concern now is that those students receive a high-quality education. What is meant by quality education? It likely includes basic scientific knowledge, critical and reflexive thinking, complex communication skills, prosocial attitudes and values, and preparation for work and civic participation. Educational reforms in the region in the 1980s and 1990s produced isolated results (UNESCO 2005). Service-learning is one strategy that has all these as potential goals, and limited research in the United States has demonstrated effects in these areas (Furco 2004a, 19–26; Billig 2004). One study even suggests that these impacts are stronger among more disadvantaged students (Brandeis University 1999). Service-learning practitioners in Latin America and the Caribbean would agree based on their experience, but there is too little systematic research in the region to demonstrate the truth of this suggestion.

In Argentina, service-learning not only considers students as the citizens of tomorrow, but also promotes their commitment and leadership in the present. In the future, it may be especially relevant for Latin American countries with a strong clientelistic history and a weak tradition of citizen participation to measure impacts of service-learning programs on civic and social attitudes. School principals in Argentina, Chile, Uruguay, and Brazil describe a common pattern. Service-learning projects have changed school climate, reduced disciplinary problems, and improved relationships between faculty and students and between teachers and school authorities who are involved in the projects. More students feel more proud of their schools, and more parents who never showed up at school meetings do so now. All these signs are encouraging, but must be more carefully documented and studied.

The third area of research is the impact of service-learning on beneficiaries and communities. In the United States and Europe, little research has examined these impacts (Furco 2004a, 19–26). Clearly it is difficult to isolate demonstrable impacts in communities after only twenty hours of student service, but again, anecdotal evidence suggests that these may occur. The Liceo Remehue program in Chile has provided hundreds of buildings for needed communities. Students at a Santo Domingo high school conducted research that located new sources of drinkable water for their community. A rural school in Uruguay ran a successful campaign to change village habits toward garbage disposal. A technical school in Argentina provided environmentally friendly, alternative sources of energy to isolated communities in the Andes. Kindergarteners have started a public library in a small village, changing the reading habits of young people and adults in just two years (MECyT 2004). These positive stories suggest that better research is needed.

A final question concerns the relationship between the quality of the service provided to the community and the educational impact on students. One hypothesis is that the more significant the service is for the community, the more significant the experience may be for students and the more they may learn from the service experience. In Latin American communities, where youth may be associated with drugs, violence, and legal violations, quality service-learning may have the power to turn potential juvenile delinquents into local heroes and to change the youths' perceptions of themselves. Again, this result is speculative until we have better research.

Even though the origins of service-learning can be traced to the beginning of the twentieth century and before, service-learning research is still under construction. "The research base, while growing, is still in need of more studies, and of studies that meet the criteria for scientifically based evidence" (Billig 2004, 24). "Although the existing studies of service-learning have been helpful in shedding light on the various potential outcomes of service-learning, the studies have not been conducted through any collective, systematic approach.

Rarely have the studies been based on prior research findings" (Furco 2003, 18). Moreover, of the research that exists, most has been conducted in the United States. In a comparative context, U.S. experiences probably occur with economic resources that may not be available in the developing world. Similar studies are needed in other countries. Producing local studies on service-learning, and showcasing inclusive models, may open a wider global framework for service-learning and civic service in Latin America and other regions.

Notes

1. Although Mexico is part of North America, it culturally identifies with Latin America.

2. NGO Web sites: Opción Colombia (www.opcioncolombia.org.co), Adopta un Herman (www.adoptaunhermano.cl), Faça Parte (www.facaparte.org.br), UniSoli (www.unisol.org.br), CVU (www.aprendiendojuntos.org), CEBOFIL (www.cebofil. org), Alianza ONG (www.alianzaong.org.), and CLAYSS (www.clayss.org).

3. Data from ongoing CLAYSS research on K–12 service-learning in Argentina.

4. Interviews done by the author with Dominican Republic Secretary of Education officers, 2002–2003.

5. For an example of a classic service-learning program, see Secretaria de Servicios a la Comunidad at www.dgose.unam.mx/ss/ss.htm.

6. Information provided by Honduras UNPD (United Nations Program for Development) officers, 2002.

7. As studied in ongoing CLAYSS research on 5,000 schools offering community service-learning in Argentina. Research funded by Washington University in St. Louis, Center for Social Development, Global Service Institute.

8. Thanks to Teresa Marshall, Director of Secondary Education at the Chile Ministry of Education, for sharing this unpublished information.

References

Billig, S.H. 2004. Heads, hearts, and hands: The research on K–12 service-learning. In *Growing to Greatness 2004: The State of Service-learning Project.* St. Paul, MN: National Youth Leadership Council.

Blanco, J. 2002. La solidaridad se puede aprender. *El Nacional*, Caracas, May 17.

Brandeis University. 1999. *National Evaluation of Learn and Serve America: Summary Report.* Waltham, MA: Brandeis University, Center for Human Resources.

Britton, F. 2000. *Active Citizenship: A Teaching Toolkit.* London: Community Service Volunteers Education for Citizenship-Deutsche Bank.

Cairn, R.W., and J. Kielsmeier. 1995. *Growing Hope. A Sourcebook on Integrating Youth Service into the School Curriculum,* 3rd ed. Minneapolis: National Youth Leadership Council.

Centro del Voluntariado del Uruguay (CVU). 2004. Press release. November.

Community Service Volunteers (CSV) Education for Citizenship. 2002. Discovering Citizenship through active learning in the community. A teaching toolkit. Created by Francine Britton with new materials in association with the Institute for Global Ethics. London: CSV Education for Citizenship-Deutsche Bank.

Conrad, D., and D. Hedin, eds. 1982. *Youth Participation and Experiential Education.* New York: Haworth Press.

Corporation for National and Community Service. 1993. *The National and Community Service Act of 1993.* www.learnandserve.org/about/lsa/history.asp.

Costa Rica University, Trabajo Comunal Universitario (TCU). 1975. www.vas.ucr.ac.cr/tcu/index.html.

Cruz, P. 2004. The experience of Faça Parte–Brazilian Volunteer Institute (Instituto Brasil Voluntário). Paper presented at the 7th International Seminar of Solidary Service-Learning, Buenos Aires, Argentina, October 6–7. www.me.gov.ar/edusol.

Dominican Republic Secretary of Education officers. Interviews with the author in 2002–2003.

Eberly, D. 1968. Service experience and educational growth. *The Educational Record.* Washington, DC: American Council of Education.

———, ed. 1988. Service experience and educational growth. In *National Service: A Promise to Keep.* New York: John Alden Books.

———. 2002. Service-learning and prosociality. In *Aprender sirve, servir enseña.* Buenos Aires: Centro Latinoamericano de Aprendizaje y Servicio Solidario (CLAYSS).

Eroles, D. 2004. Service-learning: School programs for all. Paper presented at the 7th International Seminar of Solidary Service-Learning, Buenos Aires, Argentina, October 6–7. www.me.gov.ar/edusol.

Escuela Solidaria Premio Bicentario (Solidary School Bicentennial Award). 2004. www.bicentenario.gov.cl/inicio/escuela_solidaria.

Freire, P. 1973. *Pedagogy of the Opressed.* Buenos Aires: Siglo XXI Editors.

———. 1992. *Pedagogy of Hope.* Sao Paulo: Paz e Terra.

———. 1997. *Pedagogy of Autonomy: Necessary Knowledge for the Educational Practice.* Buenos Aires: Siglo SXXI Editors.

Furco, A. 2002. Is service-learning really better than community service? A study of high school service program outcomes. In *Service-Learning: The Essence of the Pedagogy,* ed. A. Furco, and S.H. Billig. Greenwich, CT: Information Age Publishing.

———. 2003. *Service-Learning and the Engagement and Motivation of High School Students.* Berkeley: University of California, Berkeley, Service-Learning Research and Development Center.

———. 2004a. The educational impacts of service-learning. What do we know from research? Paper presented at the 7th International Seminar of Solidary Service-Learning, Buenos Aires, Argentina, October 6–7. www.me.gov.ar/edusol.

———. 2004b. Service-learning impact: State of the art: Meeting the challenges of service-learning research. Paper presented at the 7th International Seminar of Solidary Service-Learning, Buenos Aires, Argentina, October 8.

Giles, D.E., Jr., and J. Eyler. 1994. The theoretical roots of service-learning in John Dewey: Toward a theory of service-learning. *Michigan Journal of Community Service Learning* 1 (1): 77–85.

Gonzalez, A., and P. Elicegui. 2002. NYS and service-learning: What is learnt when we learn to serve? Paper presented at the 6th global conference of the Association for National Youth Service, Buenos Aires, Argentina, September 3–6.

———. 2004. The impact of the projects of learning-service in the educational quality. Reflections concerning eight experiences. Paper presented at the 7th International Seminar of Solidary Service-Learning, Buenos Aires, Argentina, October 6–7.

Gortari Pedroza, A. 2004. The Mexican social service: Model building and design. Paper presented at the 7th International Seminar of Solidary Service-Learning, Buenos Aires, Argentina, October 8. www.me.gov.ar/edusol.

Instituto Faça Parte—Brasil Voluntario. 2003. *Construindo um projeto de voluntariado.* Sao Paulo: Fundação EDUCAR Dpaschoal. www.facaparte.org.br/new/download/construindo_voluntarios.pdf.

Instituto Nacional de Estadisticas y Censos (INDEC). 2004. No. 11 of the 2001 Argentina Census Surveys.

Kendall, J. 1990. *Combining Service and Learning. A Resource Book for Community and Public Service*, vol. 1. Raleigh, NC: National Society for Internships and Experiential Education.

Kliksberg, B. 2003. *Los niños de América Latina en riesgo.* www.iadb.org/etica/documentos/kli_ninos.pdf. Originally published in La Bitácora, Montevideo, Uruguay, April 2.

Learn and Serve America. 2002. National service-learning leader schools program (news release), April 18. www.learnandserve.org/about/newsroom/releases_detail.asp?tbl_pr_id=130.

Meililo, A., and E.N. Suarez Ojeda, comps. 2001. *Resiliencia: Descubriendo las propias fortalezas.* Buenos Aires: Paidós.

Meo no R., and R. Mongecorrales. 2002. Present situation of service-learning in Costa Rica. Abstract submitted to the 6th global conference of the Association for National Youth Service Buenos Aires, Argentina, September 3–6.

Ministerio de Educación, Ciencia y Tecnología (MECyT). 2004. Aprendizaje y servicio solidario. Minutes of the 5th and 6th International Seminar: Learning and united service. Buenos Aries, Argentina: Unit of Special Programs, National Program United Education.

Ministry of Culture and Education (MCyE). 1997. *Basic Contents for Polimodal Education.* Buenos Aires, Argentina: Federal Council of Culture and Education.

———. 1998. *Community Service as School Learning. Minutes of the First International Seminar on Education and Community Service.* Buenos Aries, Argentina: Federal Council of Culture and Education, Investigation and Education Department.

Ministry of Education, Chile. 2005. Service Learning. lpt.mineduc.cl/index_sub1.php?id_contenido=679&id_portal=42&id_seccion=1417&id_padre=1328.

National Center for Education Statistics (NCES). 1999. *Statistics in Brief: Service-Learning and Community Service in K–12 Public Schools.* Washington, DC: U.S. Department of Education, Office of Educational Research and Improvement.

National Ministry of Education, Argentina. 2005. Programa Nacional Educación Solidaria. www.me.gov.ar/edusol.

National Youth Leadership Council and University of Minnesota. 1993. *National and Community Service Trust Act 1993.* Minnesota: National Service-Learning Cooperative Publication.

Nunca es Tarde (It's Never too Late). Program developed by Federación Universitaria Argentina (FUA). www.nuncaestarde.org.ar/.

Opción Latinoamérica. www.opcioncolombia.org.co/ (under construction).

Participación Solidaria para América Latina (PaSoJOVEN). 2004. *Manual de formación de formadores en aprendizaje-servicio y servicio juvenil.* www.pasojoven.org/biblioteca.htm.

Programa Adopta un Herman (Adopt a brother/sister) www.adoptaunhermano.cl/.

Programa Nacional Escuela y Comunidad. 2001. The pedagogical proposal of service-learning. Minutes of the 4th Seminar of the International School and Community.

Buenos Aires: Secretary of Basic Education, Ministry of Education of the Nation. www.me.gov.ar/eyc/publicaciones/pdf/actas_3y4.pdf.

Roche Olivar, R. 1998. *Psicología y Educación para la Prosocialidad.* Buenos Aires: Ciudad Nueva.

Sanchez Soler, M.D., coord. 2003. *La Educación Superior y el Desarrollo Local. El Servicio Social Universitario Como Apoyo a la Gestión Municipal.* Mexico City: Mexico, National Association of Universities and Institutions of Higher Learning (ANUIES).

Sberga, A.A. 2003. *Voluntariado Educativo: Jóvem Voluntário, Escola Solidária.* São Paulo: Fundação EDUCAR Dpaschoal.

Secretaría de Educación Pública (SEP). 2001. Programa Nacional de Educación 2001–2006, México.

Service Learning 2000 Center. 1996. *Service Learning Quadrants.* Palo Alto, CA: Stanford.

Sherraden, M. 2001. *Youth Service as Strong Policy* (CSD Working Paper 01-12). St. Louis: Washington University, Center for Social Development.

Sigmon, R., ed. 1996. The problem of definition in service-learning. In *The Journey to Service-Learning: Experiences from Liberal Arts Colleges and Universities.* Washington, DC: Council of Independent Colleges.

Simón Bolívar University Extension Department. 2004. Dirección de Extensión Universitaria de la USB. www.deu.usb.ve/.

Sirve Quisqueya. 2005. www.communicate.org.do/voluntarios.

Tapia, M.N. 2000. *La Solidaridad como Pedagogía.* Buenos Aires: Ciudad Nueva.

———. 2002. Civic service in South America. Paper presented at the 6th global conference of the Association for National Youth Service, Buenos Aires, Argentina, September 3–6.

———. 2003. On solidaridad. In *Service Enquiry: Service in the 21st Century,* ed. H. Perold, M. Sherraden, and S. Stroud. Johannesburg: Global Service Institute, USA and Volunteer and Service Enquiry Southern Africa (VOSESA). www. service-enquiry.co.za.

———. 2004. La juventud invisible. *La Nación,* December 15, 21.

Tapia, M.N., A. Gonzáles, and P. Elicegui. 2004. *K–12 Service-Learning in Argentina Schools.* Buenos Aires: Latin American Center for Service-Learning. www. gwbweb.wustl.edu/csd/service/SRGP_CLAYSS.htm and in Spanish at www. gwbweb.wustl.edu/csd/gsi/sp/projects/tapia_pr.htm.

Tapia, M.N., and M.M. Mallea. 2003. Service-learning in Argentina. In *Service Enquiry: Service in the 21st Century,* ed. H. Perold, M. Sherraden, and S. Stroud. Johannesburg: Global Service Institute, USA and Volunteer and Service Enquiry Southern Africa (VOSESA). www.service-enquiry.co.za.

Titlebaum, P., G. Williamson, C. Daprano, J. Baer, and J. Brahler. 2004. *Annotated History of Service-Learning, 1862–2002.* Dayton, OH: University of Dayton.

UNESCO. 2005. *EFA Global Monitoring Report 2005. Education for All: The Quality Imperative.* unesdoc.unesco.org/images/0013/001390/139002e.pdf.

UNESCO Institute for Statistics. 2001. *Latin America and Caribbean Regional Report.* Quebec, Canada: UIS. www.uis.unesco.org/TEMPLATE/pdf/ed2001/Amerique_latine_ENPDF.pdf.

Universidad Católica de Occidente (UNICO). 2005. Community Oriented Departments. www.unico.edu.sv/proysocial/ssocial.phtml.

Universidade Solidária (UniSol). 2005. www.unisol.org.br.

8

Youth Service and Elder Service in Comparative Perspective

Nancy Morrow-Howell and Fengyan Tang

In the United States, the elderly population is larger, healthier, more educated, and better off financially than ever before (Federal Interagency Forum on Aging-Related Statistics 2002). Due to the institutionalization of retirement from the formal workforce, older adults have the commodity of time, sometimes twenty or more years after leaving a career job. Older adults also have a strong desire to make vital contributions to their families and communities (Bass 1995). In short, the resources embodied in the older population are enormous and expanding. How will older adults and this society use these resources, which have been described as the only growing natural resource of this nation (Freedman 1999)?

To answer this question, some gerontology scholars and aging advocates have called for a new perspective, the productive aging perspective, which broadens our view of the potential of the later stages of human life (Butler, Oberlink, and Schecter 1990; Bass, Caro, and Chen 1993). This view calls for the active engagement of older adults in economic, environmental, cultural, political, social, civic, and spiritual spheres (Morrow-Howell, Hinterlong, and Sherraden 2001). Instead of frail and dependent elders or well-off and selfish elders, the older population is seen as a fount of workers and volunteers, the "new trustees of civil life" (Freedman 2001). The productive aging perspective highlights the current and future capacities of our aging society.

Volunteerism and service are activities that take center stage in the discussions of a productive aging society (Bass, Caro, and Chen 1993) because these service programs are likely mechanisms through which this great resource will be put to use. Elder service grows from the intergenerational movement of the last twenty years and chases the well-established youth service movement. This chapter considers the emerging institution of elder service. What is elder service? Why is elder service lagging behind youth service? What does elder service have to offer; that is, what are the known and anticipated effects of elder service? How do youth service and elder service compare? We conclude with a description of the complementary nature of youth and elder service and argue that society will benefit from well-developed service opportunities for people across the lifespan.

Service: What Does Age Have to Do With It?

We view service as "an organized period of substantial engagement and contribution to the local, national, and world community, recognized and valued by society, with minimal monetary compensation to the participant" (Sherraden 2001, 2). More specifically, service can be viewed as a subset of volunteer activities, and there are certain features of these volunteer roles that lead us to identify them as service: (1) a formal organization and structure; (2) identification as a service program (e.g., AmeriCorps; Experience Corps); (3) a defined role for service, comparable to a job description; (4) a required level or duration of commitment; (5) an articulated goal of improving a specific area of human or environmental affairs; and (6) acknowledgment and recognition as a valuable contribution (Morrow-Howell, Carden, and Sherraden 2004).

There is nothing about age in these definitions of service. However, when people think of service, they usually think of young people, taking a year or two between school and employment or involved in service-learning projects as part of their formal education. Indeed, the service institutions that have developed over the last fifty years have focused largely on youth. In a survey of 210 service programs worldwide, 77 percent engaged youth as the servers and only four programs targeted older adults as the primary server group (McBride, Benítez, and Sherraden 2003). Similarly, in a review of the literature on the effects of service programs on citizenship, Perry and Katula identified thirty-seven studies, and all but eight focused on young people's civic participation exclusively. Perry and Katula comment that "many institutions and organizations have taken up the task of orienting people, *especially youth*, toward participation in public life in the United States" (2001, 330).

Of course, older adults are part of our service programs but volunteers aged fifty and over account for only 7 percent of the Peace Corps volunteers (Peace Corps 2002), and fewer than 3 percent of AmeriCorps volunteers are over the age of sixty (Freedman 2002). Learn and Serve America is strongly biased toward youth in its organization through schools, colleges, and universities (Center for Human Resources 1999). With the exception of Foster Grandparents and Senior Companions, the largest and most widely known service programs are geared toward youth.

In sum, the elder service movement lags behind youth service, despite the potential of our aging society. Thus, we raise the question of *why* the service movement is biased toward youth. What does age have to do with it? We offer two explanations for the current situation.

Despite substantial and ever-growing evidence to the contrary, the stereotype of the physically and cognitively frail older adult prevails in this society. Older adults are generally viewed as incapable of handling important jobs or fulfilling challenging roles. The renowned gerontologist Dr. Robert Butler tells the story of his encounter with Sergeant Shriver (first director of the Peace Corps) in the early stages of the Peace Corps (Butler 1999). Butler communicated his excitement about the possibility of targeting older Americans as Peace Corps volunteers. Shriver discounted the idea, worried that an older person would be a handicap overseas. Despite the accumulated evidence about the capacity of older adults, images of the greedy geezers and dependent elders are still more prominent than the image of the competent older adult making valuable contributions to society. For example, surveys indicate that employers still hold negative perceptions of older workers, despite evidence of their positive impacts (Barth 1997; Friedland 1997). The negative stereotypes of older adults may in part explain their exclusion from the service movement.

Another possible explanation for the delay in the development of elder service is the initial ways that our society thought about the new institution of retirement. Retirement was long described as a roleless period (Rosow 1967) where, as a society, we were not sure what older adults should be doing with their time. Exit from the workforce was all-or-nothing and there were no alternative structures for productive engagement (Moody 2002). Time use studies reveal that retired American workers reallocate a large fraction of time from paid work to passive activities (watching television, listening to radio, relaxing, self-care) (Gauthier and Smeeding 2003). Retirement came to be characterized by an expansion of leisure time, a time to step into less demanding roles.

These expectations have contributed to the lag in the development of opportunities for productive engagement of older adults in later life. The fundamental viewpoint of the structural lag theory (Riley, Kahn, and Foner 1994) is that structures to facilitate productive engagement, including employment, volunteer, and educational structures, are lagging behind the potential of older individuals. In sum, our society's initial visions about retirement and the social structures (or lack thereof) that developed accordingly did not expect older adults, did not provide for older adults, to be actively involved in service roles.

Yet older adults and aging advocates are confronting the myths of aging and outmoded visions of retirement. Evidence is accumulating about the functional abilities of older adults, despite chronic health conditions that they may experience. Recent evidence suggests that a compression of morbidity is occurring and that there is great potential to remain healthy and active until much later in life (National Institute on Aging 1999; Svanborg 2001). In fact, gerontologists have divided the third age of life into the third and fourth age, thanks to extended life expectancy and increased vitality (for an example, see Baltes and Smith 2002). The third age, or young-old, may be viewed as a time of maximal capability combined with the experience of long life. Not until the fourth age, or old-old, do stereotypes of the dependent elderly become accurate and medical illness precludes active engagement in productive roles.

There may be an emerging trend toward structural lead in the area of elder service (Freedman 2001)—that is, the growth of service opportunities for older adults, under the assumption that there is a growing demand for such roles, both nationally and locally. Freedman (1999) argues that older adults themselves are taking the lead in developing structures for meaningful volunteer work. This is consistent with assertions of elder advocates that older adults are not satisfied with many of the current roles available to them and want more challenging responsibilities (Morris and Caro 1996). National surveys reveal that older adults want well-deserved leisure, but they also want meaningful engagement (Rowe and Kahn 1998). Elder service is thus emerging as part of the service movement in this country and, hopefully, service endeavors will move away from a negative age bias to age-neutral or age-as-asset perspectives.

What Is Elder Service?

There has been recent and substantial development of elder service programs, in which older adults are specifically recruited for their time and talents and there are older age criteria for inclusion. These programs support older adults in challenging activities that seek to improve human or environmental conditions; most often, the beneficiaries of the programs are children and youth. We focus in this chapter on service programs specifically designed for older adults, excluding from this analysis those programs that are age-neutral, in which all people over the age of eighteen are eligible to participate. The recruitment and deployment of older adults in those programs is another important topic that deserves serious scholarly attention. We also note that consideration of elder service possibilities outside the U.S. context is an important direction for future scholarship, but it is beyond the scope of this chapter.

The Corporation for National and Community Service organizes the two best-known elder service programs. Foster Grandparents serve as mentors, tutors, and caregivers for children and youth with special needs in such community organizations as schools, hospitals, Head Start, and youth centers (Senior Corps 2002a). During 2001, about 30,200 Foster Grandparents served over 275,000 children and youth with a total of more than 27.3 million hours (Senior Corps 2002a). The Senior Companions program matches older volunteers to frail adults who need assistance and friendship (Aguirre International 2001). In the year 2001, about half (49 percent) of the servers were sixty-five to seventy-four years old, 31 percent were seventy-five to eighty-four, 15 percent were sixty to sixty-four, and 5 percent were eighty-five and over (Senior Corps 2002b).

Public/private partnerships provide national programs, like Experience Corps, where older adults assist in urban public schools in thirteen cities across America. Through OASIS's Person-to-Person Peer Counseling program, older adults are recruited and trained to support other older adults; the program operates in over ten cities with more than 125 volunteers (OASIS Institute 2000). Temple University's HomeFriends program supports older volunteers who work with grandparents who are raising grandchildren (Temple University Center for Intergenerational Learning 2000). Then there are local programs, operating in one or two communities, where older adults take on challenging roles to confront serious community concerns. For example, in two Texas cities, Denton and Dallas, seniors work with hospitals and clinics to increase the number of children who get immunized (Center for Public Service 2001).

We are in the process of cataloging elder service programs; to date, we have described about fifty programs. Going beyond traditional volunteer activities, these service programs utilize the skills and experiences of older adults to address serious problems: failing schools, environmental degradation, youth drug abuse, and child maltreatment. Programs vary in the extent to which older adults are trained, supervised, and given recognition and rewards, including stipends, opportunity for personal growth and education, supplemental insurance, college credit, health screenings, and meals. Financial support for most of these senior service programs comes from foundations and private or corporate contributions, with some partnerships with state or local governments. Few programs receive substantial federal support, with Experience Corps, Foster Grandparents, and Senior Companions being notable exceptions.

Comparing Youth and Elder Service

A more systematic comparison of youth and elder service programs is needed, but several observations can be made from the knowledge that exists. It appears that elder service programs may be largely national programs. There are few international and transnational opportunities that focus solely on older adults, and older adults are underrepresented in these types of service opportunities (McBride et al. 2003). Also, the service programs available to older adults seem to require a different type of commitment from youth service (McBride et al. 2003). That is, fewer hours per week are requested, but for an extended period of time. For example, many of the tutoring programs request that the server commit to working with a child once a week throughout the full academic year.

This type of commitment (a few hours a week over an extended period of time) lends itself to ongoing service: mentoring, coaching, counseling, and tutoring over time. Elder service programs seem to differ from youth service programs in that they are frequently targeted toward individual people (a child, a grandparent, an older adult needing assistance), whereas youth service is often targeted toward a community development enterprise, like building infrastructure or developing community projects (Iyizoba 1982; Omo-Abu 1997; Sikah 2000). Relationship building is a key component of many services aimed at assisting young people in difficult situations, in transition periods, and in educational endeavors. This type of service cannot be done in short, intensive periods of time, but are, in fact, best done by older people who bring life and work experience and, in general, maturity and patience to the work. Research has documented that older adults are more dependable, more stable employees than younger adults, and these characteristics most likely extend to service roles (Zweigenhaft, Armstrong, and Quintis 1996). Thus, we speculate that the type of work and the type of commitment needed for the work go hand in hand and that youth and elder service may vary in the type of service work for which their physical, mental, and emotional abilities are best suited.

The differences in type of commitment, type of service, and location of service seem appropriate, given life stage differences between younger and older servers. A driving force behind the elder service movement is the factor of time associated with retirement from a career job; older adults do have more time outside of the formal workforce than younger adults (Gauthier and Smeeding 2003). Even though older adults are freer from work and childrearing responsibilities than younger adults, they remain closely involved in family life. For example, surveys indicate that over 40 percent were helping children and grandchildren and almost 25 percent were providing care for a disabled person (Caro and Bass 1992). In sum, it is difficult for an older adult to commit to a full-time or a distant job in the face of responsibilities at home. On the other hand, youth are more likely to have the flexibility to serve in distant locations and for intense periods of time.

Effects of Youth and Elder Service

Effects of Youth Service

Sherraden, Sherraden, and Eberly (1990) collected information about the anticipated outcomes of youth service and the following outcomes were of high or medium priority: promotion of cultural integration and political tolerance, expression of citizenship, increasing social development, increasing economic development, personal development and connections to adulthood for the server, education and training for the server, and employment opportunities for the server. This study highlighted the multiple effects of youth service (Sherraden 2001), which had been previously articulated by Eberly (1986), who noted that youth service is a lot of things to a lot of people: a rite of passage, a training ground for citizens, a service delivery program, experiential education, and a source of labor.

In the worldwide search and description of the 210 programs identified, McBride, Benítez, and Sherraden (2003) note that these programs are intended to benefit the server and the served, but they conclude that youth service programs are more concerned with the server. The most frequently listed goal of the programs in the survey was increasing the server's motivation to volunteer again. The next most frequently listed outcomes were increasing the server's skills and increasing the server's social skills. These outcomes were listed more frequently than any of the outcomes regarding the people or community served. In terms of the served, the most frequently mentioned outcome was promoting cultural understanding. However, this outcome is not just about the improvement in conditions of life for the served population; it still involves a positive change to the server. Three outcomes regarding the served are often cited, but with less frequency than outcomes regarding the server. Fifty-five percent of programs listed creating or improving public facilities, 50 percent listed promoting sustainable land use, and 47 percent listed improving the well-being and health of the population.

In a review of research on service, McBride et al. (2003) do not restrict their analysis to youth service programs, but these programs dominate their sample of forty-two studies. In an assessment of effects, they conclude that both the server and the served are targets of intervention, but that an overwhelming majority of the effects that are studied pertain to the individual server. They lament the lack of attention to the effects of the program on the served.

In Table 8.1 we classify the effects of youth service into two categories: effects on the server and effects on the served. It is important to note that documentation of youth effects has relied heavily on qualitative methods, including semistructured interviews and focus groups with program administrators and program participants. In the research by McBride et al. (2003),

Table 8.1

Outcomes of Youth Service for the Server and the Served

Outcomes for the server[a]
  • Increase maturity and personal autonomy
  • Become disciplined and reduce risk behavior
  • Promote social, ethnic, and cultural interactions and awareness
  • Improve understanding of self and community
  • Practice and increase skills
  • Explore career opportunities
  • Acquire human capital and educational awards
  • Increase civic knowledge and value
  • Bring change in civic attitudes and participation
  • Increase the likelihood to vote
Outcomes for the served[b]
  • Improve school children's attendance and literacy
  • Enhance manpower distribution and rural infrastructure development
  • Develop community projects and build community capacity
  • Provide better services in rural areas and a steady stream of volunteers
  • Benefit local nonprofit sectors
  • Promote personal and professional development of the individual members
  • Build inter-organizational partnerships
  • Foster a sense of national integration and cultural integration
  • Improve social infrastructures, future earnings, and productivity
  • Promote national unity and democracy

[a]Aguirre International (1999); Center for Human Resources (1999); Cohen (1997); Edwards et al. (2001); Egan (1994); Frees et al. (1995); Griffiths (1998); Hadjo (1999); Iyizoba (1982); Janoski et al. (1998); Jastrzab et al. (1996); Jastrzab et al. (2001); Kalu (1987); Macro International (1997); Newton (1992); Omo-Abu (1997); Purvis (1993); Sherraden et al. (1990); Sikah (2000); Starr (1994).
[b]Aguirre International (1999); Center for Human Resources (1999); Ekhomu (1985); Griffiths (1998); Iyizoba (1982); Kalu (1987); Neumann et al. (1995); Omo-Abu (1997); Sherraden et al. (1990); Thomson and Perry (1998); Wang et al. (1995).

twenty-four out of forty-two studies used a combination of methods (for example, survey, interview, and/or secondary data analysis), and ten studies used a survey method only. Survey questionnaires were specially designed or developed for the study, except a few program evaluations used standardized questionnaires; for example, the Physical Quality of Life Index (PQLI) was used to measure the impact of Peace Corps programs on women (Cohn and Wood 1985), and Standard Achievement Test Scores were applied in the evaluation of AmeriCorps programs (Macro International 2000; Moss, Hiller, and Moore 1999). None of the studies used an experimental design or random assignment; most of the studies were exploratory and descriptive, using convenience sampling without comparison groups (McBride et al. 2003). These methods yield the identification of the experienced or anticipated outcomes, and further quantification is in order if we are to move toward cost-effectiveness or cost-benefit analyses.

Effects of Elder Service

In Table 8.2, we list the outcomes of elder service that have been documented through qualitative and quantitative research methods. As for youth service, multiple effects are evidenced and we organize them into effects on the server and effects on the served. There is well-established literature on the effects of volunteering on older adults, documenting the positive relationship between volunteering and well-being in later life (Fengler 1984; Havighurst, Neugarten, and Tobin 1968; Herzog et al. 1989; Maddox 1968; Oman, Thoresen, and McMahon 1999; Ward 1979). Most studies are limited to nonrepresentative samples and cross-sectional designs, but several longitudinal studies with improved sampling and measurement have documented a link between volunteering and physical and mental health, mortality, and life satisfaction (Moen, Dempster-McClain, and Williams 1992; Morrow-Howell et al. 2003; Musick, Herzog and House 1999; Oman, Thoresen, and McMahon 1999; Van Willigen 2000). Quasi-experimental design and/or longitudinal data are also used in the program evaluations of Senior Companion (SRA Technologies 1985) and Senior Corp Volunteers (Gartland 2001).

Thus, these studies produce solid evidence that volunteer engagement in later life is related to improved well-being. In fact, Oman, Thoresen, and McMahon (1999) argue that the reduction in mortality associated with volunteering was larger than the reduction associated with exercising and attendance at religious services. The ability to establish causality has been limited by study design in this area of research, but Thoits and Hewitt (2001) used longitudinal data to demonstrate the reciprocal relationship between volunteering and personal well-being. Their analyses show that well-being facilitates volunteer involvement and that volunteer involvement subsequently augments well-being. A limitation of this knowledge regards the operational definition of the independent variable of volunteering. Any type of volunteer activity with any type of organization is usually included, and volunteer activities that we might classify as service are not specified.

Table 8.2 also demonstrates that elder service programs produce positive outcomes for the service recipients. Tutoring programs produce improvements in educational performance; mentoring programs produce improvements in behavior and attitude. Evaluations of elder service programs vary in rigor and completeness, but results overall are encouraging. Initially, the evaluation of intergenerational programs focused on process outcomes and how

Table 8.2

Effects of Elder Service on the Served and the Server

Source	Sample	Program	Method	Major findings
Effects on the served				
Freedman (1998)	47 pairings of older adults and at-risk youth in 5 intergenerational programs	Foster grandparent program	In-depth, semi-structured, one-on-one interview	37 out of 47 pairings form significant primary (16) and secondary (21) relationships. 3 examples of primary relationships showed strong kinship attachment and intimacy between youth and elders, and role model of elders to at-risk youth. 3 examples of secondary relationships showed elders help youth as good neighbors, reinforce the positive aspects of behavior, and have informal and public relationship with youth.
LoSciuto et al. (1996)	729 students completed in the pretest, and 562 in both pretest and posttest	Across Ages, a national drug prevention program that provides intergenerational mentoring for at-risk youth	Randomized pretest-posttest control group design; instrument based on research on Positive Youth Development Curriculum (PYDC); Statistical analysis: ANCOVA, ANOVA	Those students who received mentoring, PYDC, and community service scored better in attitudes toward school, future, and elder; and frequency of substance use was less than those who only attended PYDC and community service. They scored better than control group in attitudes toward school, future, and elder; Rand well-being scale; knowledge about older people; reaction to drug use; and community service.
Morrow-Howell, Kinney, and Mann (1999)	289 participants in OASIS	OASIS, a national network with community-based volunteer programs	A cross-sectional survey with telephone interview; specially developed instrument; Statistical analysis: ANOVA, MANOVA; Measurement: perceived benefits	85% report increased socialization; 77% increased generativity; 87% increased well-being; 90% report increased opportunities for participation in OASIS. The most perceived benefit is opportunity, followed by well-being, then socialization and generativity at the same level. Volunteers perceived more benefits in the four domains than tutors or class takers.

RTI International (2003)	155 SCP directors and volunteer station supervisors; 1520, 658, and 394 clients in 3 waves of surveys, respectively; 803, 362, and 186 eligible family/caregivers in 3 waves	Senior Companion Program (SCP)	Random sample of volunteer station staff; 3-wave telephone survey (3-month, 9-month follow-up); comparison groups of eligible clients and family caregivers; Statistical analysis: descriptive and multivariate analysis	64% agencies reported the SCP freed up their staff to do other work, and 75% agencies reported family members were better able to remain employed. 30 to 55% clients spent less on meal preparation, personal care, and transportation than before. SCP clients scored 87% higher in health; 16% lower in depression; 85% higher in life satisfaction than waitlist clients in 3-month follow-up survey. At 9-month follow-up, SCP family members reported 85% higher ADL functioning of clients than waitlist family members reported. Waitlist families were 23% as likely as SCP families to report being able to care for a relative well at 3-month follow-up.
Project STAR (2001)	Internal evaluation of 51 schools; Surveys of 70 school principals/staff and 273 teachers	Seniors for Schools, a Senior Demonstration project initiated by the National Senior Service Corps known as the Experience Corps	A standardized and non-standardized reading skills test were used in pre- and posttests. Respondents reported benefits from their opinions.	92% students increased reading skills measured by using standardized and non-standardized reading skill tests, and 85% increased measured through assessment tests. Over 81% of survey respondents showed students increased positive attitude toward reading, self-confidence in reading ability, and improved overall self esteem.

Effects on both the served and servers

Granville (2000)	45 volunteers working in 3 projects in England	Intergenerational school-based projects	Semi-structured, one-to-one interviews over 6 months	• *For the servers:* Overwhelmingly, older volunteers felt volunteering benefited their health, particularly mental health. They had a sense of purpose and direction. • *For the served:* Older volunteers became champions for young people, teaching staff, and parents. They played a part in breaking down the stereotypes of old age.

168

Source	Sample	Program	Method	Major findings
SRA Technologies Inc. (1985)	462 respondents (153 active Senior Companions, 70 waitlist companions, 179 clients, and 60 waitlist clients) in round one data collection at six sites (1980)	Senior Companion Program	Quasi-experimental research design: 3-round (5 years) longitudinal evaluation within 4-group respondents; In-person interviews using a modified version of the Older American Resources and Services (OARS)	• *For the servers:* Volunteers' financial resources increased from 0 to 50%, and the proportion of household income of at least $4,000 a year increased from 40 to 80%. The proportion of good mental health rating increased from 50 to 90%. • *For the served:* Clients reported 10% decrease in impairment of social resources, while clients who stopped participation in the SCP increased 22%. Active clients reported 22% decrease in illness, while inactive clients increased 3%.
Wheeler, Gorey, and Greenblatt (1998)	37 independent studies	All forms of volunteer activities: voluntary association membership, indirect and direct helping roles	Meta-analysis, using *r* index to test the strength of volunteer program outcome measures; Standardized, construct-qualitative, and construct-quantitative measures	• *For servers:* 70% of older volunteers scored higher on life quality measures than nonvolunteers. 12 studies show those who engaged in direct helping derive greater rewards than others who engaged in more indirect or less formally helping roles. • *For the served:* 85% of clients were less isolated and depressed as compared with non-participating clients. 3 studies show that enablement or counseling-type services have larger interventive effect than other types.
Effects on the servers Gartland (2001)	Random sample of Atlantic Cluster senior volunteers, N = 1,075	Senior Corps Volunteers	Quasi-experimental design; self-report survey	93% of respondents indicate that life is better since participation in volunteer program. Quality of life is significantly associated with income; lower income volunteers report high life satisfaction. Volunteers in Foster Grandparents programs report higher degree of positive change than volunteers in Senior Companions and Retired Senior Volunteers.
Jirovec and Hyduk (1998)	120 respondents aged 62 and over in a large metropolitan hospital	Formal volunteering in a hospital	Cross-sectional design; mail survey; inferential statistics	Volunteering is significantly associated with mental health but not physical health. Older adults who donated 500 hours (F = 3.35, p < .05) and interacted with younger people (t = 2.55, p = .01) had greater contentment.

Study	Sample	Type of volunteering	Design/Method	Findings
Kornblum (1981)	198 from the mobile, organized older people in Philadelphia in the 1st wave, and 149 in the 2nd wave (6 months later)	Retired Senior Volunteer program (RSVP)	Pre- and posttest among 3 groups: experimental, (drop out), and control groups; Standardized, repeated measures for life satisfaction index.	There are no differences in outcome measures between volunteers and nonvolunteers at Time 1. Self-perception of volunteers is higher than nonvolunteers at Time 2. There are significant differences between volunteers and nonvolunteers in 3 indicators of self-assessed health at Time 2.
Morrow-Howell Hinterlong, Rozario, and Tang (2003)	Secondary data: American's Changing Lives: 3 waves, subset to aged 60 and over, $N = 1,669$ in 1st wave	Formal volunteering in religious, political, educational, senior citizen or related organizations, etc.	Cross-sectional design; Statistics analysis: generalized estimating equations	Volunteer status positively affects late-life well-being in self-rated health, physical dependency, and depression. The impact of volunteering is at maximum at 100 hours per year.
Musick, Herzog, and House (1999)	Secondary data: American's Changing Lives: 3 waves, subset to aged 65 and over, $N = 1211$	Formal volunteering in religious, political, educational, senior citizen or related organizations and others	Quasi-experimental design; Statistical analysis: SUDAAN, Taylor series linearization procedures; Instrument: National Death Index	There is a curvilinear relationship between volunteering and mortality. The lowest hazard rate ratio for mortality occurs among those who volunteered for one organization and those who volunteered less than 40 hours. Volunteering effect was strongest among those who report low levels of informal social interaction and who do not live alone.

Source	Sample	Program	Method	Major findings
Oman, Thoresen, and McMahon (1999)	1972 older residents in California; twice—1990–91 and 1995; aged 55+	Formal volunteering	Quasi-experimental: comparison among 3 groups; Statistical analysis: Cox proportional hazard modeling	High volunteers (for two and more organizations) had 63% lower mortality than nonvolunteers. After multivariate adjustment, any level of volunteering reduced mortality by 60% among weekly attendees at religious services. Health habits, physical functioning, religious attendance, and social support partly explain lower mortality rates for community service volunteers.
Omoto, Snyder, and Martino (2000)	144 hospice volunteers from 5 organizations	Formal volunteering in hospices	Quasi-experimental: comparisons of 3 age cohorts, pre- and posttest; self-administered survey; Statistical analysis: MANOVA, ANOVA, hierarchical regression	Older volunteers reported greater overall satisfaction, more positive change in self-esteem than younger volunteers ($F = 4.32$, $p < .05$), and perceived greater relative benefits ($F = 3.97$, $p < .05$). Older volunteers experience a small increase in self-esteem, while younger and middle-aged volunteers had slight decreases ($F = 3.39$, $p < .05$).
Van Willigen (2000)	Secondary data: American Changing Lives, 2 wave; $N = 3,617$ in 1st wave	Formal volunteering in religions, political, educational, senior citizen, or related organizations and others	Quasi-experimental: comparison between older and younger volunteers; Statistical analysis: net effect models, OLS, Stata, probit-based lambda procedure	For elders, volunteering for more than one organization increases 26% in satisfaction and 63% in health. Volunteer hours are curvilinearly related to satisfaction among younger adults while linearly among seniors. Volunteer hours are linearly related to health for younger while curvilinearly for seniors; the physical benefits begin to decrease after 100 hours per year. The effect of volunteer role on health is more than 2.5 times greater for seniors than for younger adults.

senior volunteers benefited from the participation (Ward 1979). The programs listed in Table 8.2 demonstrate that current evaluation efforts surpass process analyses to demonstrate tangible impacts on the targeted issues. Evaluations document benefits to service recipients and their families. The trends in evaluation of elder service toward increased rigor and assessment of impacts should be continued.

In addition to effects on the server and the served, there are wider effects on families, communities, and society. We have yet to systematically collect data regarding these wider effects, but we gathered volunteer directors at Washington University on June 25 and July 10, 2003, to brainstorm about wider effects of late-life volunteering, and we base the following discussion on the observations that they provided. Families express satisfaction and relief when an older adult finds meaningful engagement and new social connections. Family members benefit when the older persons transfer increased compassion or appreciation for youth or computer skills to the home setting. These families benefit a great deal when an older adult maintains independence through the active involvement of service work. Indeed, maintenance of physical and mental health has a positive ripple effect beyond families to society as a whole, where the provision of care to dependent older adults has high costs. The community benefits when older volunteers transition from volunteer work into a job, and the workforce gains older workers (who research shows are more reliable and satisfied than younger workers). The host institutions, like schools or nursing homes, benefit from improved reputations in the community (Hegeman 1985). In a specific nursing home example, the staff reported that it benefited from having a volunteer service program, despite not being directly involved in the program (Goyer 1998/99). In a specific school example, children's test scores were raised by the tutoring program, enabling the school to improve its ranking and gain the subsequent benefits (Project Star 2001). Older adults are more active politically, more experienced in community affairs, and they become valuable advocates for the social causes that service programs connect them to. They are also more likely than other age groups to have financial resources to make contributions to these important causes. There are likely more of these wider effects of participation in service roles, and indeed a full cost/benefit accounting would require the consideration of these multiple effects. However, measurement is very challenging, and research designs to isolate the impact of service on these effects may be impossible.

Comparing Youth and Elder Service Outcomes

From the above review, we conclude that both youth service and elder service programs intend to produce multiple benefits and outcomes for both the server and the served. However, among youth service programs, more attention seems to be on the young servers. Service activities are intended to build servers' human and social capital—to make them better citizens, more tolerant people, better equipped for the working world, better suited to a multicultural society. The products of social and economic development are important, but these program goals are articulated less prominently, and there are fewer efforts to document effects on the served.

The opposite seems to be true among the elder service programs. The primary focus is on the service recipients, on the children, youth, and families receiving the service. The advocates of the productive aging movement come from a social development perspective. They argue that human and environmental problems remain massive in the face of dwindling public resources and that society cannot afford to ignore the growing number of older adults who have the capacity and motivation to confront these problems. They advocate transforming social structures to achieve a productive aging society not for the sake of older adults, but for the sake of the wider community (Caro and Bass 1992). As seen in the literature, many evaluations of elder service focus on a program's impact on the served. The benefits to the server are largely seen as by-product.

There is some empirical support for the idea that outcomes associated with service vary by age. Using a life-course perspective, Omoto, Snyder, and Martino (2000) tested the proposition that motivation and outcomes of volunteering vary between younger and older adults. They found that older volunteers reported greater service motivation than younger adults, who were more motivated by opportunities for social relationships. Further, the authors found partial support for the hypothesis that positive volunteering outcomes depended more on relationship experiences for younger volunteers and more on service experiences for older volunteers. These authors conclude that over the life course, there are shifting motivational agendas for civic participation, and attention to these shifts is important to achieve maximum participation and benefit.

It is clear that a primary focus of youth service is capacity building—personal development for citizenship, for the workplace. There is a future orientation, an investment in human capital. Cries of ageism might arise from aging advocates who know that older adults are avid learners and seekers of personal development (as witnessed by the huge success of the Elderhostel program and, in fact, development of service-learning programs within Elderhostel). But the productive aging movement promotes the engagement of the capacity of older adults more than the building of capacity. In fact, older adults are motivated by the opportunity to use their existing skills and knowledge, and they are rewarded when their capacities are recognized (this finding derives from four focus groups that we completed with older volunteers in spring 2003; data analysis is in progress). Indeed, the most important incentive and recognition for older adults for their services provided may be this honoring of capacity.

Further, when the capacity of older adults is used and honored, it is more likely to be maintained. "Use it or lose it" has remained a powerful guideline in fostering the physical and mental health of older adults. Research documents that they are healthier, both mentally and physically, and happier when involved in productive roles. As Moen, Dempster-McClain, and Williams (1992) have documented through longitudinal studies, older adults involved in volunteer roles maintain higher levels than other older adults who are not involved in volunteer roles of functional ability. Thus, we argue that participation in service programs also maintains capacity. Svanborg (2001) suggests that perhaps the biggest contribution of the productive engagement of adults to the individual, family, and society is the postponement of functional decline associated with aging.

Thus, we propose that youth service is about building capacity and elder service is about using, honoring, and maintaining capacity; and both groups of servers accomplish these positive ends through social and economic development activities valuable to others and society at large.

Conclusion

The nature of service activities and the emphasis on the desired outcomes of service programs may differ for servers across the lifespan, and from a life-course perspective these differences may be very appropriate. From this perspective, the life course is conceptualized as a series of transitions, varying roles, and activities that are age-specific meaning and challenges (Elder 1994). Perhaps there is service for all seasons. Young people may be less obligated to family and free to travel to distant places and commit themselves to periods of intense service. Although many older adults will relish these opportunities, they are more responsible to family and friends, and ample opportunities for local service activities will be important.

Further, older adults may be better equipped to take on certain types of service roles, where life and work experience, maturity, stability, and dependability are desired attributes. They may be better coaches, mentors, and advisers, especially on a one-to-one basis (although we must remember that older adults report that socialization aspects of service roles are important to them). Young servers may be more comfortable in group activities aimed at a community-level target, such as housing stock, infrastructures, or land use. Perhaps elder service programs are more concerned about the impact of these services on the served, rather than on the server. Developmental psychologists have posited that aging tasks include achieving generativity, finding meaning, transcending the self, and leaving a legacy (Erikson, Erikson, and Kivnick 1986). (Erikson wrote: "I am what survives of me." About fifty years ago, the American Association of Retired Persons wrote its original motto: To serve, not to be served.)

To continue to allow elder service to lag behind youth service in the United States may be shortsighted. Why limit the expression of citizenship and the use of mature workers that we have tried to spawn through youth service? When we look at a young server today, we need to be farsighted and ask, What do we want her to be doing fifty or sixty years from today? If youth service is seen as an investment in the future, then elder service must be seen as a continuing return on that investment. Youth service and elder service advocates may be most effective by working together to develop service across the lifespan.

References

Aguirre International. 1999. *Making a Difference: Impacts of AmeriCorps*State/National Direct on Members and Communities 1994–1995 and 1995–1996.* Washington, DC: Corporation for National Service.

Aguirre International. 2001. *Senior Companions: Accomplishment Report.* Report prepared for the Corporation for National and Community Service. www.seniorcorps.org/research.

Baltes, P., and J. Smith. 2002. New frontiers in the future of aging: From successful aging for the young old to the dilemmas of the fourth age. Plenary lecture prepared for the Valencia Forum, in Valencia, Spain, April 1–4. www.mpib-berlin.mpg.de/en/forschung/lip/valencia.htm.

Barth, M. 1997. Older workers: Perceptions and reality. Speech prepared for the U.S. Senate Special Committee on Aging Forum, Washington, DC, July 25.

Bass, S. 1995. *Older and Active: How Americans over 55 Are Contributing to Society.* New Haven: Yale University Press.

Bass, S., F. Caro, and Y.-P. Chen. 1993. *Achieving a Productive Aging Society.* Westport, CT: Auburn House.

Butler, R. 1999. Productive aging: Current concepts, research, and programs. Symposium presented at the annual meeting of the Gerontological Society of America, San Francisco, November.

Butler, R., M. Oberlink, and M. Schecter. 1990. *The Promise of Productive Aging.* New York: Springer.

Caro, F., and S. Bass. 1992. *Patterns of Productivity Among Older Americans.* Boston: University of Massachusetts, Gerontology Institute.

Center for Human Resources. 1999. *Summary Report: National Evaluation of Learn and Serve America.* Prepared for the Corporation for National Service by Brandies University, Waltham, Massachusetts.

Center for Public Service. 2001. Senior Volunteers for Childhood Immunization. www.cps.unt.edu/svci/.

Cohen, C. 1997. *What Service Teaches About Citizenship and Work: The Case of AmeriCorps.* Report (ED 424 183). Seattle: Washington.

Cohn, S., and R. Wood. 1985. Foreign aid at the grass roots: The interaction of Peace Corps volunteers with host country people. *Human Organization* 44 (2): 167–171.

Eberly, D. 1986. *National Service: Report of a Conference*. New York: Russell Sage Foundation.

Edwards, B., L. Mooney, and C. Heald. 2001. Who is being served? The impact of student volunteering on local community organizations. *Nonprofit and Voluntary Sector Quarterly* 30 (3): 444–461.

Egan, T.M. 1994. Youth service international: Adventure in service. PhD diss., Seattle University, 1994. *Dissertation Abstracts International* 55, 05A (UMI No. 9426424).

Ekhomu, O. 1985. Evaluation of manpower utilization in Nigeria: The case of the national service corps. PhD diss., University of Pittsburgh, 1985. *Dissertation Abstracts International* 47, 05A (UMI No. 8617174).

Elder, G.H. 1994. Time, human agency, and social change: Perspectives on the life course. *Social Psychology Quarterly* 57(1): 4–15.

Erikson, E., J. Erikson, and H. Kivnick. 1986. *Vital Involvement in Old Age*. New York: Norton.

Federal Interagency Forum on Aging-Related Statistics. 2002. *Older Americans 2000: Key Indicators of Well-Being*. Washington, DC: U.S. Government Printing Office.

Fengler, A.P. 1984. Life satisfaction of subpopulation of elderly. *Research on Aging* 6: 189–212.

Freedman, M. 1988. *Partners in Growth: Elder Mentors and At-Risk Youth*. Philadelphia: Public/Private Ventures.

———. 1999. *Prime Time: How Baby Boomers Will Revolutionize Retirement and Transform America*. New York: Public Affairs.

———. 2000. Making policy for an aging century: Expanding the contribution of older Americans through national and community service. Speech presented at the Coming of Age Conference, Warrenton, Virginia.

———. 2001. Structural lead: Building the new institutions for an aging America. In *Productive Aging: Concepts and Challenge,* ed. N. Morrow-Howell, J. Hinterlong, and M. Sherraden. Baltimore: Johns Hopkins University.

Freedman, M. 2002. *Making policy for an aging century: Expanding the contribution of older Americans through national and community service*. Coming of Age Conference, Warrenton, Virginia.

Frees, J.W., T. Hardaway, and G. Locke. 1995. *Lessons Learned from the Experience of Subtitle D Programs*. Report prepared for the Corporation for National and Community Service. www.abtassociates.com/reports/D19950015.pdf.

Friedland, R. 1997. Lesson from the past and opportunities for the future: The labor market for older workers. *Public Policy and Aging Report* 8: 9–19.

Gartland, J.P. 2001. *Senior Volunteer Participation: An Effective Means to Improve Life Satisfaction*. Report prepared for the Corporation for National and Community Service. www.nationalservice.org/jobs/fellowships/2000-01.html.

Gauthier, A., and T. Smeeding. 2003. Time use at older ages. *Research on Aging* 25: 247–274.

Goyer, A. 1998/99. Intergenerational shared site programs. *Generations* 22 (4): 79–80.

Granville, G. 2000. *Understanding the Experience of Older Volunteers in Intergenerational School-Based Projects*. Hartshill, UK: Beth Johnson Foundation.

Griffiths, C.Y. 1998. The impact of service: An exploration of the characteristics of volunteer tutors in the AmeriCorps for math and literacy program and the benefits they gained for service. PhD diss., The Ohio State University, 1998. *Dissertation Abstracts International* 59, 05A: 1411.

Hajdo, D. 1999. National service and civic education: The potential of AmeriCorps' National Civilian Community Corps to foster civic character. PhD diss., University of Maryland College Park, 1999. *Dissertation Abstracts International* 60, 12A: 4585.

Havighurst, R.J., B.L. Neugarten, and S.S. Tobin. 1968. Disengagement and patterns of aging. In *Middle Age and Aging,* ed. B.L. Neugarten. Chicago: University of Chicago.

Hegeman, C. 1985. *Child Care in Long-Term Care Settings.* Albany, NY: Foundation for Long-Term Care.

Herzog, A.R., R. Kahn, R. Morgan, J. Jackson, and T. Antonucci. 1989. Age differences in productive activities. *Journal of Gerontology: Social Sciences* 44: 129–138.

Iyizoba, W.O. 1982. Nigeria Youth Service Corps: An evaluation of an attempt to foster unity in the face of ethnic diversity. PhD diss., Rutgers The State University of New Jersey–New Brunswick, 1982. *Dissertation Abstracts International* 43, 10A (UMI No. 8305751).

Janoski, T., M. Musick, and J. Wilson. 1998. Being volunteered? The impact of social participation and pro-social attitudes on volunteering. *Sociological Forum* 13 (3): 495–519.

Jastrzab, J., L. Bernestein, L. Litin, S. Braat-Campbell, E. Stickney, and L. Giordono. 2001. *Assessment of Long-Term Impacts on Service Participation: A Profile of Members at Baseline.* Washington, DC: Corporation for National and Community Service.

Jastrzab, J., K. Masker, J. Blomquist, and L. Orr. 1996. *Evaluation of national and community service programs. Impacts of Service: Final Report on the Evaluation of AmeriCorps.* Report prepared for the Corporation for National and Community Service. Cambridge, MA: Abt.

Jirovec, R., and C.A. Hyduk. 1998. Type of volunteer experience and health among older adult volunteers. *Journal of Gerontological Social Work* 30 (3/4):29–42.

Kornblum, S. 1981. Impact of a volunteer service role upon aged people. PhD diss., Bryn Mawr College, 1981. *Dissertation Abstracts International* 43, 01A (UMI No. 8207595).

LoSciuto, L., A.K. Rajala, T.N. Townsend, and A.S. Taylor. 1996. An outcome evaluation of Across Ages: An intergenerational mentoring approach to drug prevention. *Journal of Adolescent Research* 11 (1): 116–129.

Macro International. 1997. *Study of Race, Class, and Ethnicity, Final Report.* Report prepared for the Corporation for Community and National Service. www.americorps.org/research/index.html.

Macro International. 2000. *Evaluation of DC Reads: Year 2 Final Report.* Report prepared for the Corporation for National and Community Service. www.americorps.org/research/index.html.

Maddox, G.L. 1968. Persistence of life style among the elderly: A longitudinal study of patterns of social activity in relation to life satisfaction. In *A Reader in Social Psychology,* ed. B.L. Neugarten. Chicago: University of Chicago Press.

McBride, A.M., C. Benítez, and M. Sherraden. 2003. The forms and nature of civic service: A global assessment. St. Louis, MO: Washington University, Center for Social Development.

McBride, A.M., M. Lombe, F. Tang, M. Sherraden, C. Benítez. 2003. The knowledge base on civic service: Status and directions. St. Louis, MO: Washington University, Center for Social Development.

McBride, A.M., M. Sherraden, C. Benítez, and E. Johnson. 2004. Civic service worldwide: Defining a field, building a knowledge base. *Nonprofit and Voluntary Sector Quarterly* 11 (4): 8S–21S.

McBride, A.M., M. Sherraden, M. Lombe, and F. Tang. 2003. *Civic Service Scholarship Worldwide: The Prevalence of Service and the Role of Research* (CSD Working paper 03–20). St. Louis: Washington University in St. Louis, Center for Social Development.

Moen, P., D. Dempster-McClain, and R. Williams. 1992. Successful aging: A life-course perspective on women's multiple roles and health. *American Journal of Sociology* 97: 1612–1638.

Moody, H. 2002. Is retirement obsolete? In *Aging: Concepts and Controversies,* ed. H. Moody. Thousand Oaks, CA: Pine Forge Press.

Morris, R., and F. Caro. 1996. Productive retirement: Stimulating greater volunteers' efforts to meet national needs. *Journal of Volunteer Administration* 14: 5–13.

Morrow-Howell, N., M. Carden, and M. Sherraden. (2004). Productive engagement of older adults: Volunteerism and service. In *Perspectives on Productive Aging: Social Work with the New Aged*, ed. L. Kaye. Washington, DC: NASW Press. National Association of Social Workers.

Morrow-Howell, N., J. Hinterlong, P. Rozario, and F. Tang. 2003. The effects of volunteering on the well-being of older adults. *Journal of Gerontology: Social Science* 58B (3): S137–S145.

Morrow-Howell, N., J. Hinterlong, and M. Sherraden. 2001. *Productive Aging: Concepts and Challenges.* Baltimore: Johns Hopkins University Press.

Morrow-Howell, N., S. Kinnevy, and M. Mann. 1999. The perceived benefits of participating in volunteer and educational activities. *Journal of Gerontological Social Work* 32 (2): 65–80.

Moss, M., J. Hiller, and D. Moore. 1999. *Descriptive Study of AmeriCorps Literacy Programs: State and National Final Report.* Report prepared for the Corporation for Community and National Service. www.abtassociates.com/reports/ac_literacy_1199.pdf.

Musick, M.A., A.R. Herzog, and J.S. House. 1999. Volunteering and mortality among older adults: Findings from a national sample. *Journal of Gerontology: Social Science* 54B (3): S173–S180.

National Institute on Aging. 1999. The declining disability of older Americans. *Research Highlights in the Demography and Economics of Aging* 5:1–4.

Neumann, G., R. Kormendi, C. Gardener, and R. Tamura. 1995. *The Benefits and Costs of National Service: Methods for Benefit Assessment with Application to Three AmeriCorps Programs* (Report No. CE069162). Washington, DC: Corporation for National and Community Service (ERIC Document Reproduction Service No. ED383853).

Newton, R.R. 1992. *City Volunteers: The Status of Members of the City Volunteer Corps Two Years After Program Entrance.* Fullerton, CA: Public/Private Ventures.

OASIS Institute. 2000. OASIS Intergenerational Tutoring Program. www.oasisnet. org.

Oman, D., C.E. Thoresen, and K. McMahon. 1999. Volunteerism and mortality among the community-dwelling elderly. *Journal of Health Psychology* 4 (3): 301–316.

Omo-Abu, A. 1997. Ethnic cleavages and national integration: The impact of the National Youth Corps. PhD diss., Colombia University. *Dissertation Abstracts International* 58, 602A (UMI No. 9723835).

Omoto, A.M., M. Snyder, and S.C. Martino. 2000. Volunteerism and the life course: Investigating age-related agendas for action. *Basic and Applied Social Psychology* 22 (3): 181–197.

Peace Corps. 2002. Fast facts. www.peacecorps.gov/index.cfm?shell=learn.whatispc. fastfacts.

Perry, J.L., and M.C. Katula. 2001. Does service affect citizenship? *Administration and Society* 33 (3): 330–365.

Project Star. 2001. *Seniors for Schools Evaluation Results 1999–2000 School Year.* Report prepared for the Corporation for National and Community Service. www. seniorcorps.gov/pdf/seniors_4schools.pdf.

Purvis, T.G. 1993. Partnership in cross-cultural mission: The impacts of Kentucky Baptist Short-term Volunteer Missions. PhD diss., Asbury Theological Seminary, Kentucky.

Richards, A., and L. Kemeny, eds. 1986. *National Service in the 1990s, Monograph on Youth in the 1990s. Service Through Learning: Learning Through Service.* Halifax, Nova Scotia: Dalhousie University.

Riley, M.W., R.L. Kahn, and A. Foner, eds. 1994. *Age and Structural Lag: Societies' Failure to Provide Meaningful Opportunities in Work, Family, and Leisure.* New York: John Wiley.

Rosow, I. 1967. *Social Integration of the Aged.* New York: Free Press.

Rowe, J.W., and R.L. Kahn. 1998. *Successful Aging.* New York: Pantheon.

RTI International. 2003. *Final Report of the Senior Companion Quality of Care Evaluation.* Report prepared for the Corporation for National and Community Service. www.seniorcorps.gov/pdf/final_scp_report.pdf.

Senior Corps. 2002a. Research: Foster Grandparents program review. www.senior-corps.gov/about/programs/fg.asp.

Senior Corps. 2002b. Research: Senior Companion program review. www.seniorcorps. gov/about/programs/sc.asp.

Sherraden, M. 2001. *Civic Service: Issues, Outlook, Institution Building.* St. Louis: Washington University, Center for Social Development.

Sherraden, M., M.S. Sherraden, and D. Eberly. 1990. Comparison and understanding non-military service in different nations. In *The Moral Equivalent of War?: A Study of Non-military Service in Nine Nations,* ed. D. Eberly, and M. Sherraden. New York: Greenwood.

Sikah, V.P. 2000. The Ghana National Service Scheme: Perceptions of former educational personnel, students and guardians. PhD diss., Florida International University. *Dissertation Abstracts International* 61, 10A (UMI No. 99915554).

SRA Technologies Inc. 1985. *Senior Companion Program Impact Evaluation: Final Report.* Washington, DC: ACTION.

Starr, J. 1994. Peace Corps service as a turning point. *International Journal of Aging and Human Development* 39 (2): 137–161.

Svanborg, A. 2001. Biomedical perspectives on productive aging. In *Perspectives on Productive Aging: Concepts and Challenge,* ed. N. Morrow-Howell, J. Hinterlong, and M. Sherraden. Baltimore: Johns Hopkins University Press.

Temple University Center for Intergenerational Learning. 2000. Homefriends Program. www.temple.edu/cil/Homefriendshome.htm.

Thoits, P.A., and L.N. Hewitt. 2001. Volunteer work and well-being. *Journal of Health and Social Work* 42: 115–131.

Thomson, A., and J. Perry. 1998. Can AmeriCorps build communities? *Nonprofit and Voluntary Sector Quarterly* 27 (4): 399–420.

Van Willigen, M. 2000. Differential benefits of volunteering across the life course. *Journal of Gerontology: Social Sciences* 55B (5): S308–S318.

Wang, C., T. Owens, and K. Kim. 1995. *A Cost Benefit Study of Two AmeriCorps Projects in the State of Washington.* Portland, OR: Northwestern Regional Educational Laboratory.

Ward, R.A. 1979. The meaning of voluntary association participation to older people. *Journal of Gerontology* 34: 438–445.

Wheeler, J.A., K.M. Gorey, and B. Greenblatt. 1998. The beneficial effects of volunteering for older volunteers and the people they serve: A meta-analysis. *International Journal of Aging and Human Development* 47 (1): 69–79.

Zweigenhaft, R.L., J. Armstrong, and F. Quintis. 1996. The motivations and effectiveness of hospital volunteers. *Journal of Social Psychology* 136 (1): 25–34.

IV

CIVIC SERVICE
ACROSS BORDERS

9

International Civic Service

A Step Toward Cooperation
in a Global World

Margaret Sherrard Sherraden

Although economics and terrorism dominate headlines about globalization, other global realities are beginning to receive greater scrutiny. These include social inequality between the Global South and North, immigrant and refugee flows, crime and human trafficking, and environmental challenges (Held et al. 1999). Attention has also shifted to solutions for global social issues, including emerging transnational social movements (Keck and Sikkink 1998), global civil society (Clark 2003, 1–23; Kaldor 2003), and global and regional social policy developments (Deacon 1994; Mishra 1999; Prior and Sykes 2001, 195–210).

Accompanying these developments is an upsurge in the numbers and types of institutions of international cooperation. This chapter focuses on international civic service as one example of global cooperation. The first part explores the character and growth of institutions of international cooperation. The next part identifies key dimensions of international service, followed by an analysis of one program, North American Community Service (NACS). The conclusion examines the challenges, possible benefits, and implications of international civic service as an institution of international cooperation.

Globalization and the Growth of International Institutions of Cooperation

Globalization, according to Alberto Martinelli, is a "set of related processes that interconnects individuals, groups, communities, states, markets, corporations and international governmental and nongovernmental organizations in complex webs of social relations; and more synthetically . . . the growth of networks of world-wide interdependence" (Martinelli 2003, 294). For Scholte, globalization means the "reconfiguration of social space" in which "territorial space is substantially transcended" (Scholte 2000, 46–48). The implications are far reaching, according to David Held: "Globalization can be taken to denote the stretching and deepening of social relations and institutions across space and time such that, on the one hand, day-to-day activities are increasingly influenced by events happening on the other side of the globe and, on the other, the practices and decisions of local groups or communities can have significant global reverberations" (1995, 20).

Although scholars document significant waves of globalization beginning in the late fifteenth century (Coatsworth 2004, 38–55), many argue that contemporary globalization is more potent (Robertson 1992; Martinelli 2003; Held et al. 1999). One important difference is the expansion and growing influence of institutions of international cooperation.

These institutions differ in important respects from international organizations of the past in three key ways. First, they are growing rapidly and have greater influence. In the current era, increasing numbers of powerful economic, governmental, and nongovernmental or civil society institutions operate globally. These institutions have become more influential vis-à-vis the state. As Albrow points out, "In transnational relations boundaries are being crossed, rather than maintained or negotiated by state representatives" (1998, 2).[1] At the same time, each of these institutions faces challenges from local, national, and international interests.

Powerful global economic organizations, including the International Monetary Fund and the World Bank aim to build market economies and eliminate trade and investment barriers. On a smaller scale, regional economic organizations such as the Organization for Economic Co-operation and Development (OECD), the North American Free Trade Association (NAFTA), the Association of Southeast Asian Nations (ASEAN), and the South American Common Market form possible "building blocks of a global community" (Ferge 2001, 140–141).

Organizations of global governance, such as the United Nations (UN), promote peace, human rights, international law, social progress, and improved living standards worldwide (UN 2005a). Although antecedents to the UN contributed to this agenda,[2] the scale and success of the UN have no precedent. Regional governing organizations and institutions have also emerged. The most important, the European Union (EU), has created structures that address a broad range of social and economic issues.

Global civil society organizations have also flourished since the end of World War II (Kaldor 2003), especially as nation-states and other international organizations have failed to adequately address global problems. Democracy, according to Baker, can no longer be maintained while exclusively linked to nation-states because it is "increasingly losing capacity to facilitate self-determination in a world of growing economic and cultural globalization" (2002, 929). Global civil society, according to Shaw, is comprised of (a) international social networks and social movements that focus on poverty, peace, the environment, labor, indigenous and women's rights, and other issues (Keck and Sikkink 1998); (b) formal organizations that link national institutions, such as trade unions, churches, media, and educational institutions; and (c) organizations with global missions and memberships, such as Greenpeace or Amnesty International (Shaw 1994, 650). The activities of these global civil society institutions include pressuring governments and shaping world opinion, intervening directly to benefit particular groups, and promoting structural change and creating new institutions (Ghils 1992; Baker 2002). Global civil society organizations vary widely in decision making, leadership, communications, and governance (Clark 2003, 6).

Second, contemporary international institutions of cooperation are more inclusive. For example, while the UN's predecessor, the League of Nations, did not include countries of the Global South (except for Latin America), UN membership today is more inclusive and provides greater voice for smaller and less powerful members, and a new proposal recommends even greater inclusion (UN 2005b; Farley 2005). Since World War II, regions of the Global South also have created intergovernmental organizations, including the Organization of American States (created in 1948) and the Organization of African Unity (created in 1963), which focus on regional political, economic, and social development agendas.

Nonetheless, the largest and most influential institutions of international cooperation remain dominated by a few nations. In the UN, for example, a few countries maintain veto power over key decisions made by the international body. Concerning the role of women, Schaeffer notes that institutions such as multinational corporations, the World Trade Organization, and the North Atlantic Treaty Organization are "designed by men to serve patriarchy, [therefore] it should not be surprising that it [globalization] neglects women, fails to assign them an important role in the globalization project, and dismisses adverse impacts on women as inconsequential" (2003, 14).

Women's groups and other underrepresented peoples contest this hegemony, typically through civil society organizations, where perhaps the greatest advances in inclusion have been made. Global civil society raises new concerns and gives voice to groups previously excluded from discussions of global issues. Some argue that this represents a kind of "global democratization from below" (Baker 2002, 932).

While many applaud development of institutions of global civil society as movement toward inclusion and global democracy, others are more cautious, pointing out that these institutions are neither democratic nor accountable (Scholte 2000; Baker 2002; Clark 2003, 1–28; Florini 2003). Baker, for example, argues that they represent the interests of some groups over others: "This ought to be of particular concern given that, on the basis of the uneven spread of power and resources, most global civil society organizations are actually thoroughly Western (many based in, even resourced by, Western states) and the majority of the world's citizens are more adequately conceptualized as objects rather than subjects of such organizations" (Baker 2002, 937).

A third difference between early and contemporary international institutions is that more of them address social issues (de Swaan 1994; Deacon 1994). Within the UN system, for example, the United Nations Children's Fund, the United Nations Development Program, the United Nations High Commission for Refugees, and other agencies, lead discussions about social equity and poverty. Moving beyond purely economic measures of well-\being (e.g., GDP), the UN includes social equity and well-being in its Human Development Index (Estes 1999; Florini 2003).

At regional levels, although the EU primarily addresses issues of economic integration, Leibfried and Pierson point out that a social state has progressed on several fronts (1994, 15–49). Social protections, however, have moved slowly in areas where national welfare policies dominate (Leibfried and Pierson 1994) or have been reduced in transition countries in Central Eastern Europe in the wake of privatization and a withdrawal of the state from social welfare provision (Ferge 2001, 127–152).

The growth of global civil society organizations also has led to more attention to social activism on global issues, such as the environment, human rights, and social provision (Kaldor 2003, 129). As Kaldor points out, the focus of civil society "is public affairs, not the market" and civil society provides space where people engage from below in "politics" (Kaldor 2003, 45–46, 48).

In sum, institutions of international cooperation thrive in the contemporary era of globalization, and despite limitations and lack of clear definition and conceptualization, these institutions are more inclusive and address a broader range of economic and social issues than international institutions in the past. Next, we turn to discussion of an emerging global institution that has potential for increasing inclusiveness and attention to the social and economic concerns of people at the bottom.

Figure 9.1 **Continuum of International Service Programs**

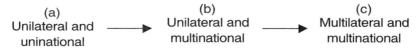

(a)
Unilateral and
uninational

(b)
Unilateral and
multinational

(c)
Multilateral and
multinational

International Civic Service

With roots in nineteenth-century missionary work and early twentieth-century international peace and postwar reconstruction efforts (Rosenstock-Huessy 1978), international civic service thrives in the contemporary era of globalization (McBride, Benítez, and Sherraden 2003; Smith, Ellis, and Brewis 2004). Here we define civic service as an organized period of engagement and contribution to the community, society, or world, sponsored by public or private organizations, and recognized and valued by society, with minimal monetary compensation to the participant (M. Sherraden 2001).

It is possible to think about international service as a continuum (Figure 9.1), using two key dimensions: (1) the first dimension is the extent to which organizations from different countries are responsible for planning and implementing the program (i.e., unilateral versus bilateral or multilateral); and (2) the second dimension is the extent to which the volunteer and host community are exposed to people from various countries (uninational versus binational or multinational) (Sherraden, et al. 2006). Unilateral and uninational programs are the least transnational, according to our definition, and multilateral and multinational programs are the most transnational. Further research is required to determine the extent to which each of these models results in specified transnational outcomes and impacts for volunteers, host communities, and sponsoring organizations.

In unilateral and uninational international service, one country sends volunteers to a host country. Using a sender-receiver model, the sending country typically defines the parameters of the program, chooses participants, is responsible for them, and provides most of the funding, although host country partners often identify projects, help place volunteers, and provide other in-country supports. This is the most prevalent and well-known type of international service. Examples include the U.S. Peace Corps and Japan Overseas Cooperation Volunteers, which send volunteers from the United States and Japan, respectively, for two-year terms of service in developing countries. Long-term unilateral service includes mission-based service by volunteers from a wide range of denominations (e.g., American Friends Service Committee, the Catholic Church, or the Church of Jesus Christ Latter-day Saints).

Unilateral programs also include short-term workcamp-type programs comprised of multinational groups of volunteers (SCI 2005). Service Civil International and International Cultural Youth Exchange are examples of networks that coordinate service across national borders, linking sending organizations with organizations that host multinational teams working in community-based projects around the globe.

In contrast, multilateral service is the least common and least familiar category of international service that sends volunteers to serve in two or more countries, often in multinational groups. Service sites sometimes include volunteers' countries of origin. A program is more transnational to the extent that program goals, management, and service involve decision making and cooperation by different countries and involve volunteers from different countries and regions of the world. Although unilateral service is far more common than multilateral service, the latter is growing in size and importance in recognition of the importance of mutuality and reciprocity in international service (Rockcliffe 2005).

North American Community Service:
An Example of Multilateral Service

Mexico, the United States, and Canada all have voluntary service programs with roots in the Great Depression of the 1930s. Programs have expanded during some eras and contracted during others, but the idea and reality of service have survived changes in administrations, budget swings, and other challenges over many decades (Furano and Walker 2000; Guevara Niebla 2000; Ninacs and Toye 2000; Sherraden 1979; M. Sherraden 2001; M. Sherraden and M. S. Sherraden 1990, 87–100).

Building on this history, knowledge, public support, and technical expertise, a consortium of organizations undertook a North American multilateral civic service demonstration in 2002–2003 called the North American Community Service (NACS) program (NAMI 2001).[3] Although Canada has several multilateral service programs, NACS is the only one in either the United States or Mexico, according to a global assessment of civic service (McBride, Benítez, and Sherraden 2003). The goal of NACS was to foster youth leadership, sustainable development, and development of a North American community. Collaborators included the North American Institute (NAMI), an organization promoting the North American community; the Universidad Veracruzana (UV), the principal public university in the state of Veracruz, Mexico; the Student Conservation Association (SCA), the leading provider of youth conservation volunteers in the United States; and Canada World Youth (CWY), an international leader in multilateral service headquartered in Montreal; along with other regional and local organizations in the three countries. A team of nine NACS volunteers rotated among three sites in North America over a period of six months. The team, composed of three participants from each country and one project group leader, began in Canada and moved to the United States and then to Mexico, spending two months in each country. The volunteers ranged in age from nineteen to twenty-five.

A steering committee included a representative from the four implementing organizations and CWY was selected to lead the project. An advisory board was made up of experts in voluntary and youth service, educators, researchers, and funders. Additional partners included the Columbia Basin Trust (CBT), a nongovernmental organization charged with promoting a sustainable environment in the Canadian Columbia River Basin, and the University of Texas at El Paso, which provided support for the Texas phase of the program. Washington University's Center for Social Development and the University of Missouri in St. Louis conducted the research.

NACS aimed "to raise awareness on the part of North Americans of shared cultural, environmental, social and economic challenges and to increase their capacity to confront these challenges in collaboration with one another" (Sherraden and Benítez 2001, 13). Objectives included (1) transforming of youth volunteers to prepare them for leadership roles in building a sustainable North American community, including cross-cultural sensitivity; increased sense of civic responsibility; increased knowledge of cultural, environmental, social, and economic issues in North America; and preparation for future employment; (2) making concrete contributions to host communities through community development and conservation services; and (3) establishing a network of youth participants and host communities committed to sustainable community development in North America.

The program consisted of community service, education, and outreach. Volunteers spent four days on a service project and one day in formal or informal educational activities per week. Other educational and recreational activities took place on evenings and weekends. Community service projects were negotiated and approved by the steering committee based on the project's relevance to NACS and the local organizational capacity to provide opportunities for service and learning.

Three Phases, Three Countries, Three Communities

The programmatic focus changed according to the phase of the project. Phase One focused on environmental preservation and sustainable development in British Columbia in three projects funded by the CBT. Volunteers lived with host families and served in a grassroots, youth-driven environmental and conservation organization, a wetlands restoration project, and a watershed alliance that operated sustainable forestry and botanical projects.

Phase Two focused on historic preservation in Socorro, Texas, where volunteers worked on the historic Socorro Mission (circa 1692) under the direction of Cornerstones Community Partnerships. Volunteers learned traditional methods of adobe construction and architecture and were immersed in the social and cultural realities of the mission and border community. They worked alongside staff, welfare-to-work participants, and volunteers, and lived in a communal facility on the grounds of the mission.

Phase Three focused on community development and sustainable development in the small mountain village of Coyopolan, Veracruz, doing community development and environmental conservation work. The principal projects, chosen by community members and representatives of UV, included building a sustainable house and garden for a local family and developing the community's greenhouses and trout stream to provide alternative income sources for the villagers. NACS volunteers lived together in the Casa de la Universidad, built by UV for outreach and service by volunteers in the university's service-learning program.[4]

Information and interviews with participants, community residents, staff, and program advisers suggest that the program affected volunteers, communities, and organizations in various ways. The following analysis focuses on impacts, illustrating the potential and challenges of multilateral civic service.

Impact on Volunteers

The five women and four men in the NACS pilot came from diverse ethnic, linguistic, socioeconomic, and geographic backgrounds. Only four had previously lived or worked with people from another country at some point. Only one volunteer had lived for an extended period outside of her country of origin. Members of each national group were similar in some important ways (due to the way they were selected). The Canadian volunteers were the youngest, had the least Spanish-language background, had relatively little international travel experience, and were least sure about their academic and career goals. The U.S. volunteers were older, had traveled more, and had some Spanish-language skills. The Mexican volunteers were the oldest and had completed professional training, but none had traveled previously to an English-speaking country or spoke English.

In interviews, the volunteers said that they developed a variety of skills and gained new perspectives as a result of the NACS experience.

Cross-Cultural Human Relations Skills

Despite their diversity, the volunteers reported that they became more effective, generous, and cohesive over time. As one volunteer stated, "I never thought [these relationships] would solidify, but [they] have become unbreakable." Another volunteer said she learned to have patience: "The experience of living in a tight group of people and working within that group to solve differences, problems and break stereotypes are lessons and skills that will help me enormously in the future. Patience, patience, patience."

Volunteers increased their ability to speak another language. In their own assessment, six volunteers progressed from almost no ability to basic ability; one progressed from basic to intermediate, one progressed from intermediate to advanced, and one progressed from advanced to proficient. The Mexicans had the greatest challenge because they were the first in the group to be placed in a language immersion situation (in Canada). By the time the group arrived in Mexico, the native English speakers had learned some Spanish from their peers and from their interactions in the bilingual U.S.-Mexican border environment in Texas. The program, as one volunteer stated, "made me realize that I like languages and I like being able to communicate with people." Several said they planned to continue their language study.

International Career Direction

The volunteers said that NACS would likely impact their career directions, and in some cases, this included considering an internationally focused career. One participant, who had already completed an undergraduate professional degree, was contemplating a change of career plans as a result of NACS: "It was through this amazing experience that I have learned the importance of fostering a sustainable society in the world. Now I wish to complete my master's degree and redirect my future. Perhaps pursue a doctorate, but in an environmental field with the purpose of applying my knowledge in the community and thus contribute to its development." Another volunteer planned to pursue graduate work in Latin America.

Knowledge and Understanding of Issues Facing North America

The volunteers gained cross-national understanding and insight into the everyday lives of people in three communities in North America. They gained understanding of people in different environments but also how institutions impact their lives. For example, a volunteer said that living "on the [Mexican-U.S.] border really made clear to me how flexible cultures can be and also how constraining society and policies can be on cultures."

On one hand, volunteers increased their understanding of issues common to all of North America. As one volunteer said, the experience made him realize that "three very distinct communities that on the cover seem so different, in reality have so many things in common." Another said that her perceptions about developed countries changed as a result of seeing challenges faced in each community:

> NACS has influenced and broken the stereotypes I had of the other countries. . . . I was able to see directly that other countries also have problems such as environmental, social, cultural problems. . . . When we see our common problems then we can relate to one another. . . . When someone tells you about his or her life . . . well, a connection is made. That's precisely what happened to us when we saw the same problem in Canada and the United States. We were able to relate and to connect. That makes it possible to [be] a North American citizen.

On the other hand, volunteers also learned how issues played out differently in the three countries, gaining a deeper and more nuanced understanding of social and economic inequities across the continent. For example, they learned how North American integration (i.e., NAFTA) affected small communities in each country, but had greater impact in some areas than in others. They discussed how negative impacts might be avoided in the future.

Global Civic Participation and North American "Citizenship"

The volunteers also said that their interest in and commitment to civic participation on global issues was enhanced. Their comments suggested several factors that contributed to a growing sense of global civic responsibility, including heightened consciousness about the reality of other people's lives, greater understanding of community and local leadership, and heightened feelings of empowerment. As one volunteer said, his belief in his own potential grew because the group members were "being spoken of as future leaders of North America . . . our accomplishments [were] acknowledged by people that I highly respect."

The volunteers also began to act on their increased knowledge of the North American context, learning how to convey what they were learning about North America to others through the NACS-sponsored community education days. Moreover, they began to develop what might be described as a North American identity. As one volunteer stated, "I no longer feel that I am from the United States or [am] what everyone calls an *American*. I am a North American!" Another concurred, "Without a doubt I now feel part of North America with the civic duty to serve and foster this citizenship." At the same time, they said that developing a North American identity did not mean giving up their national identity and their roots. As one volunteer pointed out, "I have learned to value more my personal roots."

Impact on Communities

Although more difficult to measure, interviews suggested that communities gained some tangible benefits of service (described earlier), but also less tangible benefits such as community pride, empowerment, and cross-cultural learning.

Community Pride and Empowerment

The volunteers' work invigorated and impacted community residents in part because their community was chosen as the volunteer site, but also because the volunteers worked side by side with community residents doing their daily work and contributing to valued projects in the community. A volunteer reported, for example, that in British Columbia, "people came up . . . would visit and get involved" and the volunteers were invited to present their work and the program to a session of the city council. In Texas, a volunteer pointed out that the mission workers "were looking at the work only as masonry—or disagreeable—work, but now they are impressed because we are working as volunteers. [As a result] many of them have changed their attitudes and now they value their work, [they] see their work like an art." In Mexico, initial skepticism about the foreigners was replaced by pride. Interviews with community leaders suggested that residents felt empowered by these relationships.

Cross-cultural Learning

By the end of their stay in each community, the volunteers had forged close friendships with residents. For example, in the smallest community, Coyopolan, despite villagers' initial apprehensions, "community involvement [in] this phase was amazing and the most warm and enthusiastic of any of the phases," according to one volunteer. Although community leaders in Veracruz had low expectations for the volunteers, the municipal leader stated at the end of their stay, "We have come to realize they are hardworking people and it is a shame they are going back to their countries so soon." In the words of an observer from the university, the NACS program was "something amazing to see—how people come together."

NACS volunteers may have had the greatest cross-cultural influence on children and youth, especially in Veracruz, where the proximity and presence of volunteers for eight weeks allowed a high degree of interaction, and in Texas, where volunteers worked alongside troubled youth on the mission restoration project. As one volunteer said, "It is wonderful, I think, to imagine they will not be prejudiced against foreign people, they won't have that xenophobia that [other] people have."

There was some evidence that transmission of ideas from community to community could also take place, if a program was ongoing. For example, a community leader in Coyopolan recounted that the volunteers shared some of the video footage that they had been taking throughout the program. He said:

> They showed us a video from Canada. They have over there, what do you called them? A botanical garden. I mean, if they have one of those over there, why can't we have one here? And here we have abundant vegetation! There are a lot of medicinal plants. A lot. All the years I have lived here I have learned about plants that cured me without spending one single *peso*, not one *centavo*!

North American Community Building

Several informants believed that the simple act of placing young people from three different countries together may encourage community residents to think about North American issues. As a program adviser observed, "People will be wondering why are there three people from each country coming together? . . . if we can answer that question . . . it will kind of show them that there is a connection between the three countries and this is why we're here. I think that's a major, major, thing." Despite the potential for North American community building, interviews with community leaders did not result in many comments along this vein, suggesting that more sustained efforts may be needed to encourage such outcomes.

Impact on Organizations

There was some evidence of increased interest and, to a lesser extent, capacity within the participating organizations to engage in cross-national work.

Increased Constituent Interest

NACS invigorated partner organizations. One organizational leader, for example, reported improved relations with the community, greater interaction with young people in the area, and increased visibility. She noted: "It was possible to expand the interest and knowledge of all participants about the problems of the relationship between Mexico, the United States and Canada." Moreover, the numbers of applications by young people interested in participating in NACS suggests considerable interest. SCA had 500 inquiries from its alumni pool of former leaders for just three spots. UV and CWY also reported very high interest among their alumni.

Increased International Profile

Partner and host organizations expanded their international profiles and gained greater understanding of transnational issues. Each could claim greater international involvement and an expanded profile within North America. Staff and board members developed more understanding of international issues. An organizational leader observed, "I think that [board members] got a lot out of meeting the participants and hearing what they were learning about. I think that gave them more of an understanding of why this kind of thing is important."

Challenges of International Civic Service: NACS

Research on the pilot NACS program also suggests several conceptual and practical challenges that may confront international and multilateral service programs.

Inclusion

International programs must pay attention to how inclusive they are across countries and within each country. In NACS, there were no procedures to guarantee participation of socially and economically disadvantaged volunteers within each country. Nonetheless, the pilot NACS group was remarkably diverse from a socioeconomic perspective, in part because the national sponsoring organizations covered most volunteer expenses. However, as programs grow, there may be less willingness to cover these expenses, and disadvantaged youth may find it increasingly difficult to participate. Opportunity costs and cultural issues have to be addressed in attracting a diverse volunteer corps. For instance, the opportunity costs of participation may be too high for low-income youth, and youth may have diverse views about program benefits.

Role of Communities

In NACS, interviews suggest that community members had a positive impression of NACS and the volunteers, but their involvement was not as carefully considered as much of the rest of the program. While not a major issue in the pilot, the role of community members could become a more significant issue if a succession of NACS volunteer groups were stationed in a single community. Who chooses and oversees the service projects? Who provides financial or in-kind support for the volunteer groups? These are questions that would likely be asked by local people. Perhaps more challenging is how a program like NACS can ensure that local elites do not dominate local decision making and reap project benefits (Guarnizo and Smith 1998). There should be mechanisms that ensure that international service programs provide equitable service and that local people have a role in selection and oversight. This may be more likely in multilateral service programs because of involvement by people more familiar with local circumstances.

Organizational Mission and Capacity

Some of the organizations found it challenging to integrate NACS into their mission and operations. This was particularly true for organizations whose missions were not explicitly international. For example, a representative of one organization commented, "There were definitely a lot of questions from . . . some members of our board . . . about the relevance of this kind of programming over more locally focused programs and other priorities." Questions also surfaced in international organizations. Even in NAMI, whose central mission is North American community building, there had been "some discussion on the Board of Directors about how the program fits within the larger NAMI role of serving as a convener and less as a program coordinator," according to a NAMI representative.

NACS demonstrated other complexities of managing a multilateral civic service program. It involved fairly complicated arrangements among three countries, three communities, and more than three different service projects. It took time and required great leadership skills. The challenge is to reduce complexity and yet still offer a multilateral experience. It is still not clear what kind of institutional structure is optimal for multilateral civic service.

Associated with the complexity, the NACS pilot was more expensive than other international service programs. With no economy of scale, any pilot project is expensive. But some high costs are inherent in multilateral programs, including costs of bilingual staff, travel, visas, and insurance. Local sponsoring organizations reported high expenses, which they would be unable to underwrite over the longer term. Each of the participating organizations provided funding (directly or indirectly) from existing budgets. For some, these expenditures caused relatively little strain, but for others the expense was more difficult to absorb.

Multilateral Civic Service, National Priorities,
and Going "to Scale"

Multilateral civic service may prosper or wither depending on national priorities. This became evident in the United States in the aftermath of the terrorist attacks on September 11, 2001. Heightened nationalism and xenophobia challenges the fundamental precepts of international, and, perhaps especially, multilateral service programs. Although NACS could be viewed as an effective response to terrorism for its ability to increase international goodwill and to build multinational relations, focus in the United States has been placed elsewhere. Perhaps as a result, the United States has been the most reluctant NACS partner in raising funds and generating sponsoring organization interest. An advisory board member pointed out, "No truly committed U.S. partner has yet emerged ready and situated to lead the initiative forward in the U.S. in a dynamic way. [I'm] disappointed in the difficulty in the U.S. grasping the value of the project. I would have thought it would be a 'slam-dunk'."

As a result of tight funds, the pilot project was scaled back from nine to six months and began late. "The biggest disappointment thus far," commented an NACS organizer, "has been the lack of funds available for the program, and subsequent scaling-down of the pilot."

Developing a program like NACS requires resources, probably including public funding. An advisory board member suggested, "In the longer term, scaling up and sustainability will require an investment of public funds, but the [NACS] pilot needs to be successful in order to convince public agencies to invest." Program funding must come from all three countries, although there should be recognition that, as in the EU, levels of support might differ among the nations depending on their financial ability to support the program. In the North American context, the United States might be expected to provide the greatest financial contribution to a scaled-up program, followed by Canada and then Mexico. Further, contributions by nongovernmental organizations and private partners can help support the program.

Common Goals and Shared Decision Making

A challenge for multilateral programs is how to ensure that all country partners participate equally in selecting goals and program design, implementing the program, and designing the research and evaluation. Because this was an explicit objective from the outset, NACS included all three countries equally in leadership and decision making. As one steering committee member observed, "Participants from all three nations functioned equally and well in designing the pilot project." Nonetheless, geographic distance and differences in language, culture, and resource levels made joint planning challenging.

Moreover, some differences in emphasis emerged over the course of the pilot. For example, while U.S. and Canadian planners viewed the program largely as a way to build international understanding, goodwill, and cross-cultural skills, Mexican planners emphasized economics and inequality.

They, in particular, underscored the importance of building understanding and commitment to address inequality associated with globalization. From the Mexican perspective, NACS could provide young people with firsthand knowledge of the causes and consequences of globalization and prepare young people for the challenges that lie ahead. In the words of a steering committee member from Mexico:

> The new reality of rural Mexico, its problems, its challenges, and its opportunities are closely tied to the economies and the development of the Canadian and U.S. societies. The opening of markets, the asymmetry of agricultural development in the three nations, migration and trans-culturalization are realities that require finding new forms of internationalization [in the university curriculum] that prepares professionals with a strong sense of social commitment. . . . The fight against poverty in Veracruz requires recognizing the social, economic and cultural interrelations of Mexico, Canada, and the United States.

Thus, despite a shared commitment to building a North American community, emphasis and focus differed. NACS represented a convergence, but in a context of inequality and difference. Acknowledging and addressing these differences while building common ground became the project.

Discussion

This analysis of NACS, a multilateral civic service program, suggests potential unique benefits to volunteers, host communities, and organizational sponsors. An explicit focus on transnational goals, in particular, may provide opportunities for (1) tangible contributions to sustainable social and economic development; (2) heightened global consciousness and global civic responsibility among volunteers, host communities, and organizational sponsors; and (3) support for norms of inclusion in international institutions of cooperation.

First, large-scale international service potentially could result in sustainable development of lasting social and economic value, as it has in national service (Sherraden 1979; Eberly and Sherraden 1990). Multilateral and multinational service may provide a way to incorporate mutuality and reciprocity in service (Rockcliffe 2005), resulting in more appropriate, inclusive, and sustainable development. The idea of multilateral service suggests that nations have much to learn from each other, but also that globally we confront many issues in common. Including community members and incorporating nationals and non-nationals in each group of volunteers may result in service that is more relevant and more effective.

However, because of the complexity and potentially high cost of multilateral service, it is important to consider how it can be structured and organized to simplify and reduce costs. For instance, the European Voluntary Service scheme funds cross-national service placements, and other organizations link volunteers to existing programs worldwide, but do not operate programs themselves (Sherraden et al. 2006). Such models are less expensive, but they may also be less inclusive (Schröer 2003). A comparison of models, including costs and benefits, would be helpful in order to understand how tangible benefits can be generated while meeting other international service goals.

Second, multilateral volunteer service in programs like NACS may have positive impacts that exceed other forms of international service. By serving together on an equal basis with a multinational group of volunteers in two or more countries, volunteers may gain cross-cultural skills, international understanding, and knowledge about international issues and careers, and a heightened sense of global citizenship. The perspectives of NACS volunteers, for example, contrast with what Simpson observed in interviews with gap year volunteers in the UK: "Currently the gap year industry promotes an image of the *third world other* that is dominated by simplistic binaries of 'us and them,' and is expressed through essentialist clichés, where the public face of development is one dominated by the value of western *good intentions* (2004, 690). It is likely that this type of "us and them" perspective results from the unilateral model of service and thus may be less prevalent when multinational volunteers from the Global North and South serve together in more than one country in multilateral service. Multilateral civic service may result in what Scholte calls "interculturalism," in which "different communities would encounter each other in global relations with mutual recognition, respect, responsibility and (when tensions rise) restraint" (2000, 297).

The NACS pilot suggests that multilateral service may contribute to volunteers developing "multiple civic identities" (Thompson 1998, 194) and global consciousness and skills to function effectively in a global world (Hartman and Rola 2000). The experience may be somewhat similar to the experience of immigrant youth, who according to some researchers, develop a transcultural identity and an ability to interact across ethnic groups with ease (Suárez-Orozco 2004, 194–195). According to Suárez-Orozco (2004) immigrant children are more successful academically and may be more inclined to *give back* to their community and be prepared to think creatively about cultural conflict. The ability to transcend one's nationality may be an important skill in an increasingly global world. As John Coatsworth suggests, the ability of transnational immigrants to function across national boundaries is an asset:

"In the era of belligerent and defensive nationalisms, *divided* (or worse yet, multiple) loyalties often seemed almost treasonous. In the twenty-first century, such qualities represent valuable human capital" (Coatsworth 2004, 52). Multinational service may have similar outcomes for volunteers.

Although we know much less about the impact of multilateral service on host communities and their residents, they may benefit in similar ways. Further, a question for research is whether the presence of nationals in the volunteer group helps to establish a foundation of trust, leading to empowerment of local residents. First, members of the host community may perceive the volunteer group as less foreign and more like them, engaged in similar pursuits. Second, the group itself may operate differently when outsiders do not own the truth. One possibility is that volunteers and host community residents may develop a broader (or "translocal") understanding of their condition (Suárez-Orozco and Qin-Hilliard 2004), which could develop into global understanding. Volunteers and local hosts may begin to see themselves as having a legitimate role in local—and possibly global—affairs.

At the organizational level, the NACS pilot also suggests that organizations engaged in multilateral service programs increase their international profile and capacity to work effectively cross-nationally and globally. As a result, these organizations may be in an improved position to lead bilateral and multilateral cooperative ventures, thus contributing to their institutional capacity to respond to global issues. These findings are suggestive and require more research to explore the volunteer, community, and organizational impacts of multilateral service.

Third, multilateral service may also enhance norms of inclusion in transnational policy. As we observe in multilateral civic service programs, inclusion is possible, but as John Stringham and others (EVS 2001; Schröer 2003) caution, it must be an explicit aim and resources must be devoted to these efforts. Volunteers who come from privileged backgrounds are more likely to have the resources to serve and to derive personal benefits from volunteering, but those with fewer resources (or more barriers to participation) may find volunteering less feasible and the benefits less apparent. Existing incentives and protections may not suffice. Families may need a potential volunteer's job income and help at home, and others may not have the luxury of taking time off from careers to engage in activities that may have long-term, but not immediate or clear benefits. Achieving broader participation of volunteers from all sectors of society requires more research and careful planning, possibly including education for service, stipends, access to education and skill-building opportunities.

Greater inclusion across communities, organizations, and nations also should be an explicit focus. Inclusion means not only including diverse groups of volunteers and forging multilateral volunteer programs across rich and poor nations, but also inclusiveness about mission and goals. A truly multilateral service program does not merely promote international understanding and identify commonalities; it confronts asymmetrical relationships underlying social, political, and economic realities in different countries and exposes different interpretations of what it means to build a regional or global identity. As Rohrschneider and Dalton note in their analysis of transnational activities among environmental groups:

> This is not a network of equals, with identical norms and goals, as is often implied by the global civic society literature. The resource flows follow the same North/South patterns of many other first world–third world interactions. Moreover, the resource suppliers (Western environmental NGOs [nongovernmental organizations]) often have distinct ideological and political goals that are not always shared by green NGOs in the developing world. (Rohrschneider and Dalton 2002, 529)

This comment suggests that while multilateral civic service has potential to address inequalities among nations and to contribute to greater global good, the issue is something that must be overtly addressed. Similarly, as Simpson points out in reference to the UK's gap year tradition, "As long as gap year projects fail to engage in the structural relationships between communities of the developed and developing world, they retain their myopic concentration on the individual. So that, rather than concentrating on mechanisms for increased global understanding or greater engagement between communities, they focus on individual advancement" (2004, 689). Multilateral civic service begins to achieve its goals as it deals with differences (including different interpretations of the program itself) and builds mutual understanding and common ground across countries.

Clearly, there are challenges. As Glick-Schiller, Basch, and Szanton Blanc (1995) point out, even while nations continue to move economically and socially along a path toward greater globalization, nationalism remains a powerful force and one that is not likely to support international or multilateral service. For example, recent events have underscored a narrow conception of security in the United States that currently offers little room for programs aimed at increasing global understanding and cooperation. There has been, as Scholte notes, "some increase in cosmopolitan attachment to a universal human community. However, the scale of this last trend must not be exaggerated. Globalization has to date shown little sign of supplanting particularistic group affiliations with a single world solidarity" (2000, 160). Similarly, Martinelli cautions, "Today a transnational civil society, an international public space and growing awareness of our common fate as human beings are taking shape, but a global communitarian culture is far from being achieved" (2003, 295). This reality has made it difficult to garner support and funding for large-scale multilateral service programs.

Although multilateral service could be part of a path toward global security, a way to build international understanding and to educate future leaders about the complexities of development—goals that would certainly be in the long-term best interests of democratic societies—it requires a shift in thinking about the nature of nationhood, security, culture, and progress. A vision that supports the development of institutions of international cooperation like multilateral service will be necessary before such programs can reach scale. Countries and regions that have a tradition of supporting multilateral service, such as Canada and the EU, may have to assume leadership. Like Anheier and Salamon's (1999) analysis of nations that support service, research should address those countries that support multilateral service and ask why and how this is so.

Conclusion

This analysis of international service can inform discussion about the development of institutions of international cooperation. No blueprint exists explaining how to foster the creation of such institutions, but development of international service may be a significant step. International civic service is an institution that can generate understanding of people living in different nations and also the impacts and potential of globalism. International service potentially can provide a tangible method to achieve broad access to global civic participation (Held 1998). It offers a way for people to participate in a broad array of issues that matter to communities. We propose here that international service, and in particular, multilateral service, may have the potential, as Florini writes in her book on global democracy, to "develop the habits of extensive cooperation, across cultures and issue areas that constitute social capital" (2003, 142). International institutions such as international civic service bring people together, not in an attempt to homogenize, but rather, as Bellamy and Castiglione suggest in their analysis of the EU, to progressively negotiate differences (1998, 173).

Although there is disagreement about the future of globalism, there is little doubt that it will continue to shape economic and social realities. Although we do not know what they will look like, it is clear that international institutions of cooperation will be required. One of these institutions, international civic service, could help shape approaches to solving global problems. While efforts are under way to define and garner support for international civic service, it remains largely unstudied. Nonetheless, we can begin to articulate some ways that international service can contribute (aside from well-documented effects of civic service, such as making tangible contributions to social and economic development, generating leadership skills, and encouraging future civic engagement). Multilateral civic service, particularly, could create a model for global cooperation. Because it explicitly aims to bring together groups of people of different nationalities to solve problems, it may lead to institutional forms that function well in contemporary globalization.

The second possibility is that people, particularly the young, who are exposed to the realities of globalism and to different people, communities, and countries may develop wholly different views and understandings of the world. With potentially large numbers of people engaged in multilateral service, it is possible that leadership could emerge prepared to identify and employ fruitful approaches to solving global problems and contributing to global equality, social welfare, and peace. Multilateral service may be able to help young people, along with the communities and organizations with which they work, develop new and possibly more effective ways to participate in a global world.

Although there are many challenges to global policy formation (including powerful structures that generate and maintain inequality) international civic service has the potential to offer new and fruitful approaches. These include increasing global awareness of shared circumstances and the need for solutions based on cooperation, strengthening global civic society, generating global citizenship with unique sets of rights and responsibilities, and developing mutual respect across cultures (Martinelli 2003, 319). Widespread participation by volunteers in inclusive forms of service may prepare them to think creatively about how to solve global problems. At this time, however, these remain poorly understood because of the paucity of research that conceptualizes and measures the extent, forms, and impacts of international and multilateral civic service.

Acknowledgments

I gratefully acknowledge support from the Ford Foundation for research support. For their guidance and keen insights, my gratitude goes to my research partner, Carlos Benítez, the NACS steering committee and advisory board, work supervisors, host families, and community leaders in all three countries, especially Matthew Pearce, Mario Fernandez de la Garza, Jon Amastae, Victor Arrendondo, and the late John Wirth. Appreciation also to Amanda Moore McBride, Michael Sherraden, and anonymous reviewers for their helpful suggestions. Special thanks to the nine pioneering NACSters, Jorge Alegría Torres, Zach Allison, Lakita Edwards, Adriana R. García, Jaime Llera García,

Mitch Hauptman, Hillary Schell, Julia Treu-Fowler, and Anna Wilkerson, and their talented group leader, Claudia Medina, for making the program a reality and for generously sharing their experiences and insights with us.

Notes

1. Although beyond the scope of this chapter, there is debate about the relative influence of nation-states in the context of contemporary globalization (see Glick-Schiller, Basch, and Szanton Blanc 1995; Scholte 2000).

2. The UN has its early roots in nineteenth-century and early twentieth-century international unions and discussions about preventing war and establishing rules of warfare. The League of Nations and the International Labor Organization, the UN's immediate forerunners, were established in the aftermath of World War I to promote international cooperation and peace (see UN 2005a).

3. This is a summary of the research on NACS, which was conducted on the first pilot program (see Sherraden and Benítez 2003). For the full report and discussion of research methods and results, see http://gwbweb.wustl.edu/csd/Publications/2003/ResearchReport-NACSPilot.pdf.

4. *Servicio Social* is a national policy implemented on the university level that requires college students to perform service before receiving their degrees. Service is carried out in solidarity with the nation in exchange for the education students have received. Effectiveness varies by program, with the Universidad Veracruzana implementing one of the most successful programs (see Arredondo 2003).

References

Albrow, M. 1998. Frames and transformations in transnational studies. Paper presented to the ESRC Transnational Programme Seminar, Faculty of Anthropology and Geography, Oxford, UK, May. www.transcomm.ox.ac.uk/working%20papers/albrow.pdf.

Anheier, H.K., and L.M. Salamon. 1999. Volunteering in cross-national perspective: Initial comparisons. *Law and Contemporary Problems* 62 (4):43. www.law.duke.edu/journals/lcp/articles/lcp62dAutumn1999p43.htm#H1N4.

Arredondo, V. 2003. University-based community service, foreign debt relief and sustainable development. *Service Enquiry* 1(1): 103–115. www.service-enquiry.org.za/downloads/chapter%208.pdf.

Baker, G. 2002. Problems in the theorization of global civil society. *Political Studies* 50 (5): 928–943.

Bauböck, R. 2003. Toward a political theory of migrant transnationalism. *International Migration Review* 37 (3): 700–723.

Bellamy, R., and D. Castiglione. 1998. Between cosmopolis and community: Three models of rights and democracy within the European Union. In *Re-imagining Political Community: Studies in Cosmopolitan Democracy,* ed. D. Archibugi, D. Held, and M. Köhler. Stanford, CA: Stanford University Press.

Clark, J.D. 2003. Introduction: Civil society and transnational action. In *Globalizing Civic Engagement: Civil Society and Transnational Action,* ed. J.D. Clark. London: Earthscan.

Coatsworth, J.H. 2004. Globalization, growth, and welfare in history. In *Globalization: Culture and Education in the New Millennium,* ed. M.M. Suárez-Orozco, and D.B. Qin-Hilliard. Berkeley: University of California Press.

Deacon, B. 1994. *Globalization and Social Policy* (Occasional Paper 5). Geneva: United Nations Research Institute for Social Development.

de Swaan, A. 1994. Perspectives for transnational social policy in Europe: Social transfers from West to East. In *Social Policy Beyond Borders,* ed. A. de Swaan. Amsterdam: Amsterdam University Press.

Eberly, D., and M. Sherraden, eds. 1990. *The Moral Equivalent of War? A Study of Non-military Service in Nine Nations.* New York: Greenwood Press.

Estes, R. 1999. The poverties: Competing definitions and alternative approaches to measurement. *Social Development Issues* 21 (2): 11–21.

European Voluntary Service (EVS). 2001. *Youth for Europe* and *European Voluntary Service: Evaluation Report* (Commission Staff Working Paper). Brussels: Commission of the European Communities. http://europa.eu.int/comm/youth/program/eval/sec_2001_1621_en.pdf.

Falk, R. 1995. The world order between inter-state law and the law of humanity: The role of civil society institutions. In *Cosmopolitan Democracy: An Agenda for a New World Order,* ed. D. Archibugi, and D. Held. Cambridge, MA: Polity Press.

Farley, M. 2005. Annan unveils UN reform plan, sets timer for debate. *Los Angeles Times,* March 22. http://pqasb.pqarchiver.com/latimes/access/810594831.html?dids=810594831:810594831&FMT=ABS&FMTS=ABS:FT&type=current&date=Mar+22%2C+2005&author=Maggie+Farley&pub=Los+Angeles+Times&edition=&startpage=A.3&desc=The+World.

Ferge, Z. 2001. Welfare and *ill-fare* systems in Central-Eastern Europe. In *Building a World Community: Globalisation and the Common Good,* ed. J. Baudot. Seattle: University of Washington Press.

Florini, A. 2003. *The Coming Democracy: New Rules for Running a New World.* Washington, DC: Island Press.

Furano, K., and G. Walker. 2000. Youth Service country profiles: The United States. Paper written for Worldwide Workshop on Youth Involvement as a Strategy for Social, Economic, and Democratic Development sponsored by the Ford Foundation, San José, Costa Rica, January 4–7.

Ghils, P. 1992. International civil society: International non-governmental organizations in the international system. *International Social Science Journal* 44 (133): 417–431.

Glick-Schiller, N., L. Basch, and C. Szanton Blanc. 1995. From immigrant to transmigrant: Theorizing transnational migration. *Anthropology Quarterly* 68 (1): 48–63.

Guarnizo, L.E., and M.P. Smith. 1998. The locations of transnationalism. In *Transnationalism from Below,* ed. M.P. Smith, and L.E. Guarnizo. New Brunswick, NJ: Transaction.

Guevara Niebla, G. 2000. Youth Service in Mexico. Paper written for Worldwide Workshop on Youth Involvement as a Strategy for Social, Economic, and Democratic Development sponsored by the Ford Foundation, San José, Costa Rica, January 4–7.

Hartman, D., and G. Rola. 2000. Going global with service learning. *Metropolitan Universities* 11 (1): 15–23.

Held, D. 1995. *Democracy and the Global Order: From the Modern State to Cosmopolitan Governance.* Stanford, CA: Stanford University Press.

————. 1998. Democracy and globalization. In *Re-imagining Political Community: Studies in Cosmopolitan Democracy,* ed. D. Archibugi, D. Held, and M. Köhler. Stanford, CA: Stanford University Press.

Held, D., A. McGrew, D. Goldblatt, and J. Perraton. 1999. *Global Transformations: Politics, Economics and Culture.* Stanford, CA: Stanford University Press.

Kaldor, M. 2003. *Global Civil Society: An Answer to War.* Cambridge, MA: Polity Press.

Keck, M.E., and K. Sikkink. 1998. *Activists Beyond Borders.* Ithaca, NY: Cornell University Press.

Leibfried, S., and P. Pierson. 1994. The prospects for social Europe. In *Social Policy Beyond Borders,* ed. A. de Swaan. Amsterdam: Amsterdam University Press.

Martinelli, A. 2003. Markets, governments, communities and global governance. *International Sociology* 18 (4): 291–324.

McBride, A.M., C. Benítez, and M. Sherraden. 2003. *The Forms and Nature of Civic Service: A Global Assessment* (CSD Research Report). St. Louis, MO: Washington University, Center for Social Development.

Mishra, R. 1999. *Globalization and the Welfare State.* Northampton, MA: Edward Elgar.

Ninacs, W.A., and M. Toye. 2000. Canada: country profile. Paper written for World-wide Workshop on Youth Involvement as a Strategy for Social, Economic, and Democratic Development sponsored by the Ford Foundation, San José, Costa Rica, January 4–7.

North American Institute (NAMI). 2001. *North American Community Service (NACS).* Santa Fe, NM: North American Institute.

Prior, P.M., and R. Sykes. 2001. Globalization and the European welfare states: Evaluating the theories and evidence. In *Globalization and European Welfare States: Challenges and Change,* ed. R. Sykes, B. Palier, and P.M. Prior. New York: Palgrave.

Robertson, R. 1992. *Globalization: Social Theory and Global Culture.* London: Sage.

Rockcliffe, B. 2005. International volunteering: An evolving paradigm. *Voluntary Action* 7 (2): 35–44.

Rohrschneider, R., and R.J. Dalton. 2002. A global network? Transnational cooperation among environmental groups. *Journal of Politics* 64 (2): 510–533.

Rosenstock-Huessy, E. 1978. *Planetary Service: A Way Into the Third Millenium.* Jericho, VT: Argo Books.

Schaeffer, R.K. 2003. *Understanding Globalization: The Social Consequence of Political, Economics, and Environmental Change.* Lanham, MD: Rowman & Littlefield.

Schröer, R. 2003. Voluntary service: Opening doors to the future. Comparative study on the integration of young people from disadvantaged backgrounds in transnational voluntary service. AVSO: Brussels.

Scholte, J.A. 2000. *Globalization: A Critical Introduction.* New York: Palgrave Macmillan.

Service Civil International (SCI). 2005. What is a work camp? www.sciint.org/.

Shaw, M. 1994. Civil society and global politics: Beyond a social movements approach. *Millenium: Journal of International Studies* 23 (3): 647–667.

Sherraden, M. 1979. The Civilian Conservation Corps: Effectiveness of the camps. PhD diss., University of Michigan.

Sherraden, M. 2001. *Civic Service: Issues, Outlook, Institution Building* (CSD Perspective). St. Louis: Washington University, Center for Social Development. http://gwbweb.wustl.edu/csd/Publications/2001/PerspectiveSherraden2001-October.pdf.

Sherraden, M.S., J. Stringham, S. Costanza Sow, and A.M. McBride. 2006. The forms and structure of international voluntary service. *Voluntas* 17 (2): 156–173.

Sherraden, M.S. 2001. Developing transnational social policy: A North American community service program. *Social Development Issues* 23 (3): 50–59.

Sherraden, M.S. 2001. *Developing Transnational Social Policy: A North American Community Service Program* (Working Paper 01–10). St. Louis: Washington University, Center for Social Development. http://gwbweb.wustl.edu/csd/Publications/2001/wp01–10.pdf.

Sherraden, M.S., and C. Benítez. 2003. *North American Community Service Pilot Project Research Report* (CSD Report). St. Louis: Washington University, Center for Social Development. http://gwbweb.wustl.edu/csd/Publications/2003/ResearchReport-NACSPilot.pdf.

Sherraden, M.S., and M. Sherraden. 1990. Mexico: Social service by university students. In *The Moral Equivalent of War? A Study of Non-military Service in Nine Nations,* ed. D. Eberly, and M. Sherraden. New York: Greenwood Press.

Simpson, K. 2004. "Doing development": The gap year, volunteer-tourists and a popular practice of development. *Journal of International Development* 16 (5): 681–692.

Smith, J.D., A. Ellis, and G. Brewis. 2004. *Cross-National Volunteering: A Developing Movement?* London: Institute for Volunteering Research.

Suárez-Orozco, M.S., and D.B. Qin-Hilliard. 2004. Globalization: Culture and education in the new millennium. In *Globalization: Culture and Education in the New Millennium,* ed. M.M. Suárez-Orozco, and D.B. Qin-Hilliard. Berkeley: University of California Press.

Suárez-Orozco, C. 2004. Formulating identity in a globalized world. In *Globalization: Culture and Education in the New Millennium,* ed. M.M. Suárez-Orozco, and D.B. Qin-Hilliard. Berkeley: University of California Press.

Thompson, J. 1998. Community identity and world citizenship. In *Re-imagining Political Community: Studies in Cosmopolitan Democracy,* ed. D. Archibugi, D. Held, and M. Köhler. Stanford, CA: Stanford University Press.

United Nations. 2005a. Charter of the United Nations. www.un.org/aboutun/charter/index.html.

United Nations. 2005b. *In Larger Freedom: Towards Development, Security, and Human Rights for All.* Report of the Secretary General, United Nations General Assembly, March 21. www.un.org/largerfreedom/report-largerfreedom.pdf.

Social Psychological Theory and the Potential for Intergroup and Ethnonational Cooperation in Civic Service Programs

Ronald Pitner

The field of social psychology has long examined the area of intergroup relations. This specialized area encompasses broad constructs such as stereotypes and prejudice, social identity, in-group and out-group bias, attributional biases, and ethnocentrism and ethnonational conflicts. Often, the study of intergroup relations has been a proxy for studying intergroup conflict. As a consequence, there is a plethora of knowledge development and conceptualization regarding the causes of conflict and tension between groups, with less attention focused on intergroup cooperation and conflict reduction. It is, of course, important to understand the psychology behind what causes the intractability of certain types of intergroup conflicts. Only by understanding this can we begin to develop effective conflict resolution strategies. A possible strategy that can be used to lessen intergroup conflict is civic service. This chapter examines the potential role that civic service programs and, in particular, youth service programs can play in facilitating intergroup cooperation and conflict reduction.

Civic Service and Cultural Integration

Civic service can be defined as an "organized period of substantial engagement and contribution to the local, national, or world community, recognized and valued by society, with minimal monetary compensation to the participant" (Sherraden 2001, 2). There are four forms of service programs: transnational, international, national, and local. Transnational service includes cooperative service programs between countries, international service represents programs in which volunteers provide service in a country outside their home country, national service programs are those in which volunteers provide service to their home country, and local service programs are those in which volunteers are engaged in their home communities (McBride, Benítez, and Sherraden 2003).

In a global assessment of 210 civic service programs, McBride, Benítez, and Sherraden (2003) found the following distribution across the forms of service: international service (49 percent), national service (35 percent), transnational service (10 percent), and local service (6 percent).

Service programs can also be identified by type: youth service, faith-based service, and senior service. Of these three, youth service is, by far, the most common type. McBride, Benítez, and Sherraden (2003) identified a total of eighty-six youth service programs in their study, and this list is not exhaustive. Examples of youth service programs include International Volunteers for Peace in Australia, the National Youth Service in Papua New Guinea, the European Voluntary Service scheme, the International Voluntary Workcamps in Turkey, World Youth Millennium Awards in the United Kingdom, Katimavik in Canada, Canada World Youth, the Amigos Volunteer Program in the United States, and the National Youth Service Corps in Nigeria.

The aforementioned national and international service programs have one major commonality: they place emphasis on cultural integration. These programs bring together two or more groups in order to broaden the cultural understanding of participants and to reduce participants' cultural stereotypes, biases, and prejudices. For example, Katimavik brings together Francophones and Anglophones from all regions of Canada in order to promote cultural understanding (Eberly and Sherraden 1990). The National Youth Service Corps in Nigeria brings together diverse ethnic groups within Nigeria as a way of promoting and strengthening national unity (Eberly and Sherraden 1990; Marenin 1989). Some youth service programs are also committed to broadening cultural awareness among the volunteers as well as the community members with whom they engage. But how effective is civic service at achieving cultural integration and national unity?

There is a paucity of empirical studies that examine the theoretical underpinnings of service programs designed to broaden cultural integration and national unity. Marenin (1989) is one of a few exceptions, as are Omo-Abu (1997) and Udom (1981). In his study, Marenin suggests that although the National Youth Service Corps in Nigeria has been effective at increasing awareness about cultural differences, it has been less effective at promoting national unity. Marenin defines national unity as a common destiny that members of a nation share. Achieving such a destiny is critical for any service program that aspires to strengthen cultural integration and national unity. This is even more important when bringing together groups that have long-standing antipathy toward each other. What are the challenges that civic service programs face in pursuit of these goals? How can programs be better designed to achieve such goals? In order to address these questions, it is first necessary to provide an overview of concepts and theories pertaining to intergroup conflict.

Before moving to a discussion about intergroup conflict, it is important to examine possible motives that individuals have for engaging in service. Batson, Ahmad, and Tsang (2002) suggest four motives that capture why an individual engages in service programs: egoism, altruism, collectivism, and principlism. People with egoistic motives engage in service programs in order to achieve some type of self-benefit, people with altruistic motives engage in service programs in order to benefit one or more individuals other than themselves, people with collectivist motives provide service in order to benefit the welfare of a group or collective, and people with principlist motives provide service in order to uphold some moral principle. Each of these motives has limitations, and each can be used to explain why an individual would engage in service. However, collectivist motives are the most relevant to our understanding of how service programs can be used to ease tension between groups, because they are focused directly on the common good of groups and collectives. When groups sense a common good (i.e., a common destiny), they may be more likely to work cooperatively to achieve national unity.

Intergroup Conflict: Examining the Role of Stereotypes and Prejudice

People tend to treat others unfairly based on their group membership(s). People's nationality, ethnicity, gender, sexual orientation, class, and various other social group memberships make them vulnerable to stereotypes, prejudice, and hatred from others. Social psychology is the field that examines the role that stereotypes and prejudice play in daily life. Stereotypes have been defined as the part of our attitudes that involves our beliefs and thoughts (Aronson, Wilson, and Akert 1994). Essentially, they are a way of categorizing information, in which everything within a category is ascribed the same characteristics. Stereotypes may be either positive or negative. However, stereotypes are typically referred to as *negative* attributions about an individual or group. Prejudice, on the other hand, refers to the part of an attitude that involves hostile and negative feelings toward a category, based solely on membership in that category (Aronson, Wilson, and Akert 1994). These social phenomena can exacerbate intergroup conflict and, in fact, may serve as obstacles to reductions in conflict between groups.

There are two aspects of stereotypes that make them relevant to a discussion about intergroup conflict. First, stereotypes have esteem-enhancing qualities, both at the individual and group levels (Jost and Banaji 1994). They allow people to hold negative viewpoints of others while enhancing the image that they hold of themselves. Stereotypes, however, gain their essential meanings in the context of group memberships (Bar-Tal 1997). Tajfel and Turner (1986) suggest that the core of people's self-concept is tied to the group to which they belong. As members of a group, they develop in-group and out-group bias, ascribing favorable characteristics to their own group and negative ones to out-group members. It is this *us*-versus-*them* dynamic that can make deep-rooted conflicts between groups resistant to resolution strategies.

The second important aspect is that stereotypes are normative beliefs that are perpetuated within a given culture. People within a particular culture espouse and supply negative information about out-group members. This information is internalized and becomes a common part of the language and ethos. These negative beliefs make it almost impossible to perceive the actions of out-group members in a positive light. Rouhana and Bar-Tal (1998) refer to this phenomenon as cognitive freezing. Cognitive freezing, as they describe it, is the process of making negative beliefs about out-group members resistant to change.

Cognitive freezing mainly occurs when conflicts and tensions between groups are deep-rooted. Ethnonational conflicts are an interesting example of this phenomenon. These are conflicts that occur between ethnic, religious, linguistic, and national groups within a country (Rouhana and Bar-Tal 1998). Prime examples are conflicts between Israelis and Palestinians, Muslims and Serbs, and Tamils and Hindus. In these conflicts, both groups develop strong negative stereotypes about the other (Rouhana and Bar Tal 1998), such that a person's social identity becomes dependent on the negative stereotyping of the out-group. Kelman refers to this phenomenon as a negative interdependence: such a "zero-sum view of . . . identity has in effect created a state of negative interdependence between two identities: assertion of the group's own identity requires negation of the other group's identity; each group's success in identity building depends on the other's failure in that task" (1999, 589). Thus, it becomes difficult to change information that is related to the out-group, particularly when the belief in this information goes to the core of one's own social identity. As a consequence, peaceful conflict resolutions are nearly impossible to achieve.

What causes such conflicts to become intractable? Realistic conflict theory suggests that groups are in competition for scarce resources, political power, and/or social status (Aronson, Wilson, and Akert 1994; Baron, Kerr, and Miller 1992). This, in turn, leads to feelings of inequity, which escalates prejudice and conflict between groups. In these situations, in-group members tend to develop negative viewpoints of the group they are competing with (often the out-group is perceived as the enemy). Over time, the in-group begins to perceive its own actions as legitimate and the out-group's actions as illegitimate. It is this negative interdependence that makes ethnonational conflicts so resistant to conflict resolution strategies.

Prejudice and Intergroup Conflict Reduction

Personality and Individual Differences

Prejudice is ubiquitous. As suggested, its role in establishing and maintaining intergroup conflict is both complex and multivariate. Thus, reduction in conflict is no easy task. There are, however, some constructive ways of reducing prejudice and intergroup conflict. One suggestion has been to construct prejudice reduction interventions that focus on addressing personality deficits in the prejudiced individual (Wittig and Grant-Thompson 1998). This belief that prejudice is a personality deficit was borne out in Adorno et al.'s book *The Authoritarian Personality* (1950). Although this personality and individual difference perspective has come under heavy criticism, some researchers have shown that prejudice is, indeed, related to authoritarianism (Levin and Sidanius 1997; Taylor and Moghaddam 1994). Nevertheless, this perspective is too limited to explain the complexities of prejudice. For example, it cannot explain why large groups of people (e.g., Israelis and Palestinians) hold negative viewpoints of each other. Thus, prejudice reduction interventions that are guided by this perspective are ineffective in reducing intergroup tensions caused by ethnonational conflicts.

Social Cognitive Perspectives

It is important to mention that stereotypes and prejudice are often based on distorted and faulty information. One common suggestion for reduction in prejudice and intergroup conflict is to provide individuals with accurate information about the target group. However, this social cognitive strategy does not always work (Baron, Kerr, and Miller 1992). Stereotypes and prejudice are quite resistant to change, but change can occur in the face of disconfirming information. There are three models that address the dynamics of stereotype change and prejudice reduction: bookkeeping, conversion, and subtyping (Hamilton and Sherman 1994).

The bookkeeping model predicts that stereotype change and prejudice reduction are likely to occur when there is a high frequency of disconfirming information; that is, stereotypes gradually change as the perceiver is confronted with more and more amounts of disconfirming information. The conversion model suggests that stereotype change and prejudice reduction occur radically in response to significant and critically important disconfirming information. Thus, extreme group members have an especially strong impact on perceptions of the group as a whole. The subtyping model posits that disconfirming information leads to distinctions (or subtypes) within the group.

The formation of subtypes constitutes exceptions to the group as a whole. Hamilton and Sherman (1994) contend that beliefs ascribed to the subtypes may differ dramatically from those ascribed to the group as a whole. Once subtypes become sufficiently strong, they dilute the beliefs held about the larger group. To the extent that this occurs, subtyping will lead to stereotype change and prejudice reduction.

Under what conditions do these three models lead to stereotype change and prejudice reduction? Hamilton and Sherman (1994) suggest that disconfirming information produces stereotype change and prejudice reduction only if it is associated with an individual who is prototypical of the social category. That is, the individual must be highly representative of the larger group. Hamilton and Sherman's social cognitive perspective is an important contribution to the discussion on prejudice reduction. Indeed, modifying faulty and distorted information about the target group is a necessary step toward prejudice reduction. What is unclear is whether or not target group members have to be prototypical of the larger group in order for prejudice and intergroup conflict reduction to occur. What is clear, however, is that disconfirming information is perceived only when groups come into contact with one another.

Contact Hypothesis

Earlier research suggested that exposure (i.e., contact) between groups would reduce conflict and tension (Allport 1954; Cook 1985; Stephan 1985). Gordon Allport (1954) was the first to assert that when groups who are in dispute come into contact with each other, they are exposed to more accurate information about the other. This, in turn, reduces intergroup tension and prejudice. However, this is not always the case. Sometimes exposure can lead to an escalation of tension and conflict (Brewer 1986). For instance, Forbes (1997) contends that while contact reduces conflict between individuals, it increases conflict between groups. This difference could be due to the conditions under which contact occurs.

Allport (1954) suggested that there were five conditions in which contact would lead to a reduction in intergroup conflict. First, the groups must be in situations where there is a common goal and mutual interdependence (Sherif et al. 1961; Amir 1976). Mutual interdependence refers to a situation that requires the groups to cooperate in order to accomplish the goal. This point will be elaborated below. Second, the groups must be of equal status and power. This guarantees that attention will be focused on disconfirming information, instead of on status differences between the groups. Third, members of the groups must interact with each other on a personal level (out-group members must be seen as individuals) (Wilder 1986). Fourth, groups must have multiple contacts, typically with out-group members that are prototypical of the group as a whole. Finally, the groups must foster a social norm that promotes equality and acceptance (Aronson, Wilson, and Akert 1994; Wilder 1984).

The contact hypothesis is one of the most influential theoretical frameworks used as a strategy for reducing intergroup conflict. Several studies have provided support for this perspective (Marcus-Newhall and Heindl 1998; Wittig and Grant-Thompson 1998); also, it has become the underpinning of many prejudice reduction and conflict resolution curricula. However, not all researchers are in agreement about the utility of this hypothesis. One point in question is the necessity of meeting all the conditions that Allport (1954) outlined in order for intergroup tension and prejudice reduction to occur. For example, Allport contends that groups should have equal status and power. It is possible to logistically design a program in which groups have such equal power. However, groups that are experiencing ethnonational conflicts may psychologically perceive status and power differences, regardless of the logistics of the program. It is not clear whether this condition must be met in civic service programs, or even if it can.

One condition that does seem critical in ethnonational conflicts is creating situations in which there is a common goal and mutual interdependence. This is important because such groups may not be willing to actively participate with each other. However, when the only way to achieve a desired goal is through cooperation and interdependence, then intergroup participation may occur.

Cooperation and Interdependence

Muzafer Sherif and colleagues' seminal summer camp study highlights how cooperative problem-solving strategies can reduce prejudice and tension between two groups that dislike each other (Sherif et al. 1961). Specifically, he showed that when groups work toward superordinate goals (i.e., goals that require mutual interdependence), intergroup conflict could be reduced. Years after Sherif's study, other researchers applied these cooperative problem-solving strategies to classroom settings in order to reduce racial tensions among students (Aronson et al. 1978). The strategy they employed has been termed the *jigsaw classroom*, which is "a classroom setting designed to reduce prejudice and raise the self-esteem of children by placing them in small, desegregated groups and making each child dependent on the other children in his or her group to learn the course material and do well in the class" (Aronson, Wilson, and Akert 1994, 534).

In the jigsaw classroom, children are divided into racially mixed groups. They are then given a *part* of a lesson that they must present to the entire class. Each group has different parts of the lesson to present. In order for students to understand the entire lesson, each group must pay close attention to each presenter. Under such situations, each group is motivated to help the others so that they all will be able to understand the lesson in its entirety. Aronson and his colleagues showed that the children who participated in the jigsaw classroom reduced their ethnic stereotypes about the out-group (Aronson et al. 1978). Other studies have shown similar success in reducing racial hostility in classroom settings (Johnson and Johnson 1981; Slavin 1985; Aronson and Gonzalez 1988; Aronson and Thibodeau 1992).

Cooperation and mutual interdependence work in reducing tension and hostility because they break down in-group/out-group biases. Groups become more focused on the superordinate goal and less on the conflict (Worchel, Cooper, and Goethals 1988). Although many studies have shown that cooperation and mutual interdependence can be helpful in reducing racial tensions between groups (Aronson and Thibodeau 1992), several questions remain unanswered. How enduring is the reduction of conflict and prejudice through cooperative strategies? Are prejudice and conflict completely eradicated, or do they return once groups stop engaging in mutual interdependence? These types of questions have not been adequately addressed by earlier studies. These studies mainly report results that indicate that cooperative strategies can initially reduce conflict and tensions between groups, with less attention focused on the durability of this reduction.

Another important question is warranted. Can cooperative strategies be used successfully to reduce conflict between groups that are experiencing ethnonational conflicts? Groups experiencing racial tensions in the United States are not equivalent to groups that are experiencing ethnonational conflicts. Rouhana and Bar-Tal (1998) discuss, in detail, the intractability of ethnonational conflicts to resolution strategies. They describe these conflicts as having five characteristics: (1) totality, suggesting that these conflicts permeate all aspects of personal, social, political, and cultural realms; (2) protractedness, which suggests that the conflicts tend to last at least a generation; (3) centrality, which refers to the accessibility of these conflicts in the minds of group members; (4) violence, which takes the form of terrorist acts and wars; and (5) perceptions of irreconcilability, which also tend to be pervasive among group members. Unlike racial tension, these characteristics make ethnonational conflicts very resistant to conflict resolution strategies (Rouhana and Bar-Tal 1998).

Rouhana and Bar-Tal (1998) further suggest that conflict resolution strategies must be designed to take into account the psychological foundations of the conflict and to employ psychological theories in the resolution process. This requires examining the role that stereotypes and prejudice play in the maintenance of conflict and tension. As implied earlier, ethnonational conflicts go to the heart of a person's social identity. In fact, these types of conflicts are often identity conflicts (Kelman 1999; Rouhana and Bar-Tal 1998). Social identity theory suggests that group membership is an integral part of an individual's personal identity. Given that people are motivated to establish and maintain positive self-esteem, their various group memberships have esteem implications. Stereotypes, as mentioned, are functional in that they allow people to hold negative viewpoints of the out-group while at the same time bolstering and enhancing the image that they hold of their own social group and themselves. Altering a stereotypical belief would nullify this potentially important mechanism that contributes to a positive regard for their own social group.

What would motivate an individual (or group) to engage in strategies to reduce conflict when doing so may cause a shift in how groups define themselves? Sherif and colleagues brought together two groups of campers that had animosity toward each other. Although these groups were not necessarily motivated to change their impressions of the other group, their impressions did, indeed, change once they both worked toward a common goal (Sherif et al. 1961). Other researchers have also successfully used similar cooperative problem-solving workshops to help groups move toward peaceful dialogue (Azar 1990; Burton 1987; Doob and Foltz 1973; Fisher 1997; Kelman 1992; Mitchell 1973; Rouhana and Kelman 1994). Civic service programs may provide the opportunity for cooperation, which could ease tensions between groups.

Civic Service: The Importance of Superordinate Goals

Since most service programs have objectives to alleviate negative social, economic, or environmental conditions, these objectives could be framed as superordinate goals that could potentially serve to ease intergroup tension and conflict. For example, in the transnational North American Community Service pilot program, youth from Canada, Mexico, and the United States helped restore a Texas mission founded in 1692, and they expanded community greenhouses and developed trout breeding tanks in a mountain stream in Coyopolan, Veracruz (Sherraden and Benítez 2003). Working toward these desired end states created a common group goal that eased intergroup tension; the goal required individuals to be interdependent on one another, regardless of group affiliation (Batson, Ahmad, and Tsang 2002).

Intergroup cooperation is not easily achieved, especially between groups experiencing ethnonational conflicts. Cooperation, to a certain extent, requires receiving help from the other group. When groups are experiencing ethnonational conflicts, this help may get construed as meaning that one group is dependent on and inferior to the other group (Nadler 2002). Given that people are motivated to maintain a positive image of their social identity group, it is unlikely that cooperation would occur if it ultimately leads to self-derogation. How can cooperation be achieved in such conflicts? Mutual interdependence and a common goal are possible solutions (Allport 1954). As was shown in Sherif and colleagues seminal study, distinctions between in-group and out-group were broken down when groups cooperated in order to achieve a common goal. This effect can be seen at times in the military, where everyone works together to defeat a common enemy (Sherif et al. 1961).

Strengths of This Approach

Many of the previous social psychological studies examined ways superordinate goals can be utilized to alleviate tensions between groups. As discussed, the goal of some youth service programs is not only to bring young people together in order to work toward a common objective, but also to promote cultural understanding and national unity among the volunteers. These programs, in effect, embody the contact hypothesis. Their core assumptions are that when diverse groups are exposed to each other, they will gain cultural knowledge, which will reduce prejudice and conflict, leading in turn to cultural integration and/or national unity. Research, however, does not consistently show that these programs lead to cultural integration or national unity (Marenin 1989, on the Nigerian National Youth Service Corps).

A second strength of this approach is that civic service programs tend to be intensive and last for an extended period (six months to one year). In fact, McBride, Benítez, and Sherraden (2003) reported that 81 percent of the service programs in their study required a commitment of thirty-five hours per week, with the average amount of time served being 7.3 months across all programs and 5.8 months for youth service programs in particular. Many of the cooperative strategies used in previous social psychological studies are short-term in nature, usually lasting a day or no more than a week (Sherif et al. 1961). Given that civic service programs are relatively long-term engagements, there is potential for a more enduring reduction in prejudice and conflict between groups. This is because in-group/out-group biases may be replaced as the volunteers come to see others as individuals instead of belonging to a particular social identity group. This is just a supposition, but research studies can be designed to examine this issue more thoroughly.

A third strength of this approach is that civic service programs have the potential for not only reducing conflicts between groups, but also improving the environment, physical infrastructure, organizations, and communities. In fact, this is the ultimate goal of many service programs, and when a requisite for achieving this goal is mutual interdependence, then a reduction in intergroup conflict seems possible. Quoting William James's famous phrase, Eberly and Sherraden contend that civic service programs are the "moral equivalent of war" (McDermott 1968; Eberly and Sherraden 1990). In a war, groups come together to defeat a common enemy (i.e., they come together to destroy). In civic service programs, groups come together to build. By improving the environment, infrastructure, organizations, and communities in a nation, civic service, itself, could potentially lead to national unity.

Fourth, civic service programs are recognized and valued by society. Volunteers often wear insignia, logos, imprinted shirts, hats, and other attire to signify their involvement in service. Such overt displays of unity can lead to the creation of a new social identity group. As tensions between the groups lessen, members of each group may begin to strongly identify with their service group. Wearing symbols that represent the particular service group could aid in this process.

Finally, civic service programs actually represent macrolevel applications of social psychological theory that has been applied typically at a microlevel. For example, Sherif and colleagues' seminal study sought to reduce tension and conflict between Boy Scouts at a summer camp (Sharif et al. 1961). While the study's findings were extremely important, they focused mainly on prejudice and conflict reduction that occur in small groups, with little attention focused on changes at a macrolevel. However, as already mentioned, service programs lend themselves to multiple applications and areas of impact. To the extent that these types of programs are widespread in any given country (or nation), they have the potential to reduce tension and conflict between larger groups.

There are few youth service programs that actually bring together groups who are experiencing ethnonational conflicts, but if programs were structured accordingly, this may be an innovative approach. As mentioned earlier, Kelman suggested that groups experiencing ethnonational conflicts tend to have a negative interdependence (Kelman 1999). It is argued in this chapter that youth service programs that are centered on achieving superordinate goals could potentially foster a positive interdependence between such groups. An interesting empirical question would be whether positive interdependence can overtake negative interdependence. Thus, examining various ways that service programs can be used to reduce ethnonational conflicts, as well as improve communities, is an important and fruitful line of inquiry.

Limitations of This Approach

Although there are several strengths to the use of civic service programs as a means of reducing conflict and tension between groups, there are also limitations.

These limitations are most evident when examining ethnonational conflicts. Rouhana and Bar-Tal (1998) suggest that pragmatic solutions can deflect attention away from the central issues in an ethnonational conflict and thus may be limited in reducing tension and prejudice between groups. One weakness is that service programs often do not address the central issues of the conflict. Thus, groups experiencing ethnonational conflicts may not be forced to closely examine the psychological dynamics that keep these conflicts locked in place. To reiterate, common goals and mutual interdependence could facilitate this process.

However, ethnonational conflicts are intractable largely because they are perpetuated by a conflictive ethos (Rouhana and Bar-Tal 1998); that is, negative beliefs about the out-group are reinscribed by the members of the in-group to the point that they become a necessary part of one's identity and one's society (Kelman 1999). Civic service programs may temporarily ease the tensions between groups, but the conflictive ethos could ultimately breathe new life into the conflict. Thus, service programs may be nothing more than a Band-Aid for conflict and prejudice reduction. If, however, several service programs are operating within a particular society, they may be enough to change the conflictive ethos.

Toward a Research Agenda

Researchers have designed cooperative problem-solving workshops that ease tension between groups experiencing conflicts (Burton 1987; Kelman 1992; Rouhana and Kelman 1994). Seldom have scholars theorized about the potential of civic service programs (as superordinate goals) to ease tension in conflicts. For a research agenda in this area, youth service programs should probably be the focus, because even in a conflictive ethos, young people's attitudes and prejudices may be more mutable than the prejudices of older adults.

Numerous scholars have discussed various aspects of youth service programs (Eberly and Sherraden 1990; Guevara 2000; Marenin 1989; McBride, Benítez, and Sherraden 2003; Sherraden 2001; Sherraden, Sherraden, and Eberly 1990). For this research agenda, it is important that youth service programs satisfy four criteria. First, both groups in a conflict should view the program as important for affecting collectives in a positive way. In other words, each group must have collectivist motives for engaging in the service program. It is possible that the groups may have collectivist motives for civic engagement, yet the collective they are concerned about is their own group. Their collectivist motives may therefore perpetuate in-group/out-group distinctions. Given this situation, the youth service programs with the most potential are probably those in which both groups involved in a conflict see the service as benefiting both groups.

The second criterion is that the youth service program must require mutual interdependence between the two groups. Thus, in order for the service to be conducted successfully, each group will have to cooperate with and rely on the other. The youth service therefore becomes a superordinate goal. Moreover, it will force the volunteers to concentrate on the service activity, instead of on the conflict.

The third criterion is that groups must be in constant contact with each other. This ensures that individuals will be exposed to disconfirming information about several out-group members. It is believed that constant contact and mutual cooperation will aid in reduction of intergroup prejudice and conflict. The final criterion is that the service program must last an extended period of time, at least six months, which may make reduction in intergroup prejudice more permanent. Rarely do studies examining prejudice and conflict determine how permanent is the reduction. What the evidence shows is that superordinate goals are good at *initially* reducing intergroup conflict and prejudice, but the context in which the groups pursued a common goal and mutual interdependence rarely extended beyond a week. Thus, civic service programs actually represent a novel and, again, potentially promising approach.

As mentioned earlier, it could be argued that civic service programs may only reduce conflict and tension in small groups (i.e., at a microlevel) but not at larger collective or national levels. Studying three or four different youth service programs in which activities are used as superordinate goals would further this agenda. These programs should focus on different activities, yet at the same time contribute to the improvement of social and economic development, citizenship, skill development, and/or cultural integration. It is necessary to have a sufficient number of service programs in order that change will occur at a microlevel and a macrolevel.

It has been argued that when civic service programs are conceived as having superordinate goals, they have the potential for reducing prejudice and conflict between groups—even groups that are experiencing ethnonational conflicts. Nevertheless, because ethnonational conflicts are so deep-rooted, it is recommended that this research agenda be first applied to groups whose conflicts and prejudices are not so long-standing or complex.

What are the implications of this social psychological research agenda for civic service? Foremost, program designs that aim for cultural integration may be improved. It may be that more attention should be focused on the nature of the activities implemented by the volunteers and the ultimate outcomes they work toward as a group. Designing such a program is no easy task. Nevertheless, prejudice reduction, conflict reduction, cultural integration, and national unity have greater potential for being accomplished when the activities and services that civic service programs offer are seen as the ultimate goal—the superordinate goal.

References

Adorno, T., E. Frenkel-Brunswick, D. Levinson, and R. Sanford. 1950. *The Authoritarian Personality.* New York: Harper.

Allport, G. 1954. *The Nature of Prejudice.* Reading, MA: Addison-Wesley.

Amir, Y. 1976. The role of intergroup contact in change of prejudice and ethnic relations. In *Towards the Elimination of Racism,* ed. P. Katz. New York: Pergamon Press.

Aronson, E., and A. Gonzalez. 1988. Desegregation, jigsaw, and the Mexican-American experience. In *Towards the Elimination of Racism: Profiles in Controversy,* ed. P.A. Katz, and D. Taylor. New York: Plenum.

Aronson, E., C. Stephan, J. Sikes, N. Blaney, and M. Snapp. 1978. *The Jigsaw Classroom.* Beverly Hills, CA: Sage.

Aronson, E., and R. Thibodeau. 1992. The jigsaw classroom: A cooperative strategy for reducing prejudice. In *Cultural Diversity in the Schools,* ed. J. Lynch, C. Modgil, and S. Modgil. London: Falmer Press.

Aronson, E., T. Wilson, and R. Akert. 1994. *Social Psychology: The Heart and the Mind.* New York: HarperCollins.

Azar, E. 1990. *The Management of Protracted Social Conflict: Theory and Cases.* London: Ashgate.

Baron, R., N. Kerr, and N. Miller. 1992. *Group Process, Group Decision, Group Action.* Pacific Grove, CA: Wadsworth.

Bar-Tal, D. 1997. Formation and change of ethnic and national stereotypes: An integrative model. *International Journal of Intercultural Relations* 21 (4): 491–523.

Batson, C., N. Ahmad, and J. Tsang. 2002. Four motives for community involvement. *Journal of Social Issues* 58 (3): 429–445.

Brewer, M. 1986. The role of ethnocentrism in intergroup conflict. In P*sychology of Intergroup Relations,* ed. S. Worschel, and W. Austin. Chicago: Nelson Hall.

Burton, J. 1987. *Resolving Deep-rooted Conflict: A Handbook.* Lanham, MD: University Press of America.

Cook, S. 1985. Experimenting on social issues: The case of school desegregation. *American Psychologist* 40: 452–460.

Doob, L., and W. Foltz. 1973. The Belfast workshop: An application of group techniques to a destructive conflict. *Journal of Conflict Resolution* 17 (3): 489–512.

Eberly, D., and M. Sherraden, eds. 1990. *The Moral Equivalent of War? A Study of Non-military Service in Nine Nations.* New York: Greenwood Press.

Fisher, R. 1997. *Interactive Conflict Resolution.* Syracuse, NY: Syracuse University Press.

Forbes, H. 1997. *Ethnic Conflict: Commerce, Culture, and the Contact Hypothesis.* New Haven, CT: Yale University Press.

Guevara, G. 2000. Youth service in Mexico. Paper written for Worldwide Workshop on Youth Involvement as a Strategy for Social, Economic, and Democratic Development, sponsored by the Ford Foundation, in San José, Costa Rica, January 4–7.

Hamilton, D., and J. Sherman. 1994. Stereotyping. In *Handbook of Social Cognition,* 2nd ed., ed. R. Wyer, and T. Srull. Hillsdale, NJ: Erlbaum.

Johnson, D., and R. Johnson. 1981. Effects of cooperative and individualistic learning experiences on interethnic interaction. *Journal of Educational Psychology* 73 (3): 444–449.

Jost, J., and M. Banaji. 1994. The role of system-justification and the problem of false consciousness. *British Journal of Social Psychology* 33: 1–27.

Kelman, H. 1992. Informal mediation by the scholar practitioner. In *Mediation in International Relations: Multiple Approaches to Conflict Management,* ed. J. Berkovitch, and J. Rubin. London: St. Martin's Press.

———. 1999. The interdependence of Israeli and Palestinian national identities: The role of the other in existential conflicts. *Journal of Social Issues* 55 (3): 581–600.

Levin, S., and J. Sidanius. 1997. Refining the social dominance orientation: An analysis of its context-free and context-specific components. Paper presented at the meeting of the Society of Experimental Social Psychology, Toronto, Ontario, Canada, October.

Marcus-Newhall, A., and T. Heindl. 1998. Coping with interracial stress in ethnically diverse classrooms: How important are Allport's contact conditions? *Journal of Social Issues* 54 (4): 813–830.

Marenin, O. 1989. Implementing national unity: Changes in national consciousness among participants in the National Youth Service Corps of Nigeria. *International Migration Review* 23 (1): 23–44.

McBride, A.M., C. Benítez, M. Sherraden. 2003. *The Forms and Nature of Civic Service: A Global Assessment* (CSD research report). St. Louis: Washington University, Center for Social Development.

McDermott, J.J., ed. 1968. *The Writings of William James: A Comprehensive Edition.* New York: Modern Library.

Mitchell, C. 1973. Conflict resolution and controlled communication: Some further comments. *Journal of Peace Research* 10: 123–132.

Nadler, A. 2002. Inter-group helping relations as power relations: Maintaining or challenging social dominance between groups through helping. *Journal of Social Issues* 58 (3): 487–502.

Omo-Abu, A. 1997. Ethnic cleavages and national integration: The impact of the National Youth Corps. Unpublished dissertation, Columbia University, New York.

Rouhana, N., and D. Bar-Tal. 1998. Psychological dynamics of intractable ethnonational conflicts. *American Psychologist* 53 (7): 761–770.

Rouhana, N., and H. Kelman. 1994. Promoting joint thinking in international conflicts: An Israeli-Palestinian continuing workshop. *Journal of Social Issues* 50 (1): 157–178.

Sherif, M., O. Harvey, B. White, W. Hood, and C. Sherif. 1961. *Intergroup Conflict and Cooperation: The Robber's Cove Experiment.* Norman: University of Oklahoma, Institute of Group Relations.

Sherraden, M. 2001. *Civic Service: Issues, Outlook, Institution Building* (CSD Perspective). St. Louis: Washington University, Center for Social Development.

Sherraden, M., M.S. Sherraden, and D. Eberly. 1990. Comparing and understanding non-military service in different nations. In *The Moral Equivalent of War? A Study of Non-military Service in Nine Nations,* ed. D. Eberly, and M. Sherraden. New York: Greenwood Press.

Sherraden, M.S. 2001. *Developing Transnational Social Policy: A North American Community Service Program* (CSD Working Paper 01-10). St. Louis: Washington University, Center for Social Development.

Sherraden M.S., and C. Benítez. 2003. *North American Community Service Pilot Project* (Research Report). St. Louis: Washington University, Center for Social Development.

Slavin, R. 1985. Cooperative learning: Applying contact theory in desegregated schools. *Journal of Social Issues* 41 (2): 45–62.

Stephan, W. 1985. Intergroup relations. In *Handbook of Social Psychology,* vol. 2, ed. G. Lindzey, and E. Aronson. New York: Random House.

Tajfel, H., and J. Turner. 1986. The social identity theory of intergroup relations. In *The Psychology of Intergroup Relations,* ed. S. Worchel, and G. Austin. Chicago: Nelson-Hall.

Taylor, D., and F. Moghaddam. 1994. *Theories of Intergroup Relations: International Social Psychological Perspectives.* New York: Praeger.

Udom, U. 1981. The politics of national service programs: A comparative study of the National Youth Service Corps in Nigeria and Volunteers in Service to America in the United States. PhD diss., University of Texas, Austin.

Wilder, D. 1984. Intergroup contact: The typical member and the exception to the rule. *Journal of Experimental Psychology* 20: 177–194.

———. 1986. Social categorization: Implications for creation and reduction of intergroup bias. In *Advances in Experimental Social Psychology,* vol. 19, ed. L. Berkowitz. New York: Academic Press.

Wittig, M., and S. Grant-Thompson. 1998. The utility of Allport's conditions of intergroup contact for predicting perceptions of improved racial attitudes and beliefs. *Journal of Social Issues* 54 (4): 795–812.

Worchel, S., J. Cooper, and G. Goethals. 1988. *Understanding Social Psychology.* Chicago: Dorsey Press.

V

IMPACTS AND INQUIRY

_____11

Civic Service Across Nations and Cultures

The Range of Effects and Ways to Study Them

Justin Davis Smith and Angela Ellis Paine

The past decade has witnessed an explosion of interest in volunteerism and civic service worldwide, perhaps best illustrated by the involvement of more than 130 national governments in the United Nations International Year of the Volunteer in 2001. This interest has been fueled in part by the rapid expansion of the voluntary sector, what Salamon has referred to as a "global associational revolution" (1994, 109), as well as by a growing belief among policy makers in the role of volunteerism and civic service in the building of healthy communities and democratic institutions.

The notion of civic service, in particular, as a key building block of active citizenship and social capital has underpinned public policy across the globe, from Bill Clinton's and George W. Bush's governments in the United States to Tony Blair's New Labour administration in the United Kingdom. However, despite the growth of academic research on civic service in recent years, many of the claims that have been made remain largely unsubstantiated. Anecdotal evidence abounds claiming that service can deliver a multitude of benefits for a diverse range of stakeholder groups, yet robust data on impacts lag far behind the rhetoric. As a result, as Safrit and colleagues note, "impact assessment has become a, if not 'the,' critical issue for non-profits during the last five years," (2003, 12) or, as Perry and Thomson have commented, "the greatest challenge for civic service in the twenty-first century may lie in building the capacity to evaluate carefully the impacts of service on individuals, institutions, and local communities" (2004, 2).

The demand for better measurement and impact research comes from a variety of sources: from governments determined to apply ever more rigorous tests of public accountability to the nonprofit sector, from private grant makers anxious to know what difference their grants have made, from service organizations seeking to use impact data to improve performance and leverage additional resources, from beneficiaries increasingly looking to exercise their rights as consumers, and from volunteers anxious to see their efforts used in an effective manner (Kendall and Knapp 1999; Ellis 1996; Harris, Rochester, and Hutchinson 1999).

In response to this demand, the last few years have seen an increased emphasis on research. In purely numeric terms, the volume of studies is impressive. A recent review by the Grantmaker Forum on Community and National Service (2000) identified some 997 studies on service impacts generated since 1990 in the United States alone. Yet in terms of quality, the picture is less convincing. "We are faced," Perry and Thomson claim, "with the task of comparing, contrasting, and synthesizing very different kinds of evidence" and with a body of literature "marked by a paucity of research syntheses and interdisciplinary, comprehensive reviews" (2004, 28–29). The scope of most of the research is also limited, they conclude, with a heavy emphasis on the impacts on the individual volunteer or service-giver and very little focus on institutional and community-level outcomes.

This chapter aims to move the debate forward by outlining a conceptual framework for assessing the impact of civic service and by exploring possible methodologies for such studies. The first section examines the different stakeholder groups involved in service and the various forms that impacts may take across these stakeholder groups. Drawing on work that we completed in the development of a *Volunteering Impact Assessment Toolkit,* we argue that any attempt to provide a comprehensive assessment of the impact of service must move beyond the current focus on the volunteer and the economic value of the activity to encompass a much wider range of stakeholders and noneconomic measures of benefit (Institute for Volunteering Research 2004). The second section discusses possible research methods and examines issues that will need to be considered when undertaking such research.

We acknowledge that the development and implementation of a comprehensive impact approach will not be an easy task, beset as it is by profound conceptual, methodological, and logistical issues. Kendall and Knapp argue that the voluntary sector's "very existence and form, and thus also many of its activities, challenge the assessor to seek indicators that range beyond those conventionally employed in for-profit firms and public organizations" (2000, 129). However, given the importance of the stakes, it is a task worth attempting, and as Perry and Thomson conclude, "The various faces of civic service (expressed through multiple and widely varying goals) may make the research more difficult, and it may force us to look at effectiveness measurements and standards in a new way, but ultimately, a way can be found to gauge effectiveness" (2004, 30).

Terminology

First, a note is warranted on terminology and definitions. Definitions of volunteerism and civic service and the extent to which the two concepts overlap or diverge have been explored at length elsewhere (Davis Smith 2004; McBride and Sherraden 2004). For the purpose of this chapter, we adopt the view that the concepts of volunteerism and civic service have sufficient elements in common to make it meaningful to draw on both sets of literature when exploring the issue of impacts. Both volunteering and civic service programs, we would argue, share the same range of stakeholder groups and are subject to the same range of impacts. We do not deny that some impacts may be particular to either volunteering or to civic service. For example, it is more likely that a civic service program will require a financial contribution from its participants than a more traditional volunteering scheme, thus potentially limiting the constituency from which service participants can be drawn. However, we would argue that the degree of continuity between the two concepts is such that it is legitimate to draw on both bodies of research in advancing the case for a total volunteering audit framework.

This chapter is also not the place to enter into a detailed discussion of the different definitions of the term *impact*. We are drawn to the definition developed by Blankenberg in 1995:

> [Impact] . . . concerns long-term and sustainable changes introduced by a given intervention in the lives of beneficiaries. Impact can be related either to the specific objectives of an intervention or to unanticipated changes caused by an intervention; such unanticipated changes may also occur in the lives of people not belonging to the beneficiary group. Impact can be either positive or negative, the latter being equally important to be aware of. (Adams 2001, 1)

Of particular interest in this definition is the acknowledgement that impacts can be both intended and unintended. It is essential for organizations not to overlook those impacts that arise as a by-product of the service activity, impacts that may not have been identified when the organization was developing indicators of performance and impact, but that happened as a result of the catalytic impact of the activity and that may prove to be among the most influential of all the outcomes. Blankenberg's definition is also valuable in reminding us that the impact of civic service may be negative as well as positive. Much has been written about the dark side of nonprofits and, although the recognition comes uneasily to some researchers and practitioners working in the field of service, it has to be acknowledged that such activity may not necessarily always benefit all or any of the stakeholder groups. Studies of the effects of civic service must allow space for such negative impacts to be explored.

Conceptualizing the Impact of Civic Service

Before considering the possible range of impacts, it is important to consider briefly who is likely to be affected by the civic service activity. Using the concept of stakeholder, it is possible to identify four primary groups for almost all service programs: the volunteers or servers; the organizations that run or work with the programs; the service users or beneficiaries (who are categorized most commonly as either children, youth, adults, seniors, or people who are economically and socially disadvantaged); and the wider communities in which the service takes place as well as where the servers live (during and after participation). Some authors have broken these main stakeholder groups into subgroups. For example, Rochester, in his study of the social impacts of community-based organizations, suggests that impacts be split between "members" and the "public" (Rochester 1998). Within these two main categories he identifies a number of subcategories. Members, he argues, can be split into passive members, active members, and an inner core of very active members, while the public subdivides into the narrow community, the broader community, and the wider public.

Of course, most service programs are not directed equally toward each of these groups. Some programs exist primarily to meet the needs of the volunteer, while others have as their primary focus the delivery of a quality service in the community. Work by McBride, Benítez, and Sherraden (2003) mapping the forms and nature of service schemes worldwide suggests that a majority of programs focus primarily on the volunteer. It is thus no surprise to find that most assessments of the impact of service programs to date have focused on the effect on the individual volunteer, with far less attention paid to the impact on the beneficiary or the broader community (Perry and Thomson 2004). A full evaluation of the impact of service would focus on each of the distinct stakeholder groups.

Having identified the different stakeholder groups who will be impacted by a civic service program, we turn to the different types of likely impacts. On the surface the list appears almost endless. An evaluation of the European Voluntary Service scheme, for example, found that volunteers involved in the program gained self-confidence, independence, language skills, leadership skills, and assertiveness (SOS 1999). According to a later evaluation of the same program, sending organizations found it to be a learning experience, an opportunity for intercultural learning, a chance to work with new partner organizations, and an opportunity to share information and expertise (SOS 2000). Other studies have come up with long lists of different impacts, reflecting the almost infinite variety of goals of different programs (Perry and Thomson 2004; McBride et al. 2003). In order to make sense of these impacts and to bring some coherence and rigor to the debate, it is helpful to develop a conceptual framework that brings these diverse impacts together and relates them to the four primary stakeholder groups.

Program descriptions and research suggest that, broadly speaking, five types of impacts can be identified, drawing on the concept of different forms of capital: economic capital, physical capital, human capital, social capital, and cultural capital. Each of these types of impact will manifest itself in different ways on the different stakeholder groups.

Economic Capital

A great deal of attention has been paid to the measurement of the economic impact of volunteering or service (Rochester 1998; Burns and Taylor 2000). Such measurement has assumed a number of different forms, most typically some sort of time value calculation of the amount of volunteering or service undertaken. Anderson and Zimmerer suggest that five different models in the United States have been used to estimate the dollar value of volunteering: the comparable worth method, which attempts to equate the work of volunteers to that of paid staff by using an equivalent wage rate for the job done; the minimum wage approach, which estimates the value of volunteering using the minimum wage across the economy; the average wage rate, which adopts a similar method of calculation but using an average wage rate instead of a minimum one; the living wage approach, which is based on the concept of "value based on dollars required to exist"; and the independent sector formula, a highly specific United States approach that "applies the average hour earnings of all production and non-supervisory workers on private non-farm payrolls" and then increases the rate by 12 percent to represent the estimated fringe benefits in order to arrive at the dollar value of volunteer time each year (Anderson and Zimmerer 2003, 39–44).

Such approaches have been also prevalent in studies outside the United

States. The Institute for Volunteering Research (1996), for example, has estimated that the economic value of volunteering to the UK national economy to be in the region of £40 billion per annum, using the average wage rate approach. McClintock (2004), again using an average wage approach, reports that the economic value of volunteering in Canada is in the region of $17 billion per annum. In addition to presenting the economic value of volunteering or service in strictly financial terms, some researchers have favored a person per year computation method, which values volunteering in terms of the number of full-time, year-round positions or person years that the volunteer hours would equal (Ross 1998). McClintock (2004), for example, estimates that the 1 billion hours contributed by volunteers in Canada in 2000 accounts for some 549,000 full-time jobs.

Such economic approaches, however, have their limitations. They assess the value of service only in terms of the participants' time and say nothing about other forms of economic impact. Quarter, Mook, and Richmond argue that volunteering can be given also an economic value in terms of the skills it provides to the volunteers and potentially the beneficiaries. (Depending on the emphasis, these impacts may be also considered human capital, as discussed below.) The researchers propose that in terms of skills development, undertaking a period of volunteering is equivalent to taking part in two undergraduate university courses (valued at $500 each). As such, the value of volunteering and service comes not only from the labor provided by the volunteers, but also from the economic value of the skills gained by the volunteers. In addition, many of the potential community benefits of civic service could be given an economic value. For example, if local crime rates were reduced due to a civic service program that had contributed to economic renewal, then the calculation of economic value could include the savings in police time and from reduced vandalism. Other potential effects of a civic service program, such as increased mental and/or physical well-being, could also theoretically be given an economic value (Quarter, Mook, and Richmond 2003).

More fundamentally, however, such crude calculations of the wage replacement value of volunteering and service do not tell us anything about the costs of stimulating such activity. Gaskin has identified the costs involved in establishing a volunteering program in the UK: the wages of paid staff to recruit and manage the volunteers, advertising and recruitment materials, training courses, supplies and equipment, rent and heating, travel expenses, accommodations and food, and insurance. In large organizations, wages for the staff that managed the volunteers were the single largest element of expenditure, whereas in smaller organizations, which tend to employ fewer paid staff and where volunteers themselves may undertake volunteer management, staff costs were less substantial (Gaskin 1999). In civic service programs the costs may be incurred not only by the organization, but also by the volunteers. McBride, Benítez, and Sherraden (2003) found that 33 percent of the 210 civic service programs they identified worldwide required that the server pay some or all of the costs of the experience. The average cost of the program was $600, which generally included expenses for accommodation, travel, training, and support. In other programs, volunteers received a stipend or living allowance, which also represents an economic cost that must be brought into the equation.

Physical Capital

Alongside the economic value of civic service, much of the actual work produced through such activity is also quantifiable and needs to be factored into any impact assessment. Physical capital refers to the quantifiable, inanimate objects that may result either from the direct aim of the service or as a by-product of that service (Kendall and Knapp 2000)—for example, the number of trees planted, the number of meals delivered, the number of training schemes provided, the number of leaflets produced, or the number of jobs created.

Methods to measure physical capital are relatively straightforward; an organization must simply count or calculate the physical outputs of its projects, and many organizations already keep such data as part of funding requirements. However, to complicate matters, any meaningful measurement of impact will move beyond numbers to consider the quality of the physical capital generated. Fifty trees planted that fall down after the first strong winds are clearly worth less than ten trees planted that survive the storm, and a poorly delivered training course will have little impact no matter how many times it is repeated.

Consideration also needs to be given to the appropriateness of the service for the communities in which it takes place. A comprehensive impact assessment would ask whether or not the needs of the recipient community have been taken into consideration before the project was developed. The development of a new community center, when residents have identified the need for a center and have been consulted in its design and construction, is likely to be worth more than a community center built with no public consultation.

Human Capital

The above two forms of capital involve the effects of civic service on organizations and communities, rather than on the volunteers. Human capital turns our attention toward the participants, as it encompasses the acquisition of skills and changing attitudes and behavior engendered through participation in service programs (Walker et al. 2000). Human capital is concerned with individuals—the servers, the beneficiaries, or individuals within the wider community.

Civic service can be seen to deliver positive impacts on the human capital of the servers, in terms of skills development, educational opportunity, self-esteem, and health outcomes, although the evidence in relation to citizenship and broader civic engagement is less compelling (Grantmaker Forum on Community and National Service 2000; Perry and Imperial 2001). Although Perry and Imperial's review suggests few negative impacts on human capital arising out of volunteering and service, the possibility that they may on occasion occur should not be discounted. A recent study from Australia caused some consternation in the volunteering world when it reported that volunteering, far from leading to an improvement in an individual's health, might actually lead to its deterioration (Ziersch and Baum 2004).

Social Capital

While physical capital is concerned with inanimate objects and human capital is concerned with individuals, social capital is about relationships and building bonds of trust between people (Kendall and Knapp 2000, 110). Distinct from all other kinds of capital, it cannot be owned by one person or used in isolation. Social capital is a public good as opposed to a private good such as financial capital; it is the raw material of civil society. To introduce the concept of social capital enables the impacts of volunteering and service to be considered in terms of the relationships between different people that develop (in one form or another) through participation in such activity.

Since Bourdieu and Coleman first used the concept of social capital, it has found ever-increasing popularity, especially over the past decade since the work of Putnam (Bourdieu 1986; Coleman 1990). Putnam's interpretation of social capital refers to societal features, such as networks, norms, and trust that enable and enhance cooperation for mutual benefit (Putnam 1993; Putnam 1995). In this sense social capital shapes both the quality and quantity of social interaction within a community. For Putnam, social capital is a component of civic virtue (Cox 1997, 2–7); it is accumulated through the contributions that people make to community life, including volunteering and civic service.

However, a word of caution must be added. Social capital also has its downsides. In some cases the creation of very strong community ties can serve to exclude certain individuals, barring their access to the community. As Johnston and Jowell remind us, "social capital, like financial capital, is much more available to certain people than to others" (1999, 193). Indeed, Bourdieu's conceptualization of social capital is based on the notion that people have differential access to it, with the effect of reproducing and intensifying existing inequalities within communities (see Tonkiss 2000 for a discussion).

A number of useful tools have been developed to measure social capital, which could be extended to studies exploring the impact of civic service. Krishna and Shrader (1999), for example, developed a comprehensive measurement toolkit for the World Bank in the form of a social capital investment tool. In developing this measure they field-tested a large number of indicators and methods for measuring the level of social capital in fifteen countries. The chosen methods included community profiles, household surveys, and organizational profiles. An alternative approach has been advanced by Onyx and Bullen (1997), who have developed a social capital scale, consisting of eight domains that reflect different facets of social capital, including participation in the local community, pro-activity in the social context, feelings of trust and safety, neighborhood connections, family and friends connections, tolerance of diversity, value of life, and work connections. These indicators were developed through field-testing in five communities within the New South Wales region of Australia.

Cultural Capital

Finally, when considering the full range of effects of volunteering and civic service, it is necessary to discuss the concept of cultural capital. Cultural capital refers to assets such as a shared sense of cultural and religious identity, including language, heritage, and an underlying possession of knowledge of culturally specific social meanings. These facets of cultural capital have been found to affect the level and form of volunteering and service (Dekker and Halman 2003). Volunteering and service are both ethnically and ethically guided and they both draw on our reserves of cultural capital.

Measuring the Impact of Civic Service

Due to the complexity of the conceptual framework outlined above, we argue that a multimethod approach is best suited to capture the full range of impacts and stakeholders associated with any civic service program. Employing a range of both quantitative and qualitative methods adds rigor, depth, and breadth to the process (Herbert and Shepherd 2001; Dingle 2001). Quantitative methods can be used to provide a broad overview and allow for multivariate analysis, while qualitative methods provide an in-depth understanding of values, perceptions, and processes. The mix of methods in any one study might include focus groups and case studies, participant observation, surveys, and specialized methods, such as photographic records and video (Herbert and Shepherd 2001).

A more innovative method for capturing broader public opinion is to include participatory appraisals. Participatory appraisal involves the community in the research. Participation in the appraisal of a program may engender a greater sense of awareness and ownership such that the sustainability of the project is also increased. For example, a map of the village may be drawn and people may be asked to fill in where the project has been of benefit, where it has impacted their lives, or where they have found problems.

Outstanding Issues Within Civic Service Impact Assessment

A number of issues bear on the assessment of the impact of civic service, especially in a cross-national context. First, the balance to be struck between generalizability and specificity may be difficult to achieve. Civic service takes different forms in different settings, reflecting varied political, social, economic, and cultural traditions and mores (McBride et al. 2004). In international and transnational programs, civic service occurs across national borders, with volunteers operating in often very different institutional and legislative settings. Assessing the impact of such programs requires a set of indicators that are both general enough to allow for comparisons to be drawn across geographic boundaries and loose enough to allow for specific national elements to be detected.

We recognize the importance of striking this balance by offering a set of potentially universal indicators that may have resonance in a wide variety of different settings, but which also encourages organizations to add indicators specific to individual projects or programs in their own countries (Institute for Volunteering Research 2004). Such flexibility is of value not only in a cross-national or cross-cultural context, but also in assessing the impact of programs that may be structured differently. For researchers and policy makers interested in drawing comparisons between different programs in different countries, it is important that an element of universality is incorporated into any set of indicators, while attending to national, regional, and local variations. As McBride and colleagues conclude, "A major challenge will be to keep measures general enough to allow for applications in many different contexts, in order to describe and analyse service across nations and cultures" (McBride et al. 2003, 15).

The second point is related to the issue of cultural and geographical specificity. Any impact assessment needs to take into account the different definitions and modes of language used to describe civic service. Research on *volunteering* overall has shown that different people understand different things by the term volunteering, which greatly complicates the validity of the given measure. If volunteering is restricted in the public consciousness to good works carried out within a formal setting, then the level of activity recorded in a national survey will be much lower than in countries where a broader understanding of the term is the norm. The same will be true for civic service, and this point takes on particular relevance when we consider research across nations and cultures. Different indicators (or prompts for various indicators) will likely be required given differences in cultural meaning and the need for measurement sensitivity. For example, Meijs and colleagues (2003), in their work on variations in public perceptions of volunteering across countries, discuss how certain indicators, such as the notion of volunteering to "impress" someone, were not acknowledged in some countries, such as India, and ideas of corporate volunteering were not conceivable in the Netherlands, Belgium, India, or Italy as they did not fit with cultural norms. As a consequence, the indicators used in the study had to be adapted to fit the cultural and political contexts within which the research was conducted.

Definitions of volunteering are multiple and complex. During evaluation of the International Year of the Volunteer 2001 by the Institute for Volunteering Research, over a hundred different names and terms for volunteering were found in different parts of the world (Davis Smith and Ellis 2002). For example, in Kenya the word for volunteering is *harambee,* which means "let us work together to improve our community," while in Hungary *kalaka* is largely favored, meaning mutual aid in joint agricultural projects. In French, there are two separate words for volunteering—*volontariat* and *benevolat*—the first referring to volunteering in formal, organizational settings and the second referring to time given free of charge. Once again any attempt to measure the impact of service across countries needs to strike a balance between indicators that have universal relevance and ones that are sensitive to the traditions and cultures of the countries under study.

The third issue pertains to resources—financial and human—that are needed to implement research that assesses service outcomes and impacts, costs that may be particularly high if the program spans several sites within a country or crosses national boundaries. Costs may be mediated through existing staff within the organization, who may have the capacity and skills to carry out the work, or through volunteers, who may be trained to help with the assessment. Additional considerations relate to legitimacy, which may be supported through research completed by an independent agency, unrelated to the service program. All these factors will influence the scale and design of the research.

A fourth issue is how to weigh the evidence that results from the research. Should each of the stakeholders' views be judged as equally legitimate and valid? Should each form of capital be accorded the same importance? How does one decide whether the benefits gained for one stakeholder are more important than those gained for another? For example, in some international service programs, there is evidence to suggest that while the volunteers gain, the host organization or local community benefits little, if at all. Is this outcome acceptable? How should such a judgment be made? How can conflicting results be reconciled? The answers to these conundrums lie in ensuring that the research is directly related to the program's mission and goals. An assessment of outcomes taken out of context will be meaningless and confusing, whereas an assessment set against the explicit aims of the service program will be both meaningful and constructive in assessing progress and pointing the way for future development. Thus, if the program is primarily about developing the skills of the volunteers, results that suggest that the host community does not benefit to any great extent may not necessarily be cause for undue alarm. Conversely, a program that has been established with the explicit aim of building cross-national understanding will be a disappointment if results suggest that cultural and social capital has not been enhanced as a result of the service activity.

The fifth issue pertains to causality. How can one know that the measured effects are a result of the service intervention and not some other unrelated activity? This issue is not particular to the service world. Trying to untangle cause and effect is one of the most complex tasks of the social researcher. Outside a laboratory setting, it is not possible to prove that one activity or intervention is the catalyst for change; and in a situation such as that in which civic service is operating, whereby all stakeholders are likely to come under a series of influences during the service period, *proving* that the service activity had specific impacts is extremely problematic and, in fact, impossible. All the researcher can do is provide as robust a body of evidence as possible, triangulated and cross-referenced wherever possible with alternative sets of data, to suggest that the measured changes may be attributed within varying degrees and some margin of error to the civic service activity.

Finally, there is an issue with the terminology of measurement itself. While we see outcome-based research and impact measurement as a force for good, we share the concerns of some observers about an overreliance on performance measurement, which is taking hold of the public policy arena. In particular, we stress the need to avoid the dangers of reductionism, or reducing all impacts to only those that can be quantified. Instead, we suggest there is a need to talk more about assessing impact, emphasizing the importance of both qualitative and quantitative approaches. There is also a real danger that the intrinsic value of civic service will be reduced to a bottom line on a balance sheet, which may contribute to the misleading (and damaging) notion that such activity is all about saving money.

Conclusion

This chapter has argued that knowledge of the impact of civic service is in its infancy and lags behind some of the vocal claims made on its behalf by policy makers and pundits worldwide. Many studies have been carried out to explore the effects of specific programs, but much of the research (by definition) is not rigorous enough to claim the effects and it is localized, having little to say about the wider, national (or indeed global) impact. Moreover, much of the research to date has suffered from an overemphasis on the volunteer or server and on the economic impact of the program, with far less attention paid to the effects on other key stakeholders and on the noneconomic impacts of the activity. We have argued in favor of the development of a total volunteering audit approach, which recognizes the four key stakeholder groups likely to be impacted by any service activity and the five key types of capital that may result from service. We have pointed to the need to examine both unintended as well as intended impacts and to be open to the possibility that not all impacts will necessarily be positive. We conclude by emphasizing the issues that must be addressed when carrying out research (especially cross-nationally) and offering a word of warning about the dangers of reductionism. Despite the difficulties, moving toward more rigorous research on civic service is essential. It will help organizations learn what will make service most effective and efficient, demonstrate accountability, inform and motivate staff (paid and unpaid), and assist in the development and improvement of the program's activity.

References

Adams, J. 2001. *NGO Policy Briefing Paper No. 3*. Oxford: INTRAC. www.intrac. org/docs/03ImpactAssessment.doc. Quoted by Blankenberg, F. 1995. In *Methods of Impact Assessment Research Program, Resource Pack and Discussion* (Paper for the Case Studies Phase). The Hague: Oxfam UK/I & Novib.

Anderson, P., and M. Zimmerer. 2003. Dollar value of volunteer time: a review of five estimation methods. *Journal of Volunteer Administration* 21 (2): 39–44.

Bourdieu, P. 1986. The forms of capital. In *Handbook of Theory and Research for the Sociology of Education,* ed. J. Richardson. New York: Greenwood Press.

Burns, D., and M. Taylor. 2000. Auditing the capacity of institutions and communities to deliver democratic participation. *Voluntary Action* 2 (3): 43–60.

Cnaan, R.A., F. Handy, and M. Wadsworth. 1996. Defining who is a volunteer: Conceptual and empirical considerations. *Nonprofit and Voluntary Sector Quarterly* (25) 3: 364–383.

Coleman, J. 1990. *Foundations of Social Theory.* Cambridge, MA: Harvard University Press.

Cox, E. 1997. Social capital and volunteering: How close is the connection? *Australian Journal on Volunteering* 2 (2): 4–7.

Davis Smith, J. 2004. Civic service in Western Europe. *Nonprofit and Voluntary Sector Quarterly* 33 (4): 64S–78S.

Davis Smith, J., and A. Ellis. 2002. *IYV Global Evaluation.* London: Institute for Volunteering Research.

Dekker, P., and L. Halman, eds. 2003. *The Values of Volunteering: Cross-Cultural Perspective.* New York: Plenum.

Dingle, A., ed. 2001. *Measuring Volunteering: A Practical Toolkit.* Washington, DC and Bonn: Independent Sector and United Nations Volunteers.

Ellis, S. 1996. *From the Top Down: The Executive Role in Volunteer Program Success.* Philadelphia: Energize.

Gaskin, K. 1999. Valuing volunteers in Europe: A comparative study of the Volunteer Investment and Value Audit. *Voluntary Action* 2 (1): 35–49.

Grantmaker Forum on Community and National Service. 2000. *The State of Service-Related Research: Opportunities to Build a Field.* Berkeley, CA: Grantmaker Forum on Community and National Service.

Harris, J., C. Rochester, and R. Hutchinson. 1999. *Building the Capacity of Small Voluntary Agencies: Juggling on a Unicycle: A Handbook for Small Voluntary Agencies.* Alberta, Canada: Centre for Voluntary Organizations.

Herbert, A., and A. Shepherd. 2001. *Impact Assessment for Poverty Reduction (A Spin-Off Study for Evaluation of DFID Support to Poverty Reduction).* London: Department for International Development Department.

Institute for Volunteering Research. 1996. *The Economic Value of Volunteering.* London: Institute for Volunteering Research.

———. 2004. *Volunteering Impact Assessment Toolkit: A Practical Guide for Measuring the Impact of Volunteering.* London: Institute for Volunteering Research.

Johnston, M., and R. Jowell. 1999. Social capital and the social fabric. In *British Social Attitudes, the 16th Report: Who Shares New Labour Values?,* ed. R. Jowell, A. Park, K. Thomson, J. Curtice, L. Jarvis, N. Stratford, and C. Bromley. Aldershot, UK: Ashgate.

Kendall, J., and M.R.J. Knapp. 1999. *Measuring the Outcomes of Voluntary Organisation Activities: Scoping Paper on Conceptual and Methodological Issues.* Belfast: Voluntary Activity Unit (Northern Ireland).

———. 2000. Measuring the performance of voluntary organizations. *Public Management* 2 (1): 105–132.

Krishna, A., and E. Shrader. 1999. Social capital assessment tool. Paper prepared for the Conference of Social Capital and Poverty Reduction, World Bank, Washington, DC, June 22–24.

McBride, A.M., C. Benítez, and M. Sherraden. 2003. *The Forms and Nature of Civic Service: A Global Assessment* (CSD Report). St. Louis: Washington University in St. Louis, Center for Social Development.

McBride, A.M., M. Lombe, F. Tang, M. Sherraden, and C. Benítez. 2003. *The Knowledge Base on Civic Service: Status and Directions* (CSD Working Paper 03-20). St. Louis: Washington University in St. Louis, Center for Social Development.

McBride, A.M., and M. Sherraden. 2004. Toward a global research agenda on civic service: Editors' introduction to this special issue. *Nonprofit and Voluntary Sector Quarterly* 33 (4): 3S–7S.

McBride, A.M., M. Sherraden, C. Benítez, and E. Johnson. 2004. Civic service worldwide: Defining a field, building a knowledge base. *Nonprofit and Voluntary Sector Quarterly* 33(4): 8S–21S.

McClintock, N. 2004. *Understanding Canadian volunteers: Using the national survey of giving, volunteering and participation to build your volunteer programme.* Toronto: Canadian Centre for Philanthropy.

Meijs, L., F. Handy, R. Cnaan, J. Brudney, U. Ascoli, S. Ranade, L. Hustinx, S. Webber, and I. Weiss. 2003. All in the eyes of the beholder? Perceptions of volunteering across eight countries. In *The Values of Volunteering: Cross-Cultural Perspective,* ed. P. Dekker, and L. Halman. New York: Plenum.

Onyx, J., and P. Bullen. 1997. *Measuring Social Capital in Five Communities in NSW: An Analysis* (Working Paper No. 41). Sidney: Centre for Australian Community Organizations and Management, Unit of Technology.

Perry, J., and A.M. Thomson. 2004. *Civic Service: What Difference Does It Make?* Armonk, NY: M.E. Sharpe.

Perry, J.L., and M.T. Imperial. 2001. A decade of service-related research: A map of the field. *Nonprofit and Voluntary Sector Quarterly* 30 (3): 462–479.

Putnam, R. 1993. *Making Democracy Work: Civic Traditions in Modern Italy.* Princeton, NJ: Princeton University Press.

———. 1995. Bowling alone: America's declining social capital—An interview with Robert Putnam. *Journal of Democracy* 6 (1): 65–78. http://muse.jhu.edu/journals/journal_of_democracy/v006/6.1putnam.html.

Quarter, J., L. Mook, and B. Richmond. 2003. *What Counts: Social Auditing for Nonprofits and Cooperatives.* Upper Saddle River, NJ: Prentice Hall.

Rochester, C. 1998. *Social Benefits: Exploring the Value of Community Sector Organizations.* West Malling, UK: Charities Aid Foundation.

Ross, D. 1998. *How to Estimate the Economic Contribution of Volunteer Work.* Ottowa, Canada: Voluntary Action Directorate, Department of Canadian Heritage. www.nald.ca/fulltext/heritage/ComPartnE/estvole.htm.

Safrit, R., R. Schmiesing, J. King, J. Villard, and B. Wells. 2003. Assessing the Impact of the Three-Year Ohio Teen B.R.I.D.G.E.S. AmeriCorps Program. *Journal of Volunteer Administration* 21 (2): 12–16.

Salamon, L. 1994. The Rise of the Nonprofit Sector. *Foreign Affairs* 73 (4): 109–122.

Structure of Operational Support (SOS). 1999. *Volunteers' Perceptions of the Impact of the European Voluntary Service in Their Lives.* Brussels: European Voluntary Service Pilot Action, SOS.

———. 2000. *EVS: The Sending Organizations' Perspectives.* Brussels: European Voluntary Service Pilot Action, SOS.

Tonkiss, F. 2000. Trust, social capital and economy. In *Trust and Civil Society,* ed. F. Tonkiss, A. Passey, N. Fenton, and L. Hems. New York: Palgrave Macmillan Press.

Walker, P., J. Lewis, S. Lingayah, and F. Sommer. 2000. *Prove It! Measuring the Effect of Neighbourhood Renewal on Local People.* London: New Economics Foundation. www.neweconomics.org/gen/z_sys_PublicationDetail.aspx?PID=2.

Ziersch, A., and F. Baum. 2004. Involvement in civil society groups: Is it good for your health? *Journal of Epidemiology and Community Health* 58: 493–500.

12

Directions in Civic Service Scholarship

An Institutional Perspective

Amanda Moore McBride and Michael Sherraden
with Natasha Menon

Descriptive evidence on civic service has reached a critical mass, providing a global perspective and suggesting directions for further research. In this chapter, we take stock of the civic service knowledge base, building on the global review in McBride and Sherraden (2004) and the chapters in this book. We offer tentative answers to the questions posed at the beginning of the book regarding an operational definition of civic service and influences on development, performance, and impacts of civic service. We recognize the variation in the function and forms of civic service worldwide and the influences of cultural and social, political, and economic contexts. We outline a theoretical perspective on civic service that offers specific testable hypotheses that may capture differences across service forms and contexts.

We suggest that civic service has historically been used as an "intervention," in that it has been used to address a given social condition. Also, there are indications that service may be on the verge of becoming a societal institution. As an intervention, service is considered something external, used in a given situation. As an institution, service is considered a common occurrence, a norm embedded within societal structures and cultures. Indeed, some programs have proven the test of time, surviving for decades with public acceptance through varied political administrations. Service has proliferated into different forms (service-learning, national service, and international service) across countries and cultures, and common features are easily identifiable across the different forms.

Operational Distinction: Common Features
and Possible Mediators

From this review of research, several operational features of service programs are worth noting, reinforcing the definition of service put forth by Sherraden

(2001). Service occurs through distinct programs, which have a defined role for an individual to fill. The programs focus on addressing some public issue or project, while also influencing the server in some way. We also concur with Cnaan and his colleagues (Cnaan and Amrofell 1994; Cnaan, Handy, and Wadsworth 1996) regarding the distinguishing features of volunteer programs. These features include structure, auspices and organizational host, intended beneficiaries and activities, compulsory or voluntary nature, time commitment, and remuneration or recognition. This volume does not provide examples of extreme divergence across these features, but it does reinforce underlying common denominators.

Civic Mission

Through the Global Service Institute (GSI) research initiative, we have worked with hundreds of individuals on every inhabitable continent in an effort to study civic service. As we have aimed for consensus on a definition of civic service, one that does not inadvertently create false negatives, civic engagement or collective action has emerged as a common denominator. In almost all service programs, the overall goal is to organize individuals in common pursuit and delivery of some public good—even if the individual benefits as well. Service becomes an expression of citizenship. Service embodies our connection with and responsibility to those with whom we share the planet. Through service-learning, children and youth become citizens in training; through national service, adults act in the name of the nation-state to support fellow citizens; and through international service, individuals become agents of global citizenship.

On this point of common civic mission, everyone might agree if it were not perhaps for mandatory service. There is a normative tone to civic service, but critical questions can be raised about who is to be organized, how, and toward what ends (Kuti 2004; Obadare Chapter 3). Obadare questions the rights basis of civic responsibility when national service is mandatory under authoritarian regimes. This is a cautionary perspective, though Eberly and Gal (Chapter 4) suggest that mandatory national service may eventually fade away.

Among mandatory service-learning programs, which appear to be on the rise, evidence suggests that people who participate may not view the mandatory program adversely and may actually be more likely to volunteer again than if they had not been required to serve (Metz and Youniss 2003). These programs are integral to educational pedagogy, perhaps minimizing potential negative views or effects as they are normalized. Nevertheless, the voluntary or involuntary nature of civic service remains a key feature of this phenomenon.

Inclusion

Related to mandatory service is the notion of inclusion. A mandatory program is possibly the most inclusive type of service program because all who qualify must serve. However, lack of freedom is not the most desirable feature, and it is not logistically feasible that all forms of service require individuals to serve. However, within democratic societies, an implicit value is placed on the opportunity to serve, such that anyone who qualifies and has the desire to serve would have the option to do so. In their seminal review of national service worldwide, Sherraden and Eberly propose "a universal national service in which the country tells all young people their help is needed, asks them to contribute a period of service, and makes administrative and financial arrangements such that every young person who offers to serve is able to serve" (1982, 102).

Across the chapters in this volume, inclusion is emphasized—inclusion of individuals, groups of people, and organizations. Fleischer and Gal discuss the importance of all Israeli citizens having the possibility to benefit from national service. Tapia demonstrates that service-learning in Argentina includes children of all backgrounds in service to their communities, which in many cases are low income. Morrow-Howell and Tang remind us of the graying demographic of society and the benefit of accommodating the skills and capacity of older adults in service roles. Sherraden suggests that planning and decision making across participating organizations and communities must be inclusive if international service is to become *transnational*. To be sure, however, many programs remain exclusive by virtue of their eligibility criteria or due to lack of supports, but the authors are resounding that inclusion should be a fundamental goal of service lest its mission and potential be undermined.

Service Role(s)

As we have stressed before (McBride and Sherraden 2004; McBride et al. 2003), a comparative knowledge base on civic service will rest on common concepts, terminology, and definitions, which are necessary for cross-cultural discussion and comparison. Examining research only in the United States, Perry and Thomson (Chapter 5) found that service was not explicitly defined and measured as an independent variable. We suggest that attention to the service role can help distinguish service from other types of volunteerism. This attention to the volunteer or server is warranted because the long-term, intensive, structured nature of the service role is a defining characteristic. However, in this volume, we are also reminded that the roles of auspices, organizational host, and beneficiary may be just as important.

A premium is placed on the volunteers or servers, probably because without them service would not be delivered or performed. The same could be said for those who sponsor the opportunity and those who are willing to participate in the activity, benefiting from the service. From program models to marketing materials to assessment of effects, the focus is on the volunteer. As Perry and Thomson as well as Sherraden suggest, for service to realize its potential more attention should be paid to those who also expect to benefit. Organizations get involved, either as the sending or hosting organizations, because they expect the program to help them accomplish their missions. Communities agree to let individuals from other countries or parts of their own country into their villages because they expect to gain skills, a different perspective, or a tangible result. Their incentives for involvement, forms of participation, and perceived outcomes are just as important to measure.

Service as an Institution

Multiple factors come to bear on civic service program development, implementation, performance, and effects. Many theories can and should be applied to predict and explain the influences on and effects of service. How can this range of considerations and theoretical possibilities be focused to pursue key issues across cultures and nations?

We suggest that an institutional perspective may serve as a theory of the middle range (Sherraden et al. 2001), which can be tested in its own right or which can serve to illustrate key relationships that may be best explained or predicted by more micro theories. The institutional perspective advanced by Michael Sherraden, Nancy Morrow-Howell, and others affiliated with the Center for Social Development (McBride, Benítez, and Sherraden 2003; Nagchoudhuri et al. 2005; Sherraden et al. 2001; Sherraden, Schreiner, and Beverly 2003) contends that social institutions structure human behavior and that those structures can be created and manipulated. Social institutions may largely be the result of historical timing and context as well as someone's hard work.

An institution can be thought of as a "social order or pattern that has attained a certain state or property" (Jepperson 1991, 145). Other institutions that span national and cultural contexts include voting rights, marriage, and retirement, among many others. Therefore, while organizations may implement service, the expectations for and the performance of service involves more than the auspices or organizational host. Service occurs through a complex interaction between culture, individuals, organizations, and structures, including policies. Through service there are prescribed roles for organizations and individuals (just as there are prescribed roles in the aforementioned institutions for voter, spouse, and retiree). The following pages discuss the forms and impacts of service from a role-based conception of service. The institutional dimensions are expectations, incentives, facilitation, information, and access.

We specifically extend the conceptualization and operationalization advanced in Morrow-Howell et al. (2003), who address organizational capacity for elder service in particular. We are interested in a theoretical framework that can answer questions about service across time and space for development of comparative knowledge. For example, does an institutional perspective allow us to talk about the overall status of civic service in a given region of the world, the varying impacts of national service across countries, or the impacts of international service in developing countries? The proposed institutional theory must stand the test of application.

Institutional Dimensions

Expectations

According to Morrow-Howell et al. (2003), expectations convey that service is needed and beneficial. Expectations are dependent on context. Arguably, service would not exist if there were not a societal need for the delivered service as well as for the intended impact on the volunteers. The very presence of a service program connotes need and benefit. Expectations for service also result in part from social norms regarding care and concern for others. The civic obligations that individuals have to one another are played out through mutual assistance, voluntary aid or contributions, and civic service (Menon, McBride, and Sherraden 2003). A president's speech can establish expectations through a call to service, or a disaster can reinforce our dependence on each other in times of need.

Expectations convey the role requirements or the who, what, where, when, how, and why. Jepperson states "all institutions are frameworks of programs or rules establishing identities and activity scripts for such identities" (1991, 146). Roles are created and offered by social institutions. The roles will differ in terms of their requirements; that is, compulsion, time commitments, and eligibility criteria.

Expectations may be conveyed through cultural messages and marketing. Over time, as a given service form is institutionalized, individuals come to know what is expected for role performance without even participating in the program. Expectations also moderate perceived outcomes; if volunteer host communities do not gain what they expected to gain, then perceived outcomes will be less positive. The resulting outcomes of service may then reinforce or modify expectations for service roles and performance.

Incentives

Incentives are inducements or awards for service that promote participation. Ostrom, Schroeder, and Wynne define incentives as "negative or positive changes in outcomes that individuals perceive as likely to result from particular actions taken within . . . a particular physical and social context" (1993, 8). Incentives can be thought of as intrinsic or extrinsic motivators. Incentives may motivate organizations and individuals to start or sustain role performance.

Intrinsic motivators allow the organizations or individuals to express their values or beliefs. If the mission of an organization is to create global citizens, then getting involved in an international service program may be a way to do that. For individuals, service may allow them to express their perceived citizenship obligations or engage in behaviors that will benefit others. They may also be personally satisfied, realizing the belief they have of themselves as good people.

Extrinsic motivators are awards or rewards, with the organizations and individuals advancing in some way if they participate. These incentives are part of the institutional structure and differ by program. They include community recognition and connections; increased skills and knowledge; and educational credits, awards, or scholarships. While these are incentives for service role performance, we do not know enough about the independent effect; for example, that educational awards may have on the long-term well-being of servers as an outcome of service. This example reflects the idea that service is a program bundle. There are multiple components that work together to create the service institution, but these components can be viewed in isolation for their direct effects as well.

Facilitation

Facilitation refers to support provided to the servers or volunteers for service role performance with the intention of promoting positive effects. Facilitation can take many different forms, including orientation, training, supervision, mentoring, reflection sessions, cross-group interaction, and stipends or other financial support.

Previously we have treated stipends or reimbursement for expenses as incentives (McBride, Benítez, and Sherraden 2003). However, after debate with colleagues worldwide, it is probably more appropriate to view these as facilitators or supports for service performance. They do not act as motivators, especially since they are below market wages in most cases, but instead may be necessary components to increase accessibility, facilitating involvement by those who need assistance. The same can be said for housing, childcare, health and liability insurance, and transportation assistance.

Facilitation not only increases accessibility but also may promote effectiveness. Training and supervision may sustain and improve role performance. For example, the amount of formal training has been associated with the length of engagement in volunteer programs (Grossman and Furanco 1999). Language training may be a necessary requisite for effective international service. Mentoring and reflection have been also associated with positive effects; in fact, without reflection, service-learning loses its learning distinction. As some researchers have suggested, not enough attention has been paid to the facilitation of cross-group interaction, so that the desired effects of tolerance and cross-cultural understanding are approached.

Information

Information provided by service programs gives potential volunteers crucial details about the availability of service roles, service role performance and supports, and expected service outcomes. Efforts and methods of dissemination vary greatly, with differing levels of specificity about the service role, for example, online or word of mouth, written job descriptions, and so on (Morrow-Howell et al. 2003). Dissemination strategies may favor certain groups more than others, thereby limiting accessibility. The content, degree of specificity, and methods of dissemination may influence servers' knowledge about the role they are to fill and what they may receive, conveying expectations, incentives, and facilitation.

Access

Institutional access relates to the opportunity to serve or fill the role (Morrow-Howell et al. 2003). Accessibility relates to the number of roles and available slots, as well as the cumulative, objective presence of the other institutional dimensions. For example, a stipend or educational award may increase accessibility for low-income youth, thus enabling them to serve. Accessible facilities and environments may attract potential servers with physical disabilities. Flexibility in time commitments and activity placement may facilitate involvement by different groups of people. Certain types of roles may be more accessible than others, and expectations may play a large role. Service-learning programs are implemented through the educational system and are developmental in nature with few to no eligibility criteria, such that access may be universal. International service programs, however, may have a number of requirements that are intended to bolster service effectiveness but which lower accessibility of the role.

Figure 12.1 **Institutional Determinants of Service Role Uptake, Performance, and Impacts: Service Inclusion and Effectiveness**

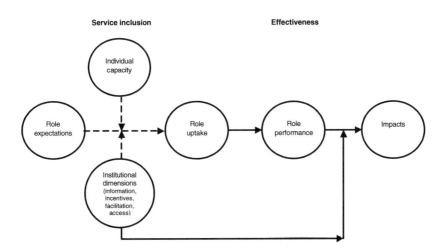

Service Inclusion and Effectiveness: Institutional Determinants

Taking these institutional dimensions together, we propose an institutional theory of service inclusion and effectiveness. We suggest examining two critical junctures: role uptake and the impacts of service role performance (see Figure 12.1.) It may be possible to apply this theory at the organizational and individual levels. For ease of exposition, we focus only on the individual here. As the constructs and variables possess variability, measurement across different cultural, social, economic, and political contexts can promote comparative study.

Role Uptake

Whether an individual decides to take up a service role is determined by expectations, institutional dimensions, and individual capacity (Sherraden, Schreiner, and Beverly 2003). In institutional theorizing, the individual's decision-making process is commonly not integrated into the model but treated as a given subjective process that is known to occur. For the purpose of assessing the inclusiveness of service, it is possible to objectively measure the institutional dimensions and the individual's capacity, thus predicting service role uptake. Objective measurement helps to identify which features most promote inclusiveness, and it also isolates the initial step necessary for service role performance. Furthermore, it captures supply and demand issues related to the service role.

Hypothesis 1:   Individual capacity moderates the relationship between expectations and role uptake.

Hypothesis 2:   Incentives moderate the relationship between expectations and role uptake.

Hypothesis 3:   Facilitation moderates the relationship between expectations and role uptake.

Hypothesis 4:   Information about the service role moderates the relationship between expectations and role uptake.

Hypothesis 5:   Access moderates the relationship between expectations and role uptake.

Role Performance and Service Impacts

Role performance is measured by the actual length and intensity of the service period and activities. The impacts of service obviously result from service role performance, but institutional supports may affect the effectiveness of service as well. Expectations or requirements for the service role will interact with a volunteer's individual capacity, influencing whether or not the role is accessible and thus performed. Accessibility also will be influenced by the incentives and facilitation provided. The incentives and facilitation provided by the program may compensate for any financial or physical challenges the potential server may face in order to meet expectations.

Hypothesis 6:   The longer and more intensive the service role performance, the more likely intended impacts will be achieved.

Hypothesis 7:   The more appropriate the role performed for the targeted individuals and community, the more likely intended impacts are achieved.

Hypothesis 8:   Facilitation moderates the relationship between role performance and intended impacts.

Hypothesis 9:   Incentives moderate the relationship between role performance and intended impacts.

Hypothesis 10:   Incentives have direct, positive impacts on volunteers.

Hypothesis 11:   Access moderates the relationship between role performance and intended impacts.

Service Impacts

Which impacts should we measure? The goals and suggested impacts of service are wide-ranging, perhaps too much so. Suggested impacts span psychological, social, educational, economic, civic, and political realms.

This range is reflected in the categories of impacts identified by the authors in this volume. In part, this smorgasbord of suggested effects is an artifact of the diversity of program structures, purposes, and goals. It also might be the result of a dual focus on the server and the served. Whatever the reasons, service scholars must wonder if the claims of effect are a bit too boundless and excessive. Might it be more productive to focus on a smaller number of key effects, especially those that may transcend program forms?

We agree with Perry and Thomson (Chapter 5) and with Davis Smith and Ellis Paine (Chapter 11) that service outcomes can be broadly classified according to their level of occurrence at the individual (volunteer and beneficiary), organizational, and community or societal levels. Although each level is conceptually distinct, they influence one another so that a benefit accrued to the individual may have an indirect or cumulative impact on community or society. Across these levels, we identify three primary areas of impact that merit focus: active citizenship and democratic values, social and economic development, and civil society development.

Active Citizenship and Democratic Values

Civic engagement has become a common measure of active citizenship and deemed the most likely service outcome. The connection is logical because service represents a chance to exercise civic muscle. However, as emerging evidence suggests, service may be most likely to develop interest and skills in social engagement, including future volunteerism and philanthropic contributions. While it is hoped that individuals would be more politically motivated as a result of service participation, there is less evidence to suggest this is the case (Abt Associates 2004; Pritzker and McBride 2005; Torney-Purta, Amadeo, and Richardson Chapter 6). Political development through voluntary contexts may require purposeful cross-group interaction and facilitation of critical reflection on the political dimensions of the participants' activities and lives.

A somewhat related concept is pro-social attitudes. We distinguish this concept from civic engagement as it relates to one's attitudes toward others, but not necessarily one's behaviors in the public realm. Pro-sociality may meaningfully capture the desired outcomes of cross-cultural understanding and increased tolerance. Again, the criterion of purposeful cross-group interaction would apply.

Social and Economic Development

Service is very much a personal experience as the individual volunteers learn their strengths and weaknesses when faced with new challenges and people different from themselves. This experience is likely no different than going to a new school, starting a new job, or joining a new group; but from this experience, individuals may increase their sense of self-efficacy, or sense of potential and effectiveness. This sense may be supported by improved interpersonal skills. Self-esteem has been commonly measured as an outcome of service, but it is a relatively fixed trait. Self-efficacy represents a more valid measure.

Increased employability of the volunteer is another area of anticipated impact, but the results are dubious. *Employability* can be defined as desirable personal qualities and skills for an employee. Beyond being able to put the service experience on one's résumé (which may be an extrinsic motivating factor that may increase one's chances of college admittance or hiring), the service experience may directly increase the skill set of the volunteer. But what skills are developed? We suggest that job-specific or topical skills are only likely to be developed when there is targeted placement, training, and supervision or mentoring, such as through national youth service programs like YouthBuild in the United States. Generalized skills, however, are more likely and might include learning and meeting professional expectations, for example, punctuality, politeness, attention to detail, and follow-through.

Social and economic impacts on service targets and host communities are too numerous to mention. Measured change should be evidenced in tangible outputs or contributions, for example, trees planted, trails built, the grades of tutored children improved, and so on.

Civil Society Development

Why do nonprofit organizations get involved in service? A very basic reason is that they view service as a way to realize their mission, to accomplish their objectives. The capacity of the organization also may be supported as it increases its visibility, viability, and sustainability. Through marketing, the organization may become more well-known, garnering more customers, volunteers, and donors. The type of service model it implements may be congruent with policy or appealing to donors and the organization may extend its connections and influence in its community.

Vogenbeck (2005) conducted a social network analysis of three organizations that host AmeriCorps National Civilian Community Corps members and found that overall these organizations increased their connectivity and leverage in their communities. If a critical mass of organizations is involved in service in a given community, then beyond any positive impact on the individual organizations the overall community may be strengthened.

Implications and Conclusion

Research

As the authors have iterated throughout this volume, impact research on the various forms of civic service is complicated and costly to develop and implement, but the field must move in this direction if service is to realize its potential. To be sure, service is just emerging in some parts of the world, and descriptive research is still necessary; but for service programs that are more established, it is important to focus research on intended impacts and determine if they are achieved. As Davis Smith and Ellis Paine point out, it is also important to pursue unintended and potentially negative outcomes.

Research Design

Questions and methods should move beyond exploration to create a more rigorous knowledge base. It is important to explicitly define and measure targeted independent (intervention) variables and dependent (outcome) variables. Pre- and posttest research designs with comparison and control groups can assess change and isolate the degree of change attributable to the service experience. Longitudinal studies that follow servers through time can gauge the presence and sustainability of effects. However, one methodological weakness that may not be overcome is the issue of self-selection bias in voluntary programs; it will be hard to develop an experimental or quasi-experimental design that allows for random assignment, but the field should be creative and aim for this goal.

Focus

As Perry and Thomson note and as was evident throughout this book, an overwhelming majority of service research pertains to the individual server. Outcomes are usually short-term effects of the service experience, mostly participant perceptions or attitudes about changes, for example, perceived social skills and civic attitudes. As such, the majority of research is attitudinal, not behavioral. To be sure, attitudes may influence behaviors, but until we know more about behavioral changes that result from service, we cannot make statements about concrete impacts. Of course, attitudinal effects are easier and less costly to assess than behavioral effects. But if policy makers, funders, and practitioners want to know the effects of service and require information for decision making, then investments in long-term, large-scale research are necessary. As for the focus of a particular study, we acknowledge that no single study can be expected to examine the effects of service on the individual server *and* on the served.

Most research is on national service programs. This emphasis may reflect the desire for accountability in public spending, thus, a governmental investment in national service research. But in our assessment of service programs worldwide (McBride, Benítez, and Sherraden 2003), international service programs may represent the most prominent form of service. If this is the case, then more research should be undertaken on different forms and their effects, especially if negative effects have been attributed to international service (McBride and Daftary 2005).

The paucity of research on the effects of service on the served fits into a pattern of limited impact assessment in the social welfare and social intervention fields overall, but this is not desirable. The impact of service on the served may result from aspects of the service role—for example, cultural training provided to the server—but it more likely results from actions the server performs, for example, economic development, disaster relief, or personal care. Much more attention should be given to the impact of the service activities on those who are served. If service objectives are not accomplished or the served are negatively affected, then some service programs may represent potentially costly or even unethical strategies. So far we know almost nothing about this possibility.

Context

The authors in this volume highlight the important role that cultural, social, economic, and political contexts play in the need for and development of service roles. It is an empirical question as to the impact that differences in context have on the functions and forms of service, both negatively and positively. There may be contexts, like multiethnic Israel, which have yet to realize the full benefit of service programs that embrace this diversity. From knowledge of the descriptive landscape, generalizable program models may be developed, and effective features for specific circumstances may be identified.

Examples of contextual determinants of the service role are evident in the history of various programs as well as recent trends. The history of national service programs in Africa as well as the Civilian Conservation Corps in the United States suggests that service roles were developed because young men needed constructive ways to spend their time when the economy did not have jobs to offer them. Able-bodied men could spend their time in service to their country through nonmilitary means. Elder service also illustrates this point, as older adults with free time and expertise can occupy service roles that are constructed to capitalize on both. As the proportion of older adults continues to increase in some countries, roles are being created for them. The gap year in the UK is another example, when youth are expected to take time to pursue volunteer and cultural pursuits between school and work as a means of personal and professional development. It also may be that cultural context dictates role requirements. In international service programs, strict enforcement of gender norms may limit the role that females can play.

There are many more scenarios that serve as examples. The object is to reach a point where hypotheses can guide cross-national research (Hodgkinson 2004). In pursuit of the impacts discussed above, comparative understanding will be enhanced through research that asks similar contextual questions regarding norms of citizenship behavior, ethnic and cultural diversity, political status, and level of economic development. Future research can examine the impact of the contextual factors, informing program development worldwide.

Policies and Programs

The authors of the chapters in this volume see potential in civic service, but each also offers a word of caution, either highlighting impediments to effectiveness or our lack of knowledge, which limits our ability to make definitive claims. While service is not the panacea it may appear to be, given its acceptance worldwide, the authors discuss ways to improve its effectiveness and efficiency.

The theme of inclusion across this volume may reflect a growing acknowledgment of the exclusivity of service. This theme suggests important implications for policy and program development, challenging practitioners to embrace their partnering organizations as cohosts and their beneficiaries as customers, for example. It also challenges programs to examine the characteristics of their volunteers and to question whether the characteristics reflect what is needed for effective service delivery or reflect those who were most able to take on the role.

As discussed above, service is only as good as the service provided. As such, critical attention should be given to the types of activities engaged in and the manner in which they are chosen and implemented. Most interventions are also only as good as the supporting management, staff, and resources are. The field should therefore aim for implementing service activities proven to be beneficial and capable of implementation by the average organization.

Also, as has been suggested by several authors in this book, service policy should be connected to other policies and institutions, such as youth education, employment policy, and retirement. Such a connection can have the benefit of integrating service within society, making it more of a social norm as well as making it more effective.

In conclusion, we suggest a long-term view of service development and evolution such that the institutionalization of service can be assessed. We should assess service integration within society, the forms it takes, its structural elements, and its resulting impacts. Service policies may ebb and flow. The ideal policies or programs for a given nation or culture may not emerge for some time. As demographics shift, political regimes change, economies fluctuate, and events occur that bind peoples together, civic service will be affected as well. By taking an institutional perspective, we have an opportunity to view service comparatively, enhancing our understanding of the emergence of civic service worldwide.

References

Abt Associates. 2004. Serving country and community: A longitudinal study of service in AmeriCorps. www.nationalservice.org.
Cnaan, R.A., and L. Amrofell. 1994. Mapping volunteer activity. *Nonprofit and Voluntary Sector Quarterly* 23 (4) Supplement 335–351.
Cnaan, R.A., F. Handy, and M. Wadsworth. 1996. Defining who is a volunteer: Conceptual and empirical considerations. *Nonprofit and Voluntary Sector Quarterly* 25 (3): 364–383.
Grossman, J.B., and K. Furanco. 1999. Making the most of volunteers. *Law and Contemporary Problems* 62: 199–217.
Hodgkinson, V.A. 2004. Developing a research agenda on civic service. *Nonprofit and Voluntary Sector Quarterly* 33 (4): 184S–197S.
Jepperson, R.L. 1991. Institutions, institutional effects, and institutionalism. In *The New Insitutionalism in Organizational Analysis,* ed. W.W. Powell, and P. DiMaggio. Chicago: University of Chicago Press.
Kuti, E. 2004. Civic service in Eastern Europe and Central Asia: From mandatory public work toward civic service? *Nonprofit and Voluntary Sector Quarterly* 33 (4): 79S–97S.
McBride, A.M., C. Benítez, and M. Sherraden. 2003. *The Forms and Nature of Civic Service: A Global Assessment* (CSD Report). St. Louis: Washington University, Center for Social Development.
McBride, A.M., and D. Daftary. 2005. *International Service: History and Forms, Pitfalls and Potential* (CSD Working Paper 05-10). St. Louis: Washington University, Center for Social Development.
McBride, A.M., M. Lombe, F. Tang, M. Sherraden, and C. Benítez. 2003. *The Knowledge Base on Civic Service: Status and Directions* (CSD Working Paper 03-20). St. Louis: Washington University, Center for Social Development.
McBride, A.M., and M. Sherraden, eds. 2004. Toward an international research agenda on civic service. *Nonprofit and Voluntary Sector Quarterly* 33 (4) Supplement.
Menon, N., A.M. McBride, and M. Sherraden. 2003. Understanding service in the context of history and culture. In *Service Enquiry: Service in the 21st Century,* ed. H. Perold, S. Stroud, and M. Sherraden. Johannesburg: comPress.
Metz, E., and J. Youniss. 2003. A demonstration that school-based required service does not deter—but heightens—volunteerism. *PS: Political Science and Politics* 36 (2): 281–286.

Morrow-Howell, N., J. Hinterlong, M. Sherraden, F. Tang, P. Thirupathy, and M. Nagchoudhuri. 2003. Institutional capacity for elder service. *Social Development Issues* 25 (1/2): 189–204.

Nagchoudhuri, M., A.M. McBride, P. Thirupathy, F. Tang, and N. Morrow-Howell. 2005. Maximizing elder service: Incentives and facilitation. *Journal of Volunteer Administration* 23 (1): 11–14.

Ostrom, E., L. Schroeder, and S. Wynne. 1993. *Institutional Incentives and Sustainable Development: Infrastructure Policies in Perspective.* Boulder, CO: Westview Press.

Pritzker, S., and A.M. McBride. 2005. Service-learning and civic outcomes: From suggestive research to program models. Paper presented at the 5th Annual International Conference on Advances in Service Learning Research, East Lansing, Michigan, November 13–15.

Sherraden, M. 2001. *Civic Service: Issues, Outlook, Institution Building* (CSD Perspective). St. Louis: Washington University, Center for Social Development.

Sherraden, M., and D. Eberly. 1982. *National Service: Social, Economic, and Military Impacts.* New York: Pergamon Press.

Sherraden, M., N. Morrow-Howell, J. Hinterlong, and P. Rozario. 2001. Productive aging: Theoretical choices and directions. In *Productive Aging: Concepts and Challenges,* ed. N. Morrow-Howell, J. Hinterlong, and M. Sherraden. Baltimore: Johns Hopkins University Press.

Sherraden, M., M. Schreiner, and S. Beverly. 2003. Income, institutions, and saving performance in Individual Development Accounts. *Economic Development Quarterly* 17 (1): 95–112.

Vogenbeck, D. 2005. Social network analysis for policy design: Collaborative discourse between nonprofit/government organizations and the resulting effect on community level social capital. PhD diss., University of Colorado at Denver. *Dissertation Abstracts International* 66/07: 2710.

About the Editors and Contributors

Jo-Ann Amadeo, PhD, is Vice-President for Programs at the Close-Up Foundation, Alexandria, Virginia. Her publications include *Civic Knowledge and Engagement: An IEA Study of Upper Secondary Students in Sixteen Countries* (2002), *Strengthening Democracy in the Americas Through Civic Education: An Empirical Study of the Views of Teachers and Students* (2004), a chapter reviewing research on service-learning, and a chapter reporting a cross-national analysis of media use among adolescents in relation to their civic attitudes.

Justin Davis Smith, PhD, is director of the Institute for Volunteering Research, London, and a visiting professor at Birnbeck University of London. His extensive research on the voluntary sector includes two national surveys of volunteering in the United Kingdom, a ten-nation European study of volunteering, and studies on youth and older adults as volunteers. Davis Smith also consults with the United Nations on volunteerism. His publications include *Volunteering and Society* (1992) and *An Introduction to the Voluntary Sector* (1995). He is the founding editor of the journal, *Voluntary Action,* and cofounder and honorary secretary of the Voluntary Action History Society.

Donald J. Eberly, EdM, has been honorary president of the International Association for National Youth Service since 1998. He founded the National Service Secretariat in the United States in 1966 and served as its executive director from then until 1994. Eberly received his BS from the Massachusetts Institute of Technology in 1950 and his EdM from the Harvard Graduate School of Education in 1960. He served in the Signal Corps of the U.S. Army from 1951 to 1953. Eberly has written numerous articles on national youth service and service-learning as well as several books including *National Service: A Promise to Keep* (1988) and *A Profile of National Service* (1966). He is the coeditor with Michael Sherraden of *National Service: Social, Economic and Military Impacts* (1982) and of *The Moral Equivalent of War: A Study of*

Non-Military Service in Nine Nations (1990), and coauthor with Reuven Gal of *Service Without Guns* (2006).

Angela Ellis Paine, PhD, is the assistant director for the Institute for Volunteering Research in London. She has been involved in evaluations of various government initiatives, including the Active Citizens in Schools pilot, and the Millennium Volunteers program in the United Kingdom. She has written a number of reports, including a discussion document on measuring the impacts of volunteering and a literature review on university-based volunteering. Ellis Paine also has been involved in a study into social exclusion and volunteering and in research consultancies for various volunteer organizations. Her dissertation looked at local participation in rural community development initiatives.

Amitai Etzioni, PhD, is university professor and director of the Institute for Communitarian Policy Studies at George Washington University, Washington, DC. He served as a senior advisor to the Carter White House and taught at Columbia University, Harvard Business School, and the University of California, Berkeley. In 1990, Etzioni founded the Communitarian Network, a nonprofit, nonpartisan organization dedicated to shoring up the moral, social, and political foundations of society. Etzioni is the author of numerous books, including *From Empire to Community: A New Approach to International Relations* (2004), *The Monochrome Society (2001), Next: The Road to the Good Society* (2001), *The Limits of Privacy* (1999), *The New Golden Rule: Community* and *Morality in a Democratic Society* (1996), which received the Simon Wiesenthal Center's 1997 Tolerance Book Award.

Nicole Fleischer, MBA, is presently the manager of European marketing at NetManage, a worldwide software company. Previously, as the director of the Carmel Institute for four years and the cofounder of the Israeli Center for Outstanding Leadership, a new spin-off of the Carmel Institute, Fleischer participated in the development of a working model for the World Jewish Peace Corps and conducted feasibility studies in South Africa and India. She has coauthored several civic service-related research projects and papers, among them evaluation studies related to the impact of national youth service on male volunteers and on the inclusion of volunteers with special needs in national youth service.

Reuven Gal, PhD, served in the Israeli Defense Forces (IDF) as a combat infantry officer (1960–1963) and commanded a reserve reconnaissance unit during the battles in Jerusalem in the Six-Days War. After completing his academic studies in psychology and sociology (BA and MA at the Hebrew University, Jerusalem; PhD at the University of California, Berkeley), Gal served as IDF's chief psychologist (1976–1982) and retired with the rank of colonel. Gal founded the Israeli Institute for Military Studies (IIMS) in 1985. In 1992, the IIMS became the Carmel Institute for Social Studies, a nonprofit research and policy-making center that studies and promotes social and psychological projects in Israel and internationally. In 2002, Gal joined Israel's National Security Council (NSC), where he serves as the deputy to the head of the NSC, responsible for domestic and social policy. Among Gal's books are *A Portrait of the Israeli Soldier* (1986), *Legitimacy and Commitment in the Military* (1990), *The Seventh War: The Effects of the Intifada on the Israeli Society* (1990), and *Handbook of Military Psychology* (1991), and, with D. Eberly, *Service Without Guns* (2006).

Wendy Klandl Richardson, PhD, is a faculty research assistant in the Department of Human Development at the College of Education, University of Maryland, College Park. She is a former social studies teacher and recipient of the Harry S. Truman Scholarship. Richardson's dissertation earned the 2004 Bruce H. Choppin Award, which is awarded to an outstanding dissertation using International Educational Achievement data.

Margaret Lombe, PhD, is an assistant professor at the Boston College Graduate School of Social Work. Lombe received both her doctoral and master's degrees from the George Warren Brown School of Social Work at Washington University in St. Louis. Her area of expertise is in international social economic development with an emphasis on social exclusion/inclusion and civic service. Lombe is also a faculty associate at the Center for Social Development at Washington University.

Amanda Moore McBride, PhD, is an assistant professor at the George Warren Brown School of Social Work, director of the Gephardt Institute for Public Service, and research director of the Center for Social Development (CSD) at Washington University in St. Louis. Her scholarship focuses on civic engagement and civic service. McBride is principal investigator for CSD's Global Service Institute research initiative, implementing an international research agenda on civic service. Recent studies examined the civic engagement effects of asset building, the role of AmeriCorps*VISTA members in asset-building programs, and the forms and nature of civic service worldwide. McBride was lead editor of a 2004 special issue of *Nonprofit and Voluntary Sector Quarterly* titled "Toward a Global Research Agenda on Civic Service," and was coeditor of an issue of *Voluntary Action* titled "International Service in the Context of Globalization." McBride also directs a civic service research grants and fellows program, which currently supports twenty fellows with research spanning thirty-two countries.

Natasha Menon, PhD, is an assistant professor in the Graduate School of Social Service at Fordham University in New York. Menon received both her doctoral and master's degrees from the George Warren Brown School of Social Work at Washington University in St. Louis and a master's degree in social work from the Tata Institute for Social Sciences in India. Her area of expertise is community development, decentralization of public services, collective action, and international social development. Menon is also a faculty associate at the Center for Social Development at Washington University.

Nancy Morrow-Howell, PhD, is a gerontological social worker. She is implementing a research agenda on the productive engagement of older adults in work, volunteer, and care-giving activities. With support from the Longer Life Foundation, MetLife, and the Atlantic Philanthropies, she is assessing institutional arrangements for older adults to engage in service as well as the effect of service on older adults. Morrow-Howell has published numerous articles and chapters in this field, including the edited volume *Productive Aging: Concepts and Challenges* (1991).

Ebenezer Obadare, PhD, is an assistant professor in the Department of Sociology, University of Kansas, Lawrence. Before his appointment, he was a visiting research fellow at the Centre for Civil Society, Department of Social Policy, at the London School of Economics and Political Science, where he completed his doctorate in social policy in June 2005, and was co-recipient of the Department of Social Policy's Richard Titmuss Best PhD Thesis Prize for the year 2005. Obadare holds undergraduate and postgraduate degrees respectively in history and international relations from the Obafemi Awolowo University, Ile-Ife, Nigeria. In 2004, he was jointly awarded the MacArthur Foundation's prestigious Research and Writing grant for a study of the short- and long-term impacts of current migratory patterns on citizenship in Africa. In 2003, through the Center for Social Development at Washington University in St. Louis, Missouri, he received a research grant to study the citizenship effects of the Nigerian national service program. A one-time award-winning journalist, Obadare's scholarship connects various themes in African governance and development, including migration, civil society, the state, religion, nongovernmental organizations, the public sphere, citizenship, youth, and civic service. His articles have appeared in books and refereed journals, including the *Review of African Political Economy* (ROAPE), *Journal of Civil Society*,

Patterns of Prejudice, Africa Development, and *The New Dictionary of the History of Ideas.*

James L. Perry, PhD, is Chancellor's Professor of the School of Public and Environmental Affairs (SPEA) at Indiana University-Purdue University in Indianapolis. His recent research focuses on public service motivation, community and national service, and government reform. His research appears in such journals as *Academy of Management Journal, Administrative Science Quarterly, Nonprofit Management and Leadership, Nonprofit and Voluntary Sector Quarterly,* and *Public Administration Review.* Perry is author and editor of several books, including *Handbook of Public Administration* (second edition, 1996). His most recent book is *Civic Service: What Difference Does It Make?* (2004), coauthored with Ann Marie Thomson.

Ronald Pitner, PhD, is an assistant professor at the George Warren Brown School of Social Work, Washington University, St. Louis, Missouri. His research interests are broadly defined in terms of social cognition, stereotyping, prejudice, race and ethnicity, cultural diversity, and children's perceptions of violence. He is particularly interested in using social psychological and developmental theories to examine and understand social issues such as violence, oppression, intergroup relations, and poverty.

Margaret Sherrard Sherraden, PhD, is a professor of social work at the University of Missouri-St. Louis, and research professor at the Center for Social Development (CSD) at Washington University in St. Louis. Sherraden's research, publishing, and teaching are in the areas of social and economic development, poverty, immigration and health, and international voluntary service. Past research includes a Fulbright-funded dissertation study of health and poverty policy in Mexico (1987), and research on birth outcomes among Mexican immigrants in Chicago. Currently, Sherraden is leading an in-depth interview study of participants in a matched savings program of individual development accounts, part of a longitudinal national demonstration at CSD (1997–2003). She is also conducting research on a trinational North American youth community service project and a children's saving account demonstration in St. Louis.

Michael Sherraden, PhD, is Benjamin E. Youngdahl Professor of Social Development at Washington University in St. Louis. He is also director and founder of the Center for Social Development (CSD). He edited two books on youth service with Donald Eberly: *National Youth Service: Social, Economic and Military Impacts* (1982) and *The Moral Equivalent of War: A Study of*

Non-Military Service in Nine Nations (1990). In his book *Assets and the Poor: A New American Welfare Policy* (1991), Sherraden articulated the concept of asset-based development, which suggests that policy should promote not merely income and consumption, but also savings and investment. He initiated the American Dream Demonstration (ADD) at CSD, a multimethod research project to test individual development accounts (IDAs), matched savings accounts for the poor. IDAs have been adopted in federal legislation and in more than forty states. An edited book titled *Inclusion in the American Dream: Assets, Poverty, and Public Policy* was published in 2005.

Fengyan Tang, PhD, is an assistant professor at the University of Pittsburgh School of Social Work. Tang received both her doctoral and master's degrees from the George Warren Brown School of Social Work at Washington University in St. Louis. Her area of expertise is productive engagement and civic engagement in later life. Tang is also a faculty associate at the Center for Social Development at Washington University.

Maria Nieves Tapia, PhD, is currently directing Argentina's federal service-learning program, "Educación Solidaria." Founder and director of Centro Latinoamericano de Aprendizaje y Servicio Solidario (CLAYSS) since 2002, Tapia has been working in the service-learning field since 1993, and has published several books on service-learning. She was the director of the Proyecto Juventud at Fundación Andina and the chief of the consultant team for the Instituto Nacional de la Juventud at the Ministerio de Salud y Acción Social in the early 1990s. Tapia has performed a consulting role for many Institutions in her career and she also held a variety of honorary titles.

Ann Marie Thomson, PhD, is an adjunct assistant professor at the School of Public and Environmental Affairs, Indiana University, Bloomington. A former national service research fellow, Thomson's research interests include inter-organizational collaboration as a national service strategy to build local communities. Her most recent work examines relationships between religion, civic engagement, and the creation of legitimate and accountable institutional structures in failed states in Africa. Besides volunteering on a number of other boards, she is also the cofounder of a nongovernmental organization that works in the Democratic Republic of Congo.

Judith Torney-Purta, PhD, is a professor of human development in the College of Education at the University of Maryland, College Park. Torney-Purta was recently awarded the national Decade of Behavior Research Award recognizing her work on young people learning to participate in democracy.

Torney-Purta's long-term interest has been developmental and educational psychology as it can be applied to political socialization and the civic engagement of youth. She served as the chair of the International Steering Committee of the Civic Education Study of the International Association for the Evaluation of Education Achievement (IEA) in Amsterdam from 1994 until 2004. *Civic Education Across Countries: Twenty-four National Case Studies from the IEA Civic Education Project* by Torney-Purta, John Schwille, and Jo-Ann Amadeo (1999) was designated by the American Library Association as an Outstanding Academic Book (the Choice Award). *Citizenship and Education in Twenty-eight Countries: Civic Knowledge and Engagement at Age Fourteen* by Torney-Purta, Rainer Lehmann, Hans Oswald, and Wolfram Schulz was published in 2001, and a volume reporting results from upper secondary students in sixteen countries was published in July 2002.

Index